Redemption:
The Life & Death of Rocky Marciano.

John Cameron.

With a forward from Angelo Dundee

Volume One:
Preliminaries
1923-1949

Dedicated to the memory of Angelo Dundee
(1921 – 2012)

For Kim, my greatest love and greatest critic and Teagan May - my greatest inspiration, plus all those who have allowed me to be a part of the greatest family I have ever known.

Finally, to Rocco Francis Marchegiano whose legend will live forever.

Acknowledgments

This project would have been made all the more difficult had it not been for the support, assistance and encouragement of the following:

Rocky Marchegiano Jr. John J. Raspanti, Bobby Bearden, Bob Yalen, Tania Grossinger, Chuck Marbry, Phil Guarnieri, Ferdie Pacheco, Luisita Pacheco, A. J. Dugger, Ian McNielly, Steve Acunto, Leo Giavagnoli, Betty Fitzgerald, Hank Cisco, Tracey Mogard, Ken White, Dennis Whitton, Clare Benfield, plus the numerous others who have not been mentioned but who have contributed with stories, support, and material, and of course not forgetting the late, great Angelo Dundee. My sincere thanks to you all….

Contents:

Forward: Angelo Dundee

Introduction: John Cameron

Part One: The Miracle of Youth - September 1923 - December 1942

chapter one: Heritage
chapter two: Hail to the Champ
chapter three: Childhood
chapter four: King of the Hill
chapter five: Earth, Wind and Fire

Part Two: The Lost Years - January 1943 - March 1948

chapter one: Private Marchegiano, Rocco F./ 31-301-298
chapter two: The Smoker
chapter three: Goodbye Uncle Sam
chapter four: Barbara and Rocky Mack
chapter five: The Dream that Died
chapter six: Crossroads
chapter seven: Lowell
chapter eight: Brooklyn
chapter nine: Goodbye Gene

Part Three: Providence - June 1948 - December 1949

chapter one:	Enter 'The Vest'
chapter two:	And Charley too
chapter three:	The Offer
chapter four:	The Birth of a Fighter
chapter five:	First Steps
chapter six:	The Tank Job
chapter seven:	Deliverance
chapter eight:	Three Gone Quick
chapter nine:	Marciano
chapter ten:	The Contract
chapter eleven:	The House of Sin
chapter twelve:	The fight that nearly never was
chapter thirteen:	One Step Forward...
chapter fourteen:	...and One Step Back
chapter fifteen:	Reflections
chapter sixteen:	Not Just a Footnote
chapter seventeen:	Artie and the Jimmy Boys
chapter eighteen:	"Uncle Mike"
chapter nineteen:	Mr. Gray
chapter twenty:	The Golden Boy and Octopus Inc.
chapter twenty-one:	Family Ties
chapter twenty-two:	The End of the Beginning

chapter twenty-three: Doubly Sure

chapter twenty-four: Tommy G.

chapter twenty-five: The Tiger

chapter twenty-six: Breakthrough

chapter twenty-seven: Carmine

Afterword: Phil Guarnieri

Forward

Rocky Marciano was of my era, I met him in his early days. Charley Goldman told me about this kid from Brockton he was training at the CYO. Shortish, stooping shoulders, two left feet, but oh how he could punch! He took me to the CYO with him and in walked Rocky with a small canvass bag, he worked out with Keene Simmons that day.

Charley moulded Rocky from the ground up, he gave him great balance, a solid and deceptive defence, he was not that easy to hit. Charley taught him to punch by bending his knees, coming up slowly and nailing his opponent with either hand.

The job of piecing together the life of a fighter is never an easy one, particularly when that fighter left us way too young, so I am pleased that he is being remembered in this new biography, for Rocky deserves his story to be told for new generations to wonder at for he is a true great, in any era, he belonged.

It is good that those who fought Rocky have been remembered too, for there were some real tough guys around back then, not everyone was a pushover, Rocky really had to work hard to beat them.

Rocky was my friend, he was a great man, he had his faults sure, but he was only human and it was this that made his achievements all the greater. I think Rocky would have been pleased that over six decades since he retired people are still interested in him. For as long as people like John continue to write about him his legacy will last forever.

Angelo Dundee. (*Tampa, Florida, February 2011*)

Introduction

> *"The great heavyweight fighters have the loneliness of the ages in their silence."*
>
> *Norman Mailer*

Friedrich Nietszche, that most astute of philosophers, once penned the maxim, "He shall be greatest who can be loneliest, the most concealed, and yet the most defiant..." If any statement summed up Marciano perfectly it was this one.

As a fighter Rocky would lock himself away for months in an almost Spartan regime of training. In fact there was an almost religious aspect to his devotion. Perhaps he was in fact a devotee to the discipline of combat. His life too was one hidden; one lived behind a veil, although not all of his own making.

The late Barney Nagler, considered to be amongst one of the preeminent boxing writers of his time, penned a piece for the May 1980 addition of *The Ring* (*a full faced color image of Marciano wearing a Mona Lisa-esque smile which seemed to be taunting us the readers to unlock his secrets, decorated the front page*). The article entitled; 'Rocky Marciano, The Man Nobody Knew' was imminently forgettable yet the title has remained with me since I first acquired the piece way back in the late summer of 1989 (*one British pound Stirling from Dave's second hand book store in my old home town - at first I mistook the cover image for Gerry Cooney*). The byline was a truth for as I was to discover few really knew Marciano, least of all the public.

By the time I began this onerous project in all seriousness some three-and-a-half years ago (*after a lifetime of being, not obsessed but rather intrigued by this man whom my father regarded as being metaphorically, 'hard as nails'*) there had been at least seven previous authors who have attempted the task before me (*I admit that I have stood on their shoulders and allowed them to carry me along as well as stretching my neck heavenward in an attempt to see a little further*) but each did not quite go deep enough into the reality of the man. Sure they told quite amply his story, at least the official one. Born, brought up, became a boxer, won the heavyweight title, retired, died.

But there is so much more to a life than mere moments, snapshots of a time. These authors told how Rocky got from A to Z but missed out how he got from C to D, from G to H, etc, etc, etc...

Every life has an evolution for someone does not, at least usually, wake up and be who they are fully formed. There is a series of events that shape and form them. Some of these take place in the mind, others swirl around them. A fall from a tree; a row with an army sergeant; a poor performance on a baseball diamond, all these redirect a life into a new path. And still more morphing occurs. A win here; a loss there; a near deat;, a close decision; all go into the making of the one in question. It is not just the believed pivotal moments, the ones that the public are familiar with for usually they are not the turning points at all. It is the little things that make the big things happen, it is the tiniest cogs that turn the face of time.

Rocky Marciano was in part a creation made by the media of the day and borne out of the second war that engulfed the world during the first half of the twentieth-century. This is a bold statement but a true one for without the Second World War Marciano would never have existed at all. Just as without the manipulation of the press during his rise to prominence in the early fifties the image we now have of the man himself would never have been formed. It is ironic that it should be this very image of the all-American poster boy from the 1950's that has threatened to bring the fighter down.

Marciano it seems really is 'A Picture of Dorian Gray' in reverse for as the image grows more wholesome over the years so the man himself seems to become corrupted and decays. You see the problem stems from the fact that there are those who would do all in their powers to protect the image, to propagate it and deny anything that would tarnish it. The problem is that this very denial has led in part to an exaggeration of the truth, a ballooning of the facts. Not in any grandiose way of making something out of nothing, of perverting what is known, but more that when a truth is exposed, due to the once perceived saintliness of the man, this truth is seen as a greater sin than it really is. Instead of stripping away the facade and seeing the real man for who he is, and he is a great man, greater than anyone has given him credit for, and his greatness stems from the fact that he is just a man, there are those who would pounce upon his deficiencies and use them against him. Why? I guess because there are those who still refuse to believe that Marciano was really as good as he was!

It is my place now to reveal the man as much as I can and in the exposing immunize the reader against believing that Marciano was something he was not. Marciano was a fighter pure and simple, it takes a certain kind of person to actually enjoy fighting and what made him such was little different from others who ascended the throne, and in many cases was in fact far tamer (*it was for this very reason that I decided to title this project 'Redemption' as in redeeming, saving someone from a dilapidated or corrupted state, returning to a better position, saving from an irreversible decline; although Peter Marciano -who before he decided to desert the cause when evidence presented did not fit with how he wished the subject to be perceived, had helped amend a very, very early draft- commented that "I do not understand, why Redemption? After all Rocky has always been at the very top to us?"*). But this is not a project that is being pieced together to appease those who venerate the very name. It is not a myth making exercise, a piece of diluted, or in extreme contrast, sensationalized storytelling, it is simply telling of a life and we all know, if we are brutally honest with ourselves, that the reality of our own lives is full of facets, some sparkling and others less than devine.

Yes Marciano has his faults, his little peccadilloes that make him human, but then so do all of us. 'Those who are without sin...' comes to mind, but again it is the perception that has been cultivated by those who, though no doubt acting with the very best of intentions, have almost destroyed the man himself. A man who is in fact two very separate people.
For one there is Rocky Marciano, the world heavyweight champion, the one whose story has been told before. And then there is also Rocco Marchegiano, the one who defied convention, the one who did not allow his perceived liabilities (*and they were many*) to get in the way of triumph, the one who was everything that Rocky was but also infinitely more, and the one whose story has never been fully explored before.

So yes, this man who ascended to the pinnacle of the hardest of sports against overwhelming odds, was the loneliest, the most concealed, and certainly the most defiant...It is my hope that when this project is finally completed we shall all know him a little better...

John Cameron

(*Exeter, UK –August 2012*)

Part One: September 1923 -- December 1942

The Miracle of Youth

part one   **chapter one**

Heritage

"I get my inner strength from my father,
And my physical strength from my mother."

Rocky Marciano

Piereno Marchegiano (*pronounced mark-a-gee-a-no*) was known by many names, Pierino, Pietro, or Puetro, considered to be his original title, and later by the anglicized Peter [1]. Yet under each of these standards he was, by the late summer of 1923 at least, a frail man as he sat cradling his new born son in the sparsely furnished apartment which he shared with his young bride of barely two years. This was a moment that he thought had passed him by after the tragedy of the previous year, for his life had up until this time been an arduous journey.

Standing barely five-feet-eight-inches tall, and weighing a meager hundred-and-thirty-pounds with a world weary face that was taut and pinched belying his twenty-nine years. This face was topped by short cropped hair that had that faint wire like quality which bespoke his origin, once jet black, yet now showing the perceptible signs of graying. Despite this however his sometime sombre brown eyes still shone with a warm steely glint that spoke volumes about the man he truly was, sure life had not always been easy, but as he sat there on this day he felt certain it could only get better.

He had been born in Italy in 1894, within the confines of the small town of Ripateatina (2). The town derived its name, it is alleged, from a traveling band of mercenaries who had been hired to protect this small community from warring factions back in the mists of time. "It is an irony," commented Marciano's youngest brother, Peter, "that everything Rocky Marciano stood for, i.e., the warrior, is representative of the naming of the town."

Piereno would speak very little about these early years, years that certainly were filled with misery which was brought about by both extreme poverty and a yearning to escape the uncertain future which lay ahead for many Europeans at the turn of the twentieth-century, an age that was charged with war and brutality. It was this uncertainty that led young Piereno, at the age of only seventeen, to follow some two-million others from his native Italy in setting sail for the new world of America united in the hope of finding, not-so-much adventure, but merely a better standard of living in which to escape the rigors of life back home.

The youth set sail from Naples on board the U.S.S Canada (3), after an arduous journey in which he, amongst some almost 1600 other passengers, had found himself traveling in the most basic of conditions he would at last witness the majestic statue of Liberty looming on the horizon on the 28th of March, 1912 . Most on board according to the reflections of those who journeyed the same path, believed that their trip had been worth the suffering. Upon arrival at the notorious disembarkation point at Ellis Island the passengers were herded down a wooden gangplank onto American soil. From here a tired, hungry and overwhelmed Piereno would be ushered up the steps of the former military defensive fortification and into the registry room, here to be inspected by a physician for any signs of disease which may preclude him from entry into this seemingly brave new world; many around him would be sent back from whence they came. Next came a testing area where he was asked to prove his ability to be able to support himself and thus, officially at least, not become a burden to the state.

Piereno was strong and robust in his youth, capable of performing the tasks laid out before him with ease. Once through these indignities he was at last cleared for entrance, his paper work completed, money exchanged, he would now pick up his meager belongings and enter his new home via New York.

From here he found himself gravitating towards Brockton, Massachusetts, a multi-cultural working class city whose heart belched out the fumes of industrial vigor. Its most famous export at this time was shoes, indeed Brockton was regarded as thee shoe making capitol of America employing some 30,000 workers with-in its multitude of factory walls. It was here that the young Marchegiano would find employment at the prestigious Stacey Adams shoe factory - his father before him had been a cobbler in his native Italy, it seemed a natural choice. So began a relationship that would endure, for better or for worse, through the rest of his working life.

These early years in his adoptive world were ones of frugality and constant work, punctuated only by a young man's desire to be entertained. Usually this came in the form of drunken brawling, proving his toughness by fighting anyone and everyone in his district, then, as now, known as Ward Two where the Italian immigrants had converged to set up their own small community. When Piereno had run out of combatants here he would often venture into a quarter of the City populated mainly by Chinese, exiles like himself, and find his excitement there. Rarely did he head home disappointed.

I had often wondered what the reason was behind Piereno's move to America. Initially I believed that it was the same as all those other itinerant workers who ploughed across the waters from Europe looking for a better life, yet the fact that he came alone bothered me at first until I understood that this was not uncommon. The eldest son, or the patriarch would travel first and create a base to bring the remaining family over to be with him, but this was something that Piereno never did, he seemed to be an island, alone, abandoned at least initially this is what I thought, That is until I made the acquaintance of one Maria Allegra and her cousin Wallace Mignault Jr. who together have helped put the pieces of a story together that brings possible clarity to his arrival in Brockton. It was perhaps not merely a quest to escape poverty and build a better life, but more a quest to find his family!

Peter Marciano assured me that Piereno never knew his father. I have not been able to establish whether this man died or abandoned his son, yet the fathers name was never forgotten for it would be immortalized in his grandson, Rocco Francis Marchegiano.

Piereno's youth is enigmatic; from what I can garner he was raised by relatives whose identities have remained a mystery, at least to me

At first in an effort to find the reason for his move to America I was garnered with the tale that Piereno had come because he had fallen in love with on older widowed Italian lady who had immigrated to America, so besotted was he that he followed her to Brockton, whereupon the lady in question immediately fled back to Italy! Yet there were holes in the story, the lady in question had arrived in 1908, fully four years before the seemingly love struck young man, if this tale were true why did he wait so long to follow her? Thus what had begun so filled with promise seemed to be leading to an almost inevitable dead end. That is until Maria spoke to her aunt who still resides in Italy and the pieces began to fall into some kind of order.

Maria's great-grandmother was named Giuseppina Barbarosa Distasi, this was the widow in question whom Piereno was believed to have fallen for. Yet it was not the boy at all, it was, or so it seemed, his late father who had, or at least attempted to have, a tryst with Giuseppina who at the time lived in Foggia, Italy, an agricultural town situated approximately at the heel of Italy's famous boot.

In Maria's own words, "A gentleman named Rocco Franco (*sic*) Marchegiano was very much in love with her. He came from (*the*) Abruzzo region." This is where the two stories became intertwined for it seems that Giuseppina spurned the elder Marchegiano and that was all the elderly-aunt could recollect, however Maria introduced me to her cousin, Wallace Mignault Jr. Wallace believed that Rocky Marciano was his cousin [4] for he recalled the then champion visiting his father Wallace Mignault Senior during the fifties [5] and it was here that he first learned that his father and Marciano were believed to be related in some way through, so it was rumored, Giuseppina.

That the pair were close is testified to by Marciano's constant contact with the senior Mignault even during the former champions retirement. Was this connection that kept Marciano and Mignault Sr close for the remainder of Rocky's life and explains Piereno's arrival in Brockton something deeper than mere friendship or mutual appreciation. There is a rumor amongst some in the extensive, and oftimes convoluted family descent that Giuseppina may perhaps be Piereno's mother for there are those who believe, particularly in the older generations, that Giuseppina did not spurn the elder Marchegiano at all, at least initially; but that is supposition, not the stuff that this project can rely too heavily upon. However there is strong support for some form of familial link that winds its way through the Marchegiano and Mignaults line which hails from Giuseppina Barbarosa DiStasi herself. So it does appear that the young adventurer did indeed have some form of family awaiting him in Brockton, at least through some tentative, or perhaps even illegitimate, thread.

There are still so many loose ends however, who did Piereno stay with when he first came to Brockton? Why did his possible matriarch return to Italy? What? When? Where? Why? How? These are all questions that may never be answered. The works that have come before paint a picture of a very lonely man in Piereno. Whilst Marciano's mother is surrounded by family for his father there is only a vague reference here and there. His life before enlistment is shadowy, so much so that sometimes one wonders if he ever really existed at all.

Piereno's story becomes solidified only in 1916 when the Great War which had been raging in Europe for almost two years, had at last hit America and she now found herself deeply embroiled. It was thus in this year that Piereno, with a sense of adopted national pride, and perhaps feeling that at last he could leave his mark on life, signed up, becoming in the process the first, so it is claimed, Italian-American from the city of Brockton to do so.

Piereno would later comment on his experience of everyday life during his short military career:

> No privata soldier 'e no nothing about a war. I know even lessa than any other, on accounta I don't even spika the sama language as the guys who are supposed to be onna my side! (*sic*)

Upon enlistment he found himself serving under the Second Marine Brigade, with whom he saw action in amongst other places, *Chateau-Thierry*, it was here that he would earn his first battle star when receiving wounds in action due to a grenade which exploded in his vicinity, the shrapnel piercing his left cheek and wrenching out three of his teeth. "Didn't bother me though," he said later, "spit 'em out and kept going, I'm tough too."

It is difficult now to imagine the true horror that faced young Piereno as he fought in the trench scarred and muddied fronts of Europe for this war was a war like no other, millions went to battle for a cause that very few really understood, even fewer could have comprehended what awaited them. "My company commander, Lieutenant Massbauer, had been at the front for one hour when he was shot through the head," wrote a young German soldier Private Paul Hub in his diaries, before continuing. "Pale and close to death, he was carried past me. Today, Sunday (*31st October 1914*), I stood at his modest grave and joined in a prayer.

"That's how it is. All around me, the most gruesome devastation. Dead and wounded soldiers, dead and dying animals, horse cadavers, burnt-out houses, dug-up fields, cars, clothes, weaponry - all this is scattered around me, a real mess. I didn't think war would be like this."

Hub seemed to be speaking for the average soldier on all sides, for others wrote too of the horrors, of wading knee deep through the dead, of praying that if they were to be shot then rather they be killed outright than being left in agony, spending days rotting away slowly in the blood spattered foreign fields of what is now becoming a tragically forgotten war. Patriotism and freedom seemed to be a price that was paid for by the bodies of an entire generation. Later most would reluctantly agree that it was a price worth paying, but at the time many felt, through their mourning tears, that the price was way to high.

Piereno was one of the, on the surface, fortunate ones for he survived, yet ostensibly not in one piece (*aside from his missing teeth*). It would be whilst deployed against the German forces in the Muesse-Argonne Offensive of September 26th 1918 (*known as the 'Path of*

Fire') that the real damage was done. It was here Piereno would inhale the insidious mustard gas with which the Germans enveloped the Argonne forest in the hope that this would assist them in winning this most brutal and crucial of battles. Despite the Axis powers best efforts it was the Allies however who took victory in what became the prelude to the end of the First Great War. Yet due to being consumed in that cloud of bilious gas Piereno would join the millions of other casualties who wore their wounds on the inside. Eventually the effects of that day would lead to his suffering from emphysema, a disease of the lungs which would leave him drained and struggling for breath whilst he coughed and choked. In later life he could be found habitually sucking on hard candy in an attempt to take away the foul taste that lingered in his mouth, it was an almost daily battle against his health that Piereno would wage for the remainder of his life.

Its harrowing effects however did not necessitate an immediate return to civilian life, for after a short convalescence he would find himself at the conclusion of the war in 1918 serving out the terms of his enlistment in Coblenz, Germany, which was now under the Army of occupation. Here Piereno remained until his discharge in 1919. It was whilst serving here, so legend would have us believe, that Piereno, although suffering from the effects of the gassing, joined the regiments boxing team, where, it is said, he remained undefeated (6).

Upon his return to that which he now called home, Piereno would find himself once more at the Stacey Adams Shoe factory which he had left behind some three-years earlier. For his commendable war time efforts he was presented with a ring by the factory officials to mark their appreciation. He would also take part in a parade held by the people of Brockton to welcome home their heroic service men and pay tribute to those who had been left behind.Piereno was singled out by the then Governors' daughter in order to receive a media friendly kiss on the cheek, he would look back on this moment as one of the proudest of his life often enlarging the tale into the entire parade being held in his own singular honor, it seemed to be a trait of his that he wished to be seen and thought off as someone who was more than a mere factory employee.

This yearning to be more than he was in life was evident at his own home where he would leave for work in his smartest civilian clothes, change at work, then re-attire himself for his journey back afterwards. Perhaps it was the loneliness of his youth that served up in him the need for acceptance now - soon he would find that acceptance in a family that was most definitely his own.

Within just a few short weeks of returning to America, Piereno, neatly tailored in his Marine uniform would be escorting his friend, Salvatore Picciuto to a private party held at the home of Salvatore's family. He was looking forward to tasting the wine that he was told was made from the vines that grew in the yard of the house and participating in a game of *Scopa (sweep in English)*, a card game which usually degenerated into a form of controlled violence with the participants butting each other akin to clashing rams. But what he did not expect was to be greeted on the porch of the house at 80, Brook Street on that humid August night of 1919 by a young Seventeen year old girl, who four years later, would become his wife.

Pasqualena Marchegiano, later to be shortened to Lena, was the archetypal Italian Mom, large and homely, with a generous, caring nature which shone through in everything she did; in the myriad photographs that she would appear in later in her life, always she was depicted with a smile that was as deep as it was infectious, many of these images concentrated on her feeding her then famous son huge almost overgenerous portions of spaghetti and meatballs *(see above)*, always the matriarch devoted to her family, always the caring mother, and always that smile. She had grown into a big woman through the birth of seven children, a fondness for Italian food *(inherited by her eldest son)*, and genetics, for her father was a mountainous man (7). Yet on that August night on the porch of her family home she had been young and slim, with long flowing strawberry blonde hair and piercing light brown eyes.

Like Piereno, she too had been born in Italy, in the quaint village of San Bartolommeo, on the outskirts of Naples in the year 1902. Unlike her future husband however her roots are far easier to trace.

She was the sixth child of Luigi and Concetta Picciuto (*later to be softened to Piccento*). Initially the young vivacious Pasqualena harbored dreams of becoming a teacher, but was forced to give up her learning when her father (*who had come to America alone in 1914*) summoned her to be with him in 1916. Settling first in Milburn, New Jersey, where she and her elder Sister Ermilinda quickly found work in nearby Newark at a textile factory. Here they would remain until the spring of 1917 when Luigi found better paid employment as a Blacksmith in Bridgeport, Connecticut. It was a move that was to prove both fruitful and appallingly sad.

This new location allowed the sisters to gain better employment for themselves at a munitions factory making the casings for bullets that were being shipped to the Allied forces overseas. Through a process of contributing to their fathers wages (*both girls were given an allowance of fifty cents a week the rest went into a pot*), the remaining members of the Picciuto family were able to make the arduous journey from Italy to join them in 1918, it would take them a month to arrive.

At first their time spent together following their arrival would be a relatively happy period, but tragedy was to strike, for in the New Year of 1919, Pasquelena's youngest brother Nicholas would be killed whilst riding on a cart his father had made for him that very Christmas. The poor boy had gone under the wheels of a truck, death was instantaneous. Crushed by the loss of his beloved son, and prompted by the marriage of his eldest daughter

Carmella to a young Brocktonian by the last name of Cappiello whom she had met whilst he had been stationed at a forces base near to her Connecticut home, Luigi, as the patriarch, made the decision to move the whole family to this Massachusetts City. It was a move that was to be the last and most decisive upheaval the family would make, for soon they were to set up home in the whitewashed brick house on Brook street where Pasqualena and Piereno were destined to meet.

For the couple it was the proverbial love at first sight, "Mamma mia, this man's for me," Pasqualena was to confide to her work colleagues at the garment factory where she was then employed. However their courtship was complicated by two things, first the differences in their ages, Piereno was some eight years older that his prospective bride, also, the Italian custom of the day did not allow the couple to spend time on their own before they were married, thus preventing the risk of any pre-marriage mishaps, a child born out of wedlock was heavily frowned upon. Thus it was that they found themselves chaperoned wherever they went, usually by Luigi himself, and then only being allowed together twice a week. "Work comes first," Luigi would tell the prospective suitor, Piereno had no option but to comply.

The couple were engaged in 1920, the proposal coming whilst they, with their ever present chaperone, were attending the Boston Opera house enjoying a performance of *Pagliacci* by the great Italian tenor Enrico Caruso. But it would it would not be untill they attenmded a funfair in Lynn, Massachusetts later that same year that Piereno was able at last to steal the first kiss from his bride to be. The pair had managed to break away from Luigi who, upon their return, was fuming at the temerity of his charges until they broke the news that they had set a date to be married.

The Wedding took place at St. Patrick's Church in Brockton on the seventh of August, 1921. The popularity of the newly married couple was attested at the reception which was attended by more than 150 guests and held at the Families Brook Street house. It was here that Luigi, who was the proudest man in all of Brockton that day allegedly, toasted the Groom and Bride with these very astute words, "May you and my beautiful daughter live to be 100…and may your first born be very famous."

Notes:

1. *Later still he became simply 'Pop'.*

2. *Province of Chieti in the state of Abruzzi.*

3. *Cost of ticket $30.*

4. *Marciano was definitely Mignault's god-father.*

5. *Mignault Sr. had himself, under the ring name of 'The Brockton Blonde Bomber', been a talented boxer previous to the outbreak of the Second World War.*

6. *Many regard this as a familial tale which is invoked from time to time to instill a kind of certainty about his own eldest son's future, even though Piereno himself always denied that he had ever boxed at all.*

7. *"Everything about him was big, he played big, worked big, gambled big, he drank big and ate big, he even talked in a big voice," Rocky would later recall.*

part one   **chapter two**

Hail to the Champ

"Figlio Mia, Figlio Mia, Corra de mama!"

(My Son, My Son, heart of my life -Trans.)

Pasqualena Marchegiano

The young newlyweds settled quickly into their fresh life together first finding themselves a small modest apartment on the corner of Warren Avenue, not far from the heart of Brockton's Italian district. With its wealth of food markets, its own social club, of which Piereno was already a paid up and well regarded member, and just as importantly, easy access to St. Patrick's church where Pasqualena would regularly pray, they were both devout Catholics. The area was perfect. Finances however were tight, as they would be for several years, thus they would forgo a planned honeymoon to Niagara falls, preferring instead to spend their meager savings on furnishing the apartment. Piereno returned to the No. 5 bed-laster machine, the most arduous task at the shoe factory, and Pasqualena found herself once again back at the garment factory where she labored sewing buttons on blouses. Life settled into a calm normality for the pair. That is until one day, approximately nine months after their marriage, Pasqualena greeted her husband with the news that she was expecting, both were delighted as each, especially Piereno, yearned for a large family.

The need for financial security however spurred the naïve expectant mother to continue her work at the factory long past the time she should have been resting. Pasqualena actually continued to toil until a mere two-weeks before the expected delivery date. To make matters far worse, fearing being pressured into giving up her job thus losing a much needed source of income before she was ready to do so she concealed her pregnancy by wearing a tight fitting corset to restrict the swelling of her expanding belly, this was to have heartbreaking consequences for the family.

When the child was eventually born, it was to suffer immediately from breathing difficulties brought about it was believed by the restrictive corset which had not allowed the child to develop naturally in the womb. Tragically the baby died only a few short hours later. Pasqualena was distraught, forever blaming herself for the loss. The family physician, Dr. Josephat Phanuef on his post-natal inspection of the now grieving mother announced the dire news that in all probability she would not be able to carry again. It was news that was greeted with dismay by the entire family who had congregated about the mournful mother and her husband.

Pasqualena however soon began to display her deep resolve, a tenacity which would be inherited by her famous son. She recovered quickly from the loss, so quickly that her husband was astounded by her capacity. It was decided that, despite the prognosis, they would try again for the child they so desperately sought, so ardent was her desire to be a mother and prove the doctor's verdict incorrect.

"If God want me to have a baby, then I have a baby," she reflected later. Her stubbornness and faith paid off when, just three months later, she again was to announce to her overjoyed, albeit anxious husband, that once more she was expecting. This time there would be no concealment for as soon as the news was confirmed she gave up her job at the garment factory, and would never return.

At one a.m on the morning of September 1st, 1923, Pasqualena once more began to experience labor pains. Piereno was not at home at this time as he was working the graveyard shift at the factory and was therefore beyond communication, thus she called her father who immediately summoned Dr. Phanuef from his slumber to attend to his daughter. The labor would not be a long one for at two-thirty that very morning Pasqualena gave birth to a thirteen-pound baby boy. All present held their collective breath as Dr. Phanuef and the nurse in attendance checked him over. This time there would be no repeat of the previous years tragedy, the baby was pronounced strong and healthy. Later that morning Piereno, oblivious to the nights events, would return to be greeted by the wailing cries of his newborn, he would name him, as agreed, after his own father; Rocco Francis Marchegiano.

Legend maintains that to celebrate the birth of the Marchegiano's eldest surviving child, they were presented with a card which was decorated with two miniature boxing gloves, the message on the front read, "Hail To The Champ". Marciano himself later recalled however, "One of the first congratulation cards mom got had little boxing gloves hanging on it above a picture of a baby, it said, 'Welcome to another champion'." The name of the sender is not recorded, but Piereno would carry the card with him always.

For the first eighteen-months of young Rocco's life his parents had no reason to think that they had anything but a strong healthy boy in their beloved son, a son they gave thanks to daily. However it soon became clear that young Rocco was ailing. The infant began to refuse his food, growing pale and weak, again Dr. Phanuef was called to the small apartment. His expert prognosis was that Rocco had contracted Pneumonia, at one stage the child's temperature broke 105. In those depression hit days when antibiotics were not so readily available this illness could prove fatal.

"Whatsa matter, God no want me to have kids," Pasqualena wailed as she kneeled before the icon of Saint Anthony that decorated a wall of the apartment. "I give you my ring if you save my son." She was referring to her diamond engagement ring, the most precious item she owned and which in her desperation she had nailed to the wall beside the icon of the Saint. Father Langly of the nearby St. Patrick's church had even been called upon to perform a small ceremony dedicated to her ailing son's health, yet still his condition worsened. That is until one fateful day when the family were visited by an elderly relative, a Mrs. Paolina Mangifesti.

This ancient spinster approached the now dangerously frail Rocco armed with but a small spoon filled only with warm water, forced the boy's lips apart and began to feed him the liquid, to the amazement of all gathered in vigil the child fed. Paolina advised the infants mother to feed him regularly on chicken broth, to force it down his throat if necessary. It worked, Rocco recovered, the first instance of his displaying the kind of fortitude that would be amongst his trademarks later on in life. Shortly thereafter, Mrs. Mangifesti herself passed away, never to see the child grow. The Marchegiano's saw the arrival of the elderly relative who seldom came before that day, as a manifestation of St. Anthony's aid, and they would forever recall it. This belief was further cemented in their minds when Pasqualena went to retrieve the ring from its place on the wall to donate it to the local church as promised, only to find that the ring had "mysteriously" gone.

Rocco would forever remain acutely aware of how close he had come to death as a baby, "As long as I can remember, mama and poppa told me about the good St. Anthony's intervention saving my life by a miracle."

Throughout the remainder of Marciano's life this "good Saint" was kept busy protecting this son of a shoe maker, but in the end even the patience of a Saint must run out.

Part one   **chapter three**

Childhood

"My mother said I was always destined to be a fighter as I looked so much like one as a young boy."

Rocky Marciano

For the first few years after Rocco's battle with pneumonia he would remain a sickly child. Dr. Phanuef maintained that it was a "medical miracle" that he had survived at all. Thus due to a genuine concern for their grandchild's health and still haunted by the earlier loss, Luigi and Concetta persuaded their daughter and son-in-law to give up their apartment and move into the Brook street house that was the family home. It seemed to make sense for Pasqualena would get help with caring for her son, whilst financially too it would ease the burden placed on Piereno now that he was the only one bringing in an income to care for the expanding family, especially as their second child, a daughter they named Alice, had arrived in 1925. Over the next sixteen years four more children would be born to the Marchegiano's giving them the large family after which they had yearned, two more Daughter's, Concetta, (*or Coonjie*) named after Pasqualena's Mother and known as Conge, in 1927, followed by

Elisabeth "Betty" in 1931, then another son Louis "Sonny" named after Luigi in 1933, and finally some seven years later in 1940, Peter, named after his father, arrived.

In order to accommodate the rapidly expanding family Luigi had converted the top floor of his home into a self-contained flat with living room, kitchen and two small bedrooms where the Marchegiano's could still find some relative privacy. The home itself however was not fitted with the convenience of central heating, hot running water, nor even a bathtub. In its place a large washtub was situated in the kitchen where the children would bathe on a Saturday night, the boys one week, girls the next. To keep warm in the cold winter months the family would leave their upper doors open to catch some heat emanating from the two coal stoves that Luigi would keep burning in his quarters downstairs, one placed in the kitchen and the other in the living room close to the stairs.

It was to be the home where Rocco would spend the majority of his childhood, and as the family grew space would be the only issue that would concern the growing boy. "When am I going to get my own room?" he would ask his mother constantly, her reply was reassuringly optimistic, "Don't worry, someday we'll have a nice big house with your own bedroom." But that big house was a long way off for now, thus he had to make do with sleeping on a mattress in the living room. As Rocky recalled, "There was a rolling bed in the closet, but I only used the mattress. I pulled it out every night and slept on the floor beside a wide-open window, even in the middle of winter. I always liked plenty of air." It was worse for his brother Sonny though who was forced to sleep downstairs!

By the age of four young Rocco would regularly wander from the stoop of his grandparent's house to the facing James J. Edgar playground, a park area that took up the equivalent of an entire city block and was fitted with a full sized baseball diamond, here he would forgo the few toys that had been bought for his pleasure and while away his hours watching the older boys playing ball. For the toddler this was to be his introduction to a sport that he would spend the majority of his formative years obsessing about. If it had been up to his parents however their young son would have gone down the musical route, wishing their son to have a chance that they never had themselves they set about organizing accordion lessons, this soon came to an end nevertheless when they discovered the prohibitive cost of an actual instrument.

At the tender age of Seven Rocco had found himself his first means of earning money. The financial side of life and the process of earning, and more importantly keeping it, would always be a major part of the Marchegiano make up (*"The dollar was his God," observed Al Weill, Rocky's manager in later years*). This side of his nature was due in part to his family's financial struggle; he had learned to respect the value of the almighty dollar and to never squander. "We never knew we were poor though," his brother Sonny would later reflect, "we always ate well." To add to their diet the children would pick dandelion leaves from the local lawns [1], and in the summer months mushrooms from the nearby woods, placing a coin in the pan with the mushrooms, if the coin changed color then they were unfit to eat.

Rocco began by doing chores for the neighbors, all he would earn from these small labor's he un-grudgingly handed over to his parents, save the obligatory fifty-cents for himself, a hangover from his mom's earliest days in America. Once, whilst washing a pair of his pants, his mother found his fifty-cents, when she enquired why he had not spent it on some little luxury, young Rocco would reply, "If I spent all the money, I would have nothing in my pocket, I want to save it so I can buy you and pa nice things." Soon he would be able to present his mother with a necklace that he had bought with these savings, it was an item she would forever treasure.

His first foray into the world of organized work was through delivering the local city paper, *The Brockton Enterprise and Times.* Each and every morning for the next three years he would deliver his cargo to over one-hundred customers who were contributing to his earnings the grand sum of eight-dollars a week. Thus he could be found trudging through rain and snow, hauling the bag up hills and stairs whilst occasionally being castigated for his poor timekeeping (*again something that would follow him into adulthood*), he would offer meek apology only to be late again the following day. On Fridays though, his payday, he would be invited into certain homes for milk and cookies, it was a small perk and besides he enjoyed being out in the open and the feeling of physicality it gave to his still growing body. The only real downside, at least at the beginning, was that his mother insisted that his sister Alice accompanied him on his route. "But my Mamma got over that after a little while," reflected Rocky, adding, "…especially after I had to fight a couple of guys who teased me because of it."

Around this time Rocco was beginning to build up around himself a pack of loyal friends, many of whom would stay with him for the rest of his life. These included such notables as Izzy Gold and Eugene Sylvester who would entitle themselves 'The Terrific Three' based on a Comic strip in the paper Rocco delivered. Together they would plan elaborate get rich quick schemes in Izzy's basement which doubled as their den. To add to this triumvirate there was also Eugene's brother, Nicky Sylvester, a boy with dreams of world stardom as a funnyman, he would act as the groups comic, and later as Rocky's unofficial camp jester. These were joined by a neighbor of his by the name of Vinnie Colombo. Together these boys would prowl the ball park at James J. Edgar, playing as often as they were able, Rocco usually hogging the bat, until some older kids would come along and he would be forced to give up the plate.

By this time he was now growing into a stocky, powerfully framed boy, one who was proving to be a well-rounded athlete, he could hit the ball beyond the boundaries of the park (*some 375-feet*), and was a proven catcher, yet his build did not lend to running. "I learnt to hit the ball as hard as I could so I didn't have to run too fast," he would reflect later.

Baseball was the be-all-and-end-all for the boys back then, they dreamt of being like their heroes Babe Ruth, Joe DiMaggio, and Ted Williams, big league players with big league salaries, they were fed up seeing their father's toil and sweat long hours for lousy pay, they wanted better for themselves and their families. "We were always scared of being stuck in the shoe factories for cheap money the rest of our lives," commented Eugene.

As the boys chased their dreams Rocco was the one who seemed to chase it a little harder, he appeared to be a natural athlete displaying huge amounts of courage and determination even then, always taking the lead, whether at baseball, or the fast growing sport of football. Outside of sports however Rocco was remembered as a rather shy boy, someone who would rather in the shadows. Never a natural academic he would daydream in his classes imagining himself back at the ball park hitting yet another home run, for in sports Rocco always played hard, and he played to win.

"He was a lousy loser, the only thing that mattered was to win," remembered Izzy Gold. "He always wanted to play the best…never the easy games. But if we were losing he would get all fired up…Lots of times he'd win the game for us…But if the Rock ever struck out or…missed a tackle…you couldn't talk to him…he wouldn't be satisfied until he played…again and won…Like in everything, Rocky was more determined than any of us, he was never a good sport about losing."

Added Izzy Gold, "There were guys around Brockton who were bigger and built better than Rock, but they didn't have his determination and guts. I always knew he'd be a winner. He was the kind of kid who wouldn't allow himself to lose. But I figured he'd be a winner in baseball."

Rocco Francis Marchegiano never wanted to be a fighter as a kid. "If he ever expected he was going to be a pro-fighter he'd have been working at it from the time he was ten years old," recalled Izzy again. There was a YMCA in the city that taught the rudiments of boxing, but Rocco never went as he was growing up, often he would see an old grizzled former fighter make his way around the streets, the old pro was suffering from a condition commonly referred to as punchy, his head involuntarily twitching, and his eyes constantly blinking. Rocco would comment to his friends on the unfortunate mans' afflictions; "Jesus, didja see the way his head jerks? See how he has to blink all the time? Nobody should ever let someone hit them in the head. It's the worst thing; it can really screw you up."

He loved to wrestle though, and hit hard in football, always trying to test his strength against the next guy, he yearned to be the strongest kid in the neighborhood. In order to achieve this he had begun secretly to train in the mornings after his paper route, he would begin by running up a steep hill near his home to build his legs and then return to work on his arms and back using an old chest expander that he eventually bent out of shape. Once his friend Eugene came round to see him earlier than usual and found him doing chin-ups from a tree in the backyard, "It embarrassed him," said Eugene. "He never liked the guys to know he was exercising."

Yet as a child, due to his build and roughhouse tactics, young Rocco would occasionally find himself pushed into a fight that he didn't really want. "He never started things, Izzy and me pushed the Rock into just about every fight he ever had. Sometimes he'd even argue that he didn't even want to go after a guy, but we could always talk him into anything," stated Eugene. "He wasn't a fighter," reiterated Izzy, "It took an awful lot to get him mad."

Rocky's first unofficial bout took place when he was eight, and he got mad. Whilst making his way home from school with his friend Vinnie Colombo, they somehow became embroiled in an argument with each other over a rubber ball. Each lay claim to the bouncy jewel and neither was prepared to give it up. Soon words escalated to pushing and shoving, then the inevitable brawl ensued. They battled 'till shirts were torn and knees scuffed and bleeding, Rocco suffered a bloody nose to add to his misery. The fight was eventually declared a draw when both boys broke apart and ran crying to their respective homes. "It was a real brawl alright, there was blood all over Brook Street, and most of it was mine," Vinnie reflected.

Rocco ran weeping to his sympathetic mother, yet he was startled by his uncle John Picciuto, Pasqualena's younger brother who at the time was still living at the house and had been standing out of sight. . His uncle, who had heard the whole sorry tale, did not share his sisters sympathy and accosted Rocco for running home crying when he should have stayed to finish the fight.

The next morning Rocco returned from his paper route to find his uncle John awaiting his arrival. The pair were very close, often they would accompany each other to ball games and wrestling matches in Boston. As Rocco explained, "My pop was always tired after work and never took me anyplace. I went everywhere with uncle Johnny." One time, in late 1933, the young impressionable boy would attend an exhibition of boxing with his uncle at the old Centre Street Arena that was refereed by the then Heavyweight Champion of the World, Primo Carnera, a fellow Italian. "On the way out, Carnera walked right by me and I reached out and touched him,…I really did," Rocco would wistfully recall years later [2].

His uncle had taken the day off from his job at the factories especially to teach his battered nephew the rudiments of self-defense. In order to do this he hung an old army duffel bag packed with rags and sawdust from a rafter in the basement of the house and ordered Rocco to hit it. "For years I punched this bag every day. On account of the ceiling was so low, I had to crouch and hit the bag with a chopping motion. I knocked out Archie Moore and Ezzard Charles with a chop, and it was the same punch I used when I hit that punching bag in my cellar," Marciano mused in his retirement.

Back when he was still a boy hitting the bag he had been encouraged to use both hands at all times by his uncle who himself was unable to use his left due to an accident as a young boy when he had fallen down the stairs of his family home in Italy leaving left his arm withered and virtually useless.

Soon Rocco was adding this newly acquired routine to his growing list of exercises, ostensibly to improve his throwing arm for baseball, but also to bolster his confidence, knowing that if he needed to he could now fight to a finish. It was in fact around this time that he took part in his first real semi-organized bout, it was on July 4th, 1931, in a midget boxing match. As Rocco recalled, "I was eight at the time,…I went into the ring with three other kids my age all of us blindfolded. The idea was that the one left standing was the winner," then as if to answer our question, "No, I didn't win."

There was another, a few years later, this time promoted and organized by a close friend and immediate neighbor who would play a big part in Rocky's future by the name of Allie Colombo. Allie was the older brother of Vincent. The bout took place in a make-shift ring in Colombo's backyard against a local boy named Jimmy DiStasi. "I was about twelve years old, and I already had a reputation of being the strongest kid around." DiStasi was, continued Marciano, "…older and bigger than me. We couldn't hurt each other, because we used great big gloves, but it was a good fight just the same. It was supposed to be a three-round fight, but neither of us got tired after three, so we kept going for ten." Rocky would amusedly add of this off the record bout, "He used to go around after I became champ saying he went ten with Rocky Marciano."

Eventually however his newly acquired fighting skills would be put to the test outside of the ring, and they would leave a lasting impression on his friends.

It happened one winter when the boys had gone to local Flagg Pond which had frozen over in order to ice-skate. At this time they had just started to become interested in the local girls, and knowing Eugene was always the one with the snappy lines they sent him over to one in particular that the budding lothario who was Rocco had taken a particular interest in, yet due to his innate shyness he was unable to approach himself. Thus Eugene skated over and engaged the girl in conversation. Soon however, a large looming presence was seen coming up to the skinny, bespectacled Eugene with a look of thunder, it was the girls erstwhile boyfriend, and he had only one thing on his mind, thumping this upstart who dared speak to his beloved. A short Max sennet-esque chase ensued. As Rocco saw the two hurtling towards him, with his friend wearing a frightened and imploring look, he lost all thoughts of play and launched himself at the bigger boy, battering him with both hands, just as his uncle John had taught him. The fight was over in less than a minute with the larger boy lying helpless on the ice, blood pouring from a vicious gash over his eye. Rocco looked down at his conquest with a look of sorrow apparent on his face, immediately sorry for the damage he had caused. His friends looked aghast at the carnage.

"Once Rocky was enraged, he was like an animal, he really punched the crap out of guys, knocked them right down, blood all over the place, I'd be saying to myself, 'Jeez, why'd I send the Rock after this kid. I've got to be careful who I get him mad at, the Rock's really dangerous'," recalled Eugene.

They would often see the boy around and he would forever sport the scar above his eye. "We always felt really bad about this guy getting scarred up like that," added Izzie. Around this time Rocco's father recalled that his son, "…told me he didn't like to hit anybody for fear of hurting him bad." His Mother added, "Rocco was the best natured child you ever see. I used to spank him for fighting. He never liked it, to hurt anyone. And I no like him to hurt anyone, or maybe be hurt himself."

It was not only his fighting that kept the young Rocco's mother concerned about his behavior as a boy however, for despite being regarded as a generous, caring, thoughtful child he was certainly no angel. "If he had have been he would never have become champion of the world," insisted his youngest brother Peter. Indeed there was a devilish streak in him that was visible then, but would lay dormant throughout his professional career as though vented, yet would inextricably raise its head again in his retirement years.

As his ruggedness with his fists became more apparent he would become filled with bravado leading him to push the boundaries of his own abilities. Once, whilst he and his friends were climbing a tree loaded with ripe cherries, Rocco climbed higher and higher, consuming the small fruits as he went. Suddenly a branch that he was using to support his weight gave way sending him tumbling some twenty-feet to the ground below, breaking several branches on his way down until eventually he landed heavily on his back. His friends assumed he had at the very least broken something, yet Rocco stood straight up and just shrugged off the fall, the pilfered cherries were worth it [3].

The boys now had found that food not paid for was far tastier, they would often turn their hands to lifting a few quarts of milk from the steps of the more affluent area of Brockton, which they would use to wash down the day old doughnuts they had managed to beg off the local baker. Added to the banana's they had stolen from the local store owned by Mike

Delarosa, who once chased the boys down the street brandishing an iron pipe, they regularly feasted well. Later in an act of revenge against Delarosa the gang smashed his storefront window with a baseball. Yet this escapade backfired on them all for although the boys swore it was an accident they would be forced to pay for the damage, yet Mike Delarosa proved to be a decent sort in the end. The families concerned were hard pressed to amass the twenty-five dollars to pay for a new window, so Mike put the lads to work unloading fruit, of course a few went missing, but Delarosa turned a blind eye to that.

Nicky Sylvester, who was two years Rocky's junior recalled in an interview with journalist Rich Bergeron how they would treat themselves to candy when they took a trip to the movies. "We would go to a candy store next to the theater in Brockton, I knew the manager of the theater...and he would let us in. But before we went to the theater I would steal peanuts or boxes of chocolates with Rocky and Rocky would always manage to wear a long coat. He knew I was going to grab a box of chocolates and he would have that coat wide open and I would throw them (*the pilfered goods*) to him full speed and he would lock up the coat and we (*would*) exit (*for*) the theater. We sat chewing on (*the chocolate*) together. Naturally he would be taking three to my one of chocolate."

Eventually their pilfering would rise to the more serious theft of equipment to aid their baseball careers, usually mitts and balls. They stole, not for malice, nor for the sheer hell of it, but because they had no other means of obtaining the things they felt they needed. Most of the younger Marchegiano's would wear hand me down clothes and find themselves at the thrift stores and public assistance offices claiming their coupons that could be traded in for food. There would however come one event that started out as sheer kicks but would lead the boys away from their mischievous ways.

One Sunday after the erstwhile gang had attended Church they were moseying around with little to do when they came upon the idea of ringing the Church's fire alarm. It had been decided that all in attendance would do it so that if they were caught each would rightfully claim that they were as guilty as the next. Rocco rang the bell first, however it made such a horrendous noise that the boys immediately fled. Rocco, accompanied by Izzy Gold, sought refuge in a nearby chicken coop where they were shot at by the enraged owner believing a dog had attempted to feast on his brood. In their speed to get away Rocky ripped the new trousers that his mother had bought him the day before, a rare treat for the boy, and eventually each one of the miscreants were rounded up for they had all been seen by someone who had recognized them.

They were turned over to appear before the local Judge who gave them a stern talking to, and to add to the punishment the boys received a hiding from their fathers, yet the admonishment of the judge, and beating at the hands of his father was as nothing compared to the anguished feeling that he had let down his mother. "It was the worst feeling of my life and an embarrassment to me even now, I guess that was a turning point for me," admitted Rocky. Indeed young Rocco would try never to do anything to embarrass his mother again, from now on in aid to earn a few honest dollars on top of his paper route Rocco would shovel snow in the winter months, and in the Summer he would assist his grandfather in producing wine.

"My grandfather spent most of the time he was around the house taking care of his vineyard. Once a year he bought maybe 175 crates of grapes. It made eleven or twelve barrels of wine. I used to help take the crates off the truck down into the cellar…There was a grape masher in one corner of the cellar, which had a very low ceiling. You'd dump a crate of grapes into it, and then a guy had to push a handle with one hand. I remember I used to do one with the left hand and one with the right. It was quite a thing to be able to squash a whole crate with your left hand." He loved the way it made his arms swell as they worked, he would use this as a method of training, anything that made his muscles work he enjoyed. When his arms felt as if they could no longer go on he would squeeze one more turn from them.

He felt that helping his grandfather in this way not only reinforced his work ethic, but also helped to make up for the time he had tried to fleece him out of fifty-cents by wrapping a small piece of metal in silver foil so that it resembled the coin his grandfather had given him to buy a cigar earlier in the day. Rocco had pocketed the coin and lied that there had been no cigars at the store, relying on his grandfather's poor eyesight he had perpetuated the subterfuge, but his grandfather was no fool and admonished him for attempting to pull such a stunt.

There had of course been other times in which he had successfully fleeced the old man, like the time he and a close pal, Izzy Gold again, stole some grapes from his grandfather that were being delivered to top up his own supply (*it seemed that Rocco was not yet fully redeemed from his pilfering ways*). As the truck pulled up and the driver and Luigi were engaged in conversation away from the precious load the boys crept away with a couple of crates. Luigi and the Irish driver nearly came to blows over the discrepancy in the number of crates paid for as to the number actually delivered. The truck driver tried blaming the boys he had seen hanging around the truck earlier. "Imagine the nerve of the Irish bastard trying to blame my Rocco and his friends," commented Luigi; it would not be the last time that Marciano would be absolved of his actions through a kind of mythic disassociation.

Notes:

1. *This was a practise which Piereno would maintain even when his Son became champion, as recalled Hank Cisco a friend of those who was a close friend of those who steered Rocky to the throne and a regular guest at the camps, "the Rocks father and I used to go outside out front and the side of the house and pick dandelion....he would take it and give it to the cook...and would tell him " YOU, YOU COOK THIS FOR MY SON"....he claimed the broth from the dandelion is good for your blood..."*

2. *It was around this time that he would allegedly tell his father, "Someday when I grow up, I'll be the heavyweight champion and make a hundred-thousand-dollars and take care of you and ma."*

3. *In later life Marciano suffered severely with often debilitating back problems the origins of which may be traceable to this very incident.*

part one   **chapter four**

King of the Hill

"That guy made such a fool of me that he almost made me never want to box again!"

Rocky Marciano

Julie Durham was an inordinately large boy for his age, added to his size was his being one of the few African-Americans then living in the neighborhood consisting mostly of second generation Europeans, he inevitably stood out. But more than this he was tough, many thought the toughest kid on the block. Renowned for his fighting skills he held the coveted title of 'King of the Hill', a mythical title but one worthy of his status and few would lay claim their right to challenge for it.

Julie had been hired by the then manager of the Taunton Lumbar company semi-pro baseball team, one Joe Downey who later was to become a respected Mayor of Brockton. Durham had been placed in the dual roles of both mascot and ball boy, his main task to retrieve the balls that had been fouled beyond the boundaries of the park in which they played. Thus far he had rarely come back empty handed, but on this particular day Izzy Gold decided he needed a new ball. What the hell did he care that big Julie would be running for it as well for Izzy had Rocco.

Eventually the moment came. A fly ball hammered hard and scooting towards the boys who had held out in the near-by Foster Street woods behind the field where the big game was taking place. Inevitably there was Julie, running like a bull to retrieve the ball. When he saw it in Izzy's hands he came right up to the skinny youth and demanded its return, yet this kid, in a moment of extreme bravado offered to fight for it, Julie agreed. Izzy however knew he would not really have to fight for Rocco interjected offering to do battle in his place, it was a response that had been calculated upon.

Thus the two squared up to each other, but, reflected Rocky, "By this time there were fifteen or twenty people around, and someone said, 'You guys can't fight here. There's a ball game going on across the street, why don't you go up to the clearing and fight?' So Julie and me went right up there and starting fighting."

Julie though, despite expectations, did not rush at Rocco throwing unruly punches as the other boys had. Instead he stood his ground and affected a boxing stance, i seemed that he knew what he was doing. Rocco swung wildly, but instead of breaking this boy apart as he had to all the others who had the temerity to assume they could battle 'The Rock' Julie merely slipped the wild, swooping swings, popping his own perfectly timed punches back. One of these swift executed blows caught Rocco flush on the nose knocking him to the ground and causing a trickle of blood to flow down to the now enraged Rocco's lip. He picked himself up as, unbeknown to the battling duo, a large crowd had gathered about them comprised mostly from spectators at the game. Even the players themselves had abandoned their sport and joined the throng to see what all the commotion was about, now they too added to the raucous cheering for the show the boys were eagerly staging.

For a while it seemed like a mismatch, with Julie's fast and accurate fists peppering the young Marchegiano's face red raw. Suddenly, as if a precursor of what was to come later in his life, Rocco launched a looping overhand right that connected flush on the superior fighters jaw and sent him crashing to the floor.

"And when he got up he was spinning and staggering around like a drunk," remembered Rocco. The crowd cheered, and with that one perfect punch Rocco was hailed as the new 'King of the Hill.'

"Now I was the neighborhood big shot," he recalled, "I was still only about twelve." He would continue, "I remember I felt like I just won a world's championship or something. I never got so much attention in the world…From then on, every time one of the kids in my gang got into trouble, someone would yell, 'Hey Rocky!' and I was expected to straighten things out."

Three years later however all bravado and confidence in his fighting ability would take a severe literal not to mention physical battering when that faint spark of interest he had been showing in the sport of boxing would be all but extinguished.

It happened at the tender age of fifteen. Rocco had begun attending the Knights of Columbus Gym in downtown Brockton with his uncle John, a small but well attended temple of exercise that the teenaged Rocco used for training with the weights kept there to improve his strength and agility. It would be here that the young impressionable Rocco received some seemingly bad advice when an un-named bodybuilder informed him that he should stay clear of lifting weights unless he wanted to get muscle bound which in turn would inhibit his agility. Rocco immediately abandoned the idea of training with weights for fear of impairing his performance [1].

The fact that Rocky took this advice so readily onboard is not that surprising for when it came to training methods Marciano could be easily swayed. He would willingly take the advice of anybody who cared to mention a particular technique for self-improvement. As the late Everett M. Skehan would record in his excellent work, 'Rocky Marciano: Biography of a first son':

> Rocky would listen to anybody's advice. If someone told him he should throw in a slightly different way, grip the bat in a certain fashion, or do special exercises to develop his strength, Rocky would devote himself to doing it. And it made no difference if the person had the expertise. A skinny little kid with arms like toothpicks could give Rocky a method for developing his biceps and Rocky would try it, figuring the kid was so self-conscious of his small arms that he had studied every possible way of developing them.

The Knight's of Columbus gym was not just used by weight lifters and locals keen to improve themselves, it was also attended by a small collection of professional boxers who used the place to work themselves into shape for their forthcoming bouts in nearby Boston. Rocco, weighing in at a solid 150lbs [2] at the time was spotted by the proprietor Pop McGowan who felt the rugged boy would make good sparring material for a promising middleweight boxer who used the gym on the odd rare occasion. Full of the exuberance of youth Rocco agreed to spar, what did he have to fear, wasn't he 'King of the Hill.'?

For the first few moments the middleweight, whose name is lost to memory, took it easy on the young man in front of him. Using the willing opponent to perfect his moves as he bobbed, weaved, feinted this way and that, practicing his combination punches, all pulled, all perfectly gentlemanly. At least it was until the youth decided to unload on the man in front of him who was not fighting in the way Rocco thought a fight should be but appeared to be almost dancing with the youngster. This was when all hell broke loose on the upstart as the professional proceeded to teach this kid the hard way what happens when you mistake your ambition for your capabilities.

"That middleweight was a good scrapper," said Rocco later. "The little son-of-a-gun did a real job on me. He made me think twice about the glory and reward of being a pro fighter." At least this was the public claim years later when the youth was the champion of the world, directly after the event however he was disgusted by his own ineptness. "Afterwards, I figured it out, this guy was a pro and I had no business putting the gloves on with him. For a while though, I wasn't to sure I ever wanted to fight again."

Notes:

1. *See footnote 1. Chap. Crossroads.*

2. *Some reports state he was closer to 200lbs which has the ring of truth about it as shall be explored later.*

part one   chapter five

Earth, Wind and Fire

"When the Rock played football or baseball, he would take a physical beating…He cracked his fingers, broke his nose and had his teeth knocked out, but he'd never cry or complain."

Peter Marchegiano

Father Jeremiah J. Minihan was not just the tutor at St. Patrick's Sunday school where Rocco and his friends would be taught the fundamentals of the Catholic faith (*a faith that Marciano maintained throughout his turbulent life*), he was also the coach of the St. Patrick's Church baseball team within which Rocco was a star turn, both as catcher and batter, therefore he held Rocco's baseball career in his hands.

It was through these sandlot games that the teenaged Marchegiano was fulfilling his dreams of baseball stardom for apart from playing on the church team he would also find time to play for the local American Legion team, plus the local Italian Community team. In an attempt to squeeze in as many games as he could in a day he would finish one, quickly run home to change his attire into the colors of the next team and run off to bat once more. Yet it was to the St. Patrick's team that he owed his main allegiance, and particularly to Father Minihan who showed great confidence in the teenagers' ability, often tutoring the lad as he played ball at James Edgar park, and constantly heaping praise upon him.

All the youths from the area respected this man of the cloth, despite the fact that in a community of mostly Italians, he was of Irish descent. Yet in his youth Father Minihan to had been a ball player of great renown, now though, he had devoted himself to his teaching, but still propagated a love of baseball through the boys on what he viewed as his team.

On the afternoon of May 6th 1938, his faith in his star pupil's ability would bear fruit. The boys of St. Patrick's had reached the finals of the prestigious archdiocese championship, they would be playing Holy Name from Cambridge, Massachusetts, at their home ground of James Edgar. The bleachers were full to bursting to witness this close game, a game won by young Rocco Marchegiano when, with the score level at eight each, and with the last hit of the game, Rocco hit a home run. The ball traveled over 375 feet clear out of the park, the first time anyone, man or boy, had managed the feat.

Commented Rocco later, "It was a hanging curve the pitcher threw me, I saw it coming and as it dipped over the plate, I swung and hit the ball solid. It kept going up in the sky like a golf ball and disappeared."

A later contrasting version of this tale would relate that the game was merely a C.Y.O League game and that Rocco won the game not by hitting a home run, but by blocking the plate and tagging out the player who was about to score a certain winning run. I mention this despite Rocky's own recollection because it seems that this is a constant theme of Rocky's early life. For each tale, legend, nostalgic recall, there is always another version which runs parallel yet relates it in a different way which often makes the job of biographer almost impossible.

That which is however established is that later that same year, Rocco and the boys who made up his clique would incur the wrath of Father Minihan, and find themselves almost kicked off their beloved team.

Rocco had for several weeks, along with Eugene, who also played on the team, been skipping Sunday school lessons in order to accompany Izzy Gold, and another uncle of Rocco's by the name of Mike Piccento, to the woods at the back of James Edgar ball park in order to watch their participation in the various games of bootleg gambling which were taking place there. Mike had once won two-hundred dollars on the turn of a card so the bets were high, but totally illegal.

The games themselves were run by a notorious character from near-by Providence who went by the provocative name of 'Peg leg' Pete due to a limp he had mysteriously picked up some time in his nefarious past.

"He brought one of those folding chairs and he sat right down," Rocco recalled. He added, "…then he opened up a chart with odds on it, like in a regular gambling joint, and spread it in front of him. After that he pulled out a pistol and laid it down beside him, just to make sure everyone knew who was boss."

This individual intrigued the impressionable Rocco who always admired toughness in a man; it was a trait, at times almost an obsession that would follow him into adulthood. Indeed it was his own innate toughness which brought him his greatest pride, although he had not realized this in himself until he and his pals were taking part in a game one winter in which one lad sat astride a snow summit and the rest tried to usurp him from his perch by any means necessary. Rocco was the boy astride the summit this day and no-one was able to unseat him. As he was walking home alone in the dark he recalled, "I heard one guy say, 'Gee that Rocky sure is tough,' they didn't see me as it was dark, I knew then that everything was gahna (*sic*) be alright. Before that I didn't really see myself as having anything special, but from then on I knew I had something."

Back to the illegal games held in the woods however and occasionally the boys would be allowed to participate if they brought along enough money. Rocco himself once won fifty-four dollars on a thirty-dollar stake that he had saved out of the earnings from his paper route, but his uncle Mike advised him to gamble it all on the next turn, he did, and blew the lot. Another time the triumvirate of Marchegiano, Sylvester, and Gold, on losing heavily previously, came up with a radical get rich quick scheme which involved alerting the police to the illegal games, and, by means of hiding out near the unsuspecting gamblers, they would, on the arrival of the police, rush out and grab as much money as they could as the gamblers dropped it to evade capture. The scheme didn't quite make them rich, but it did net them a few dollars, before they too had to run or be caught themselves. "The gamblers never figured out who reported them," confided Izzy.

On this one particular day, as they were making their way back from the game, they were spotted by none other than Father Minihan himself who immediately accosted Rocco and Eugene, inquiring why they had not been attending Sunday school. The two boys shame-facedly admitted that they had been gambling, for neither had been brought up to lie, especially to a priest. Father Minihan's Irish temperament came to the fore as he berated the boys for being, 'Heathen's and full of Sin,' not just missing their teachings, but gambling on the Lords day. He threatened to suspend them from the St. Patrick's baseball team, a punishment calculated to hit right at the nerve center of the young blasphemer's. From then on they attended Sunday school every week; they knew the threat was serious. However they continued to go to the gambling games as well, the promise of easy money was far too tempting.

It was it seemed a temptation that paid off for one day Izzy Gold got lucky; he left a game with a little over five-hundred-dollars crumpled up in his sweating hands. As the three of them had clubbed together to scrape enough for a stake that day the winnings were split three ways, this they stuffed into a cigar box and hid from prying eyes until the Brockton Fair arrived in early September, when they promptly went out and blew every penny and for a week were kings.

It was whilst here that the young Rocco would chase down a balloon for the burlesque Queen Sally Rand who was rehearsing her infamous bubble dance which had seen her arrested no less than four times at the recent world's fair in Chicago for indecency. Rocky recalled that, "She had all her clothes on though." There is no mention as to whether this disappointed him or not.

It was also at around this time that the Marchegiano's finally moved into their own home at 168 Dover Street. Built in 1925, this two-story, 10-room, 4-bed wood shingled house which was literally across the road from the old residence they shared with Luigi over on Brook Street, and more importantly for Rocco a mere stone's throw from the entrance to James J. Edgar Park, would remain the Marchegiano family home for decades to come.

Finally the family had seemed to have settled into a kind of peaceful normality. Piereno was the patriarch in his own house now, and they would all live by his rules, which were, in his mind at least, simple plain and fair. No talking at the dinner table, food was to be eaten and enjoyed, there was plenty of time for talk later, one glass of wine for each family member after the main meal of the day, even the children, but only one. Piereno made it quite plain what would happen if he caught the children drinking more than this. And most important of all, never, ever do anything that would bring shame on the good name of Marchegiano. Yes it seemed like the worst was behind them now, yet come late September of that very same year, they were lucky to be left with a house to live in at all.

On the morning of Wednesday September 21^{st,} 1938, the Marchegiano's, along with the rest of the state of New England, had awoken with a strange sense of foreboding. There was very little sound, no bird song to fill the breakfast silence, and that sky; it was almost yellow in appearance. As the day wore on they would watch the clouds in that sky race by, not float as usual, whilst keeping one ear to the broadcasts emanating from the radio that were warning the residents of Brockton to brace themselves against the incoming 'Long Island Express', the name that has in retrospect been tagged to the worst Hurricane in the state's history, a natural disaster that in the ensuing hours would claim almost 700 lives.

Brockton, in the face of it, would be relatively lucky, for the city sat on the edge of the destructive path. Yet still they experienced winds of up to 121 MPH.

The Hurricane had landed first on Long Island at three-thirty in the afternoon, torn through the outer edge of New York where a cinema playing a matinee performance had been wrenched from the ground. The Hurricane carried not just the cinema but also twenty people with-in, including the projectionist, some two miles out to sea, where all were drowned. It then scythed a path through Connecticut, Rhode Island, and into Massachusetts at approximately half-past five, before moving on to New Hampshire, Vermont, and finally dissipating over artic Canada at about ten-o-clock that evening.

At its peak the eye of the storm was some 50 miles in diameter, and the force of its winds stretched out to an astonishing 500 miles in radius; measured as a category 3 on the Saffir-Simpson Scale, it caused waves of destruction as it smashed through the mostly wood shingled houses that stood in its path, tore down bridges and left the residents of near-by Providence under some thirteen feet of water. Those in Brockton would recall seeing tree's literally ripped out by their roots, and the white-washed buildings turned green by the debris that had been churned up by the winds, yet Rocco's small kingdom had escaped relatively unscathed.

"We were lucky," recalled Rocco, adding, "I remember seeing tree's blown down and tiles scattered about from the roofs, but compared to the scenes we witnessed in the papers of Providence we had nothing, it was fun for us kids, but not for them (*in Providence*)."

With the storm now over, the youngsters of Brockton could get their minds back to their schooling for they had enjoyed a brief vacation due to the closure of the school's whilst the surrounding area's had been cleaned up in the Hurricanes aftermath. For Rocco (*now sixteen*), this meant the approaching football season. He was at that time in his sophomore year at Brockton High School, when he approached the School's football coach Marion Roberts about a place on the varsity eleven team. Coach Roberts rarely played sophomore students in his team, but was impressed by Rocco's ruggedness, prompting him to cast the teenager as a center on the team during the 1939-1940 season.

Remembered former assistant coach Charlie Holden, "He (*Rocky*) played nearly sixty minutes a game all season, he was a rough, tough, powerful kid…who never got tired and never got hurt."

It had thus far been a disappointing start to the season for the team who were at that time the defending state champions, they had seen a record twenty-two game winning streak slump to only five wins in their last ten games. The inclusion of Marchegiano wearing the Red and Gold jersey of his team, and sporting the Number 1 on his back, would not however herald an unparalleled turn in events, but he would bring the fans to their feet during a game on Columbus day (*October 12th*) against New Bedford when he intercepted a pass and ran 65 yards for the only touchdown of his short career.

"When he intercepted that pass he wanted to score a touchdown. I never saw him run that fast. He dodged and weaved to avoid being tackled, and when he reached the end zone," remembered Izzy Gold, "he was so pooped, he laid on the ground and huffed and puffed. What determination he had."

Rocco himself recalled it more realistically. "I was lucky in that I intercepted the pass over by the sideline and ran straight down the line, I needed help though, and I got it. One guy even blocked out two guys for me. Even at that, however, I didn't score the only touchdown of my career standing up. I was so slow that I was nailed from behind on the one-yard line and fell over the goal line."

Shortly after the conclusion of the football season in the Fall of 1940, as the main display window outside the offices of the *Brockton Enterprise* on Main Street would declare, a minor earthquake had been felt in and around Brockton. Rocco, on the other hand would make his own earth moving announcement, it would be amongst the most important decisions of his life as he broke one of his father's cardinal rules and announced to his parents one morning over the meal table that he was quitting school.

His decision had been determined through several factors, firstly there was the plain fact that he just didn't care that much for school and was struggling with his studies. As assistant coach Holden reflected however, "He could have studied, he could have made better marks, he was capable of it." Another reason though was that he had been offered a place on the Brockton High baseball team, but the coach of the squad had a rule that forbade the boys in his team from playing for any other team thus Rocco, being deeply indebted to Father Minihan struggled with the thought that he would have to stop playing for his beloved St. Patrick's. Plus there were the sandlot and semi-pro games in both baseball and football to be played where Rocco could earn up to fifteen-dollars a start. "That's where I got this busted nose, not fighting, but getting stepped on by one of my own guys in a sandlot football game," Rocky Marciano would recall; yet the deciding factor that caused Marchegiano to sever his ties to schooling was a purely financial one.

For a while now Rocco's fathers hours at the factory had been limited because of his recurring illness due to the gassing he had received during the war, thus family finances had taken a turn for the worse. Rocco was already toying with the idea of getting some extra hours on top of his paper route in order to contribute to their welfare when his uncle John informed him that there was a vacancy with the local coal merchant which would bring him in four dollars a day.

"He said I was getting nowhere at school, which was true, and he pointed out that I could really help at home by bringing in a few dollars."

Rocco took the advice, soon he found himself loading coal and delivering it all over Brockton. It was work that he enjoyed, for he was using his muscles all day plus working out in the open, but his mother was beside herself. She wanted to see her eldest graduate and achieve a good education, yet despite Rocco's promise that he would attend night school and graduate there, it was to cause friction for a while between Pasqualina and her brother John, one that would be eased only by Piereno's interjection. He could see the sense in what his son was doing, and it made him proud that he had brought up his child to put his family first for they all desperately needed the money that an extra income would bring, beside, wasn't Rocco destined to be a great athlete someday, a baseball star as big as Joe DiMaggio.

"Just remember, don't you ever let yourself end up in the shoe shops. Now, promise me you won't do that," said Piereno sternly, It was a promise that Rocco would make, but could not keep.

He would remain at this job for the next three months, yet the daily grime bothered him immensely. Eventually he would quit to work in a candy factory mixing the chocolate in large vats at 60-cents an hour. He would regret this move almost immediately referring to it as, "Like being in jail, they kept the windows shut all day, and the smell of the candy made you sick."

The situation became desperate for Rocco to the extent that he was forced to enter a vocational training program in, of all things, shoe making. After all his promises Rocky found himself working with his own father at the Stacey Adams factory, that very place he had vowed never to end up. As a child he had delivered his father's dinner here, standing on the street he had launched a wrapped roll of sandwich to the waiting Piereno who was leaning out of a second-story window, yet up until this time he had never been inside.

At first he enjoyed the work, starting at the very lowest rung as a floor sweeper he soon worked his way up to 'last puller' which involved pulling the leather shoes off the wooden shoe shaped molds. He loved the feeling of power this tedious job gave him in his arms. Daily he would attempt to perform this duty faster and faster, pumping up his arms and upper body. Despite the unexpected bonus of working side-by-side with his father, and the feeling of camaraderie he developed with the older Italians in the factory he began to suffer symptoms of claustrophobia and an allergy to the leather dust and smell of the curing ovens. At first he tried to alleviate his suffering by daydreaming about his prospective baseball career, for this was still his biggest dream, however within a month of starting he was forced to quit the factory vowing never to return, this time it was a vow he was to keep.

For now though he was to go from one job to another in quick succession, work in a wire factory, a dish washer, a short order cook (*where he could eat all the food he wanted*), and next onto work as a landscape gardener which he enjoyed.

"I liked the pick-and-shovel work a lot better than being in the factory. I couldn't stand being cooped up all day; I had to be out in the air. I saw what the factory had done to my father and I didn't want that to happen to me, but there didn't seem to be much for me."

Once Rocco landed a plum job digging ditches, but to do so meant you had to pay dues to the workers union, the foreman told him that he would pay the costs and that Rocco could pay him back out of his wages each week, eventually Rocco paid back his dues, and was then laid off. Eventually however he would land a job in a construction gang paying $1.25 an hour.

"We could work as long hours as we liked, and I made big money overtime. Once I gave mom the closed envelope and she opened it up and counted out 150-bucks. I felt sorry for pop that day. He sort of hung his head when he saw me, a seventeen-year-old kid, come home with all that money. Until then, the most he ever made in a week was about forty bucks."

The pay at last was good as America had by this time recovered from the economic collapse of the early thirties only to enter the Second World War, a war that had been raging in Europe since 1939, as a consequence of the Japanese attack on Pearl Harbor. Rocco was put to work first clearing brush ground for a blimp hangar, "I got to swing a sickle all day. It (*was*) terrific exercise for my arms and legs." Then he would move on to help to build Camp Myles Standish Embarkation depot in nearby Taunton; it was a place he would get to know well in the very near future.

"But all this time I kept playing ball - baseball in the summer, football in the winter - as many as eight games a week. After all, I was still only a kid - sixteen, seventeen - and only out for a good time off the job." A good time off the job meant dates. Young Rocco, although ostensibly shy, was still quite a hit with the ladies. He would take them to dances or the movies, usually, but not always, escorted by his sister Alice. One date that never happened would however remain indelibly stuck in his mind.

"It was 1941 and I was due out on this date, I don't remember her name now, but we were due to go to the theater to see a movie, the boys were bulling me about it, so I called the date off, I'm glad I did, as the theater burnt down that night."

The theater in question was the Strand Theater, a building with a 1,685 capacity. Fortunately at the start of the blaze at approximately half-past midnight, the place was empty. It was however to be the worst catastrophe for American Firefighters until the horrific events of 11th September 2001 for some thirteen would lose their lives that night as the roof of the building collapsed on top of them. No one is sure how the blaze started, it is believed that a smoldering cigarette butt could have been to blame for patrons who had earlier sat through the movie 'Secret Evidence', a crime drama, had reported smelling smoke. Nonetheless however it started the event remains the worst single tragedy to hit Brockton, and a monument now stands on the spot today.

Rocco continued to be mindful of his promise to become a big-league ball player. Over the ensuing years of his youth he would continue to strive towards his dream, however as 1943 moved into view there were no scouts for the major-league teams hammering down his door with offers and contracts, thus he resigned himself for the time being to his work, hoping for a brighter future. It was a future though that even he had never dreamt off, and it would all begin in March of that very same year.

Part Two: January 1943 -- March 1948

The Lost Years

part two **chapter one**

Private Marchegiano, Rocco F. / 31-301-298

"The Army was just kicks to me, it beat the hell out of working for a living."

Rocky Marciano

The war in Europe had been raging for almost four years before the teenaged Rocco received his calling up papers in February of 1943. It was a day that his mother had been dreading but ultimately expecting.

Over the final few weeks before his departure Rocco acted as if all was normal, not for him the cares of going to war which seemed to so affect his mom. "I kept telling her not to worry, that everything would be fine, but it didn't help," said Rocco, continuing, "…even telling her that I'd go there and show that Hitler a thing or two."

In fact the carefree youth looked towards his time in the Army as just another job. "I almost thought it was a soft-touch since it meant 'steady' employment with a nice big allotment check going home every month," he would admit later. "I figured whatever they made me do it would be easier than the long list of lousy jobs I had been slaving at before I was inducted."

On the morning of Thursday March 4th, Rocco Marchegiano marched alongside 52 others (including his close friend Vincent Colombo) from the City Hall where the day before they had posed for a group photo with the Mayor of Brockton himself who had addressed them with the usual diatribe about doing their best and how proud the City was of them. The Marchegiano family followed his march to the Brockton railroad station to await their eldest son's departure. A band was playing the Glenn Miller hit of the time, 'Don't sit under the Apple Tree' a rather melancholy tune about the pitfalls that would befall a sweet-heart if they were to cheat on their estranged love whilst away. "Don't worry, ma," Rocco was reported to have said in trying to reassure his mother again. "Look at these other guys going with me, I'm no better than them, I'll be okay." Yet as the train pulled out of the station at 7:27 a.m and headed towards the embarkation center at Camp Myles Standish, the very place Rocco had labored to erect only a few months previously, none of the family gathered there knew when, and indeed if, they would see their beloved boy again.

This new, very raw, recruit would spend his first week at Myles Standish undergoing the most basic of preliminary training before moving on to the main training depot at Fort Devens, Massachusetts. Here he would be given his physical exam before being assigned to a brand new outfit, the 150th Combat Engineers. "They must have taken one look at my thick neck and type cast me as a 'worker'…and boy did we sweat. All we were was ditch diggers in uniform."

Due to the shortage of officers a staff-sergeant was placed in command of the platoon which was broken down into three squads, the tallest man in each group being appointed leader. His badge of rank, a piece of white tracing tape tied around his arm!

It was here that Rocco, now a buck-private, and for the first time in a long while merely another nondescript name in a vast throng of soldiers would be taught the rudiments of warfare whilst being schooled in his role of maintaining and preparing track-ways and ditches for the troops under battle conditions. He was not a front-line soldier, yet was prepared to fight should the need arise.

Whilst at Ft. Devens it was not all work, although very little furlough was given, the men would occasionally sneak out under an unprotected perimeter fence into the nearby town of Devens itself, other times they would be treated to shows brought in especially for the entertainment of the troops.

A break of sorts to the almost monotonous routine would also arrive when Rocco was involved in the building of an entire training village at Camp Edwards, near Cape Cod in Massachusetts, the whole undertaking taking a mere three days. First land was cleared, then buildings erected, finally came the painting and realistic settings to be put in place. The project was completely laid out as would a genuine German town be, even the street signs were in German.

Tragedy would also be introduced to young Private Marchegiano here too when, on August 19th, two men drowned whilst practicing an assault crossing of the Merrimack River in New Hampshire. The boats were overloaded with men and equipment, their combined weight forced the front end of one boat to submerge whilst the force of the engines pushed the stricken craft completely under.

With-in just a few short weeks of this disaster Rocco would again be on the move back to Myles Standish. Whilst here would occur a turning point in his life, although seemingly innocuous at the time.

It all started simply enough. Rocco, at seeing a skinny private being berated by his overtly aggressive supply-sergeant, as he had done so many times before in civilian life, stepped up to intervene (1). The sergeant, wishing to teach this insubordinate soldier a lesson issued an offer to fight him in the camps gym later that evening, away from prying eyes. Marchegiano was not one to turn down such an offer and unhesitatingly agreed. However, as fate would have it, the units captain heard about the proposed affray and intervened to the extent of demanding the affair be settled in the boxing ring with gloves and all rules obeyed, both assented.

"I wasn't boxing at the time," Rocky would recall many years later, "But I had gained a reputation of being a tough guy because I was pretty rough in football and baseball. I also fooled around with a couple of wrestlers who tried to pin me, but they couldn't. So I agreed to fight this guy in the ring as the captain suggested."

At the bell an eager Rocco rushed at his foe with both fists pumping and with-in seconds all arrogance had been beaten out of the now suppliant sergeant as he lay on the canvass and informed the captain, acting as referee, that he didn't want to continue. "I hurt the guy pretty badly," remembered Marciano.

Impressed by this soldiers savagery in the ring, the captain offered to make him part of the post's boxing team, "…it was either doing KP (*kitchen police*) or boxing in the Army, and you know how I like to eat…and how I don't like to do the dishes," Rocky wrote to his mother. But before Rocco could take full advantage of this offer he became one of the numerous recruits who were used to bolster an already flagging unit, and was duly re-assigned to the 348th Combat Engineers under the leadership of one second-lieutenant William Roy, known affectionately as 'Boots'.

He would get little time to settle in before he was moved swiftly by train to Halifax, Nova Scotia, in Canada, arriving on 29th October, 1943; his departure overseas was now immanent. The following day, loaded with full pack, Rocco would board the former British luxury liner, HMS Mauretania, now made over into a troop carrier upon which he, along with the myriad other GI's *(over 1400 men in total)* set sail for England. Pvt. Marchegiano would not set foot on American soil again for over a year.

The journey itself took almost ten days to complete. The liner, sailing without escort and zigzagging every seven minutes so as to minimize any possible U-boat attack, was no longer luxurious. It was also vastly overcrowded meaning most on board had to sleep where they could, on the floor, on dining tables, a few lucky ones were even able to find themselves boxes to sleep in, thus affording themselves a very simple privacy.

In order to while away the tedium of time at sea, Marchegiano decided to enter a game of blackjack. Borrowing 25-cents from a buddy he experienced a winning streak, turning that quarter into eight dollars. Riding his luck he proceeded to stake his money in a poker game garnering a return of fifty dollars. Feeling now that luck truly was on his side he threw it all into the massive game of dice that involved most of the men, including the crew aboard the Mauretania. It was a gamble that paid off for he would walk away with a little over $1,300, more money than he had ever seen in his life. He was not destined to keep hold of any of it for long however for as he explained to author Bob Cutter in 1954;

> I learned a good lesson from what happened to that dough. When we landed in England, every guy in my company put the touch on me since I was the only fellow left with any money after the crossing. Like a dope I loaned away

almost every dollar, but few of them ever returned. I paid the guy who loaned me the quarter a good share of my winnings and he ended up way ahead of me when it was all over. But it was all worth it because it really brought back to me the value of money, even when it's easily gotten. - I had always been thrifty when I was a kid, but I had forgotten myself in the heat of winning all that money (2).

Finally arriving at the docks of Liverpool, England on the night of 9th November, Marchegiano, along with the rest of his company, disembarked with their full field packs consisting of M-1 rifle, blanket, mess kit, changes of clothes, personal items, wool overcoat and helmet. To a man there is little doubt that they were glad to finally be ashore.

Hardly had the sea-weary soldier time to breathe though before he was quickly ushered aboard a troop train heading for the coastal town of Swansea, Wales, and from there in quick succession on to a double-decker bus to camp Manselton, a small village on the Mumbles, just outside of Swansea itself. Here he would engage in amphibious training consisting of boat embarkation, bridge building and maintenance (*both pontoon and bailey*), planting and recovering mines and general preparation for the expected invasion that was to come.

Occasionally he would find himself wrapped in a green wool blanket perched atop a palliasse-mattress which was no more than a potato sack stuffed with straw, whilst sequestered on the near-by Mumbles pier overlooking the Bristol channel for any signs of German ships. At the time the United Kingdom was still braced for a possible invasion by the German forces. Swansea itself still bore the scars from her bombings only the year before.

It was not the most comfortable of times for young Rocco, as then second-lieutenant Roy would recall in 1990, "The fog and cold of Wales was so penetrating, I can feel it yet. Seldom did we see the sun that winter." He would continue, "We marched over the countryside several times each week. Most of our marches were twenty-five to thirty miles at a time with full field packs and carrying our rifles. Needless to say we were in excellent physical condition." This may go some way to explaining an older Rocky's obsession with walking, for he would think nothing of hiking some fifteen miles in the morning before his real training began. Recalled his future trainer, Charley Goldman, "It got so's I had to force him to sit down and rest before he exercised, the guy would just get up and walk out the door and not return for a couple hours, I swear he was shorter than most 'cos he wore his legs down with all that walking."

But back in the winter of 1943/'44 it wasn't all work and no play for the now twenty-year old private for along with occasional games of soccer played on the sandy beaches there would also be baseball, a popular pastime which would be watched by the local children who would return lost balls with the reward of a stick of chewing gum, candy, or even the trophy of a felt cap worn under the helmet of the American servicemen [3]. On several occasions trips to London were organized where Rocco would sleep in billets (*British barracks*) and tour the sights of Big Ben, Tower of London, the Wax Museum and Piccadilly Circus. For the first time young Marchegiano found himself free to indulge in the passions of youth. There are rumors he played the part of the archetype American serviceman, over-paid, over-sexed, and over-here, to the full.

"Oh yeah he liked the girls," reported a former GI who served with the future champion [4]."And more than that, he loved to fight, both in the ring and out (*a prelude perhaps to his turbulent retirement years*)."

Amongst the alleged skirmishes that Marchegiano was involved in include knocking another soldier through a glass frontage of the Forte Ice-Cream parlor in Mumbles; flooring no-less than four Military Policemen who arrived to stop a fracas between himself and another soldier outside the Castle Hotel in Maenclochog; breaking up a bar brawl in a Swansea pub by knocking cold nine soldiers before 'the snow-drops', a term used for the Military Police who wore white helmets, arrived and they all ended up in prison, the list goes on.

Most of these events can be taken with the proverbial pinch-of-salt however, legends which have grown up over time since his ascendancy to the heavyweight throne and beyond by locals eager to fuel his status in Wales. One such is the myth regarding his supposed feat of knocking out a cart-horse with a single punch to settle a bet. However one such incident is attested to by Rocky himself, and it was yet another brawl in a bar.

"The pub was called the Adelphi, I wrote the name down just in case (*anyone*) had anything to say on the matter," asserted Marciano who was at the bar drinking variously milk or coke according to the accounts, when he was accosted by, "…the biggest fellow I've ever seen before or since. I guess he was as tall and as well set-up physically as Primo Carnera.

"Well, this guy had a few drinks in him and clearly didn't like 'Yanks'. He insulted us at every opportunity and, when he called me a name that no red-blooded man can ignore, I took action.

"First I objected and asked him to apologize. He roared another insult, got off the bench and rushed at us. One of my pals yelled, 'You're the fighter - take him'. I discovered that the big guy could box well and hit hard. I had to get him in a hurry or take a beating for sure, so I threw a wild haymaker. Lucky for me, it landed on his jaw. He went down like a log and stayed on the floor, blood pouring from his mouth.

"Just then a couple of Australian soldiers, drawn by the uproar I guess, entered and looked at the fallen giant in amazement. One of them asked how many of us it took to kayo him, and when they learned that I had done it alone, they were flabbergasted. After we had explained how it had happened, we brought the big guy to his senses. He turned out to be a pretty good sport and shook hands with me. Told me he was the Australian regimental champion, which I hadn't realized because he was dressed in civvies, and that he had never been kayoed even though he had fought some pretty good English and Australian pros. I was mighty glad I had landed the first sock, you can be sure."

There is also evidence which suggests that around this time Rocco was taking part in organized, although unrecorded amateur bouts for his Regiment, for to do so meant he was allowed the weekend off during which he would, as Rocky himself recalled to the novelist John Summers in 1965, "…get the Mumbles train into Swansea and get off at Rutland Street in the centre of town and make for a gym that a Welsh heavyweight called Jim Wilde used to run just by Swansea railway station."

Later, when this nondescript serviceman had found fame as heavyweight champion of the world there were those who came forward to relate their tales of forgotten bouts against the then champion in those hazy days during the war. Included amongst them was one Irwin Moidel, Deputy Sheriff of Anderson, Indiana, who recalled fighting Marciano in England and winning a decision over the future titlist [5].

The vast majority of sources for these alleged bouts however are purely anecdotal yet most are believed to have taken place in the market hall of Haverfordwest against Welsh and British servicemen.

There were bouts too held in the RAF base at near-by St. Athan's where, famously, one Jack Matthews, who would go on to represent both Wales and Britain in international Rugby during the 1950's remembered facing the then Marchegiano.

"I was part of the boxing team of the Welsh National School of Medicine at Cardiff University. We went to St. Athan to box the RAF team and Marciano was in the team. As I climbed into the ring inside the St. Athan gym, his team-mate told me 'Rocky has knocked out his last six opponents.' I replied, 'well, he won't make it seven.' And I was true to my word!

"It was a four-round contest and no winner was declared," recalled Matthews with a hint of pride in his eyes. But the remarkable Dr. Matthews, who was eighty-eight when he related his story to an eager Welsh Media back in 2008, quickly pushed this pride to one side as he continued, "I can't remember much about the fight, I don't think about it. It's just something I did. I only fought a few fights. I didn't tell my parents because they didn't like me boxing. I don't know if many people know about it."

Many years later, whilst Rocky was guest of honour at a boxing function in London he gave a short speech in which he admitted that he had lost the first amateur bout in which he had taken part whilst stationed in Wales, that he had either lost or drawn his second, but had won the remainder. Unfortunately there was never any mention of how many or against whom, thus this part of his life, like so much of his time during 1943-1946 is left to speculation and rumour, it is the task of this biographer to piece it together from the fragmentary remains of lost archives, records, and memories; truly a mountainous task.

As that desolate winter moved on into a kinder spring of 1944 training for the now approved invasion of France was stepped up a pace. In April Rocco would join his company in Dorchester, England in preparations for maneuvers at Slapton Sands on the outskirts of Plymouth, Devon. Whilst at Dorchester however half the company came down with food poisoning and were forced to withdraw from the planned exercise that would be code-named 'Exercise Tiger'. This was to be a stroke of fortune for all those who had been taken ill, for the event would go down in history as one of the most bungled operations of the entire war.

In order to get the men involved in the operation used to the realities of invading under heavy fire a command was issued that live shells were to be used by the training vessels stationed off the coast, the only means of precaution to safe guard the men on shore was a piece of white tape stretching the entire length of the beach which denoted the area in which the live fire would be centered. Many were totally oblivious to this 'safety feature' and pushed on past the 'safe' point. Their fate was sealed. It is believed that more men died in this fiasco than were lost in the actual invasion to come.

Rocco Marchegiano had escaped this misadventure, but he would not escape Normandy.

When the men of the company had sufficiently recovered they were moved to Weymouth in Dorset, there to await deployment onto the beaches of France in what was now being referred to as 'D-Day'. Initially the day of reckoning was set for June 4th, as Rocco was not part of the front line fighting force he was due to move out on the following day in order to assist in the moving of equipment and supplies. The actual landings were however postponed for two days due to poor weather conditions, meaning the main wave moved out on the morning of the $6^{th.}$. Twenty-four hours later Rocco himself boarded a boat and headed out to France, some ten-miles from shore he would change over to the landing craft that would carry him and the remainder of his company on to shore at Omaha beach.

They had equipped themselves with bulldozers in order to clear pathways on the beach for trucks and men to move more freely, in this endeavor they cut down trees and used rocks to fill in blast holes that had been gauged out of the sand so that they were more level for the bulldozers to roll over them as they pushed through everything from charred wood to wrecked tanks to, inevitably, decaying bodies. On the following day Rocco's time was spent láying down mesh for the oncoming vehicles, replacing it when it became worn, plus unloading landing crafts as they came in. Rocco spent two-weeks on the beach, he helped to fashion hut-like structures from branches and tarpaulin for he and his buddies to sleep in, and took part in the unpleasant task of picking up the dead Allied soldiers who littered the beach, the job of collecting the German dead was left to German prisoners, all were taken to a local cemetery for burial.

Rocky would speak little openly about his experiences during the war, in fact about his military career in general, it was a period of his life that seems almost to be a time that he wished swept aside. Even in his own ghosted memoirs published in *The Saturday Evening Post* between September and October 1956 he barely makes mention beyond the usual story of his loaning most of his winnings on the journey over to Wales and the public house fracas.

In piecing together Marciano's time during these crucial years I have relied heavily on the recollections of others, many of whom wished to remain nameless, which left me in the unenviable position of having information that could not be completely verified and unverifiable material is ofttimes useless. However, as more became available to me from high sources I realized why so many involved in sharing their information were so unwilling to have their names associated with it (*this is true not just of his service years but of his whole life in general*).

Rocco's military records have been lost, a fire allegedly back in 1972. Nevertheless some of his medical files are still extant, they make fascinating reading and help piece together his whereabouts at a particular time through hospital visits and Doctoral appraisals; for instance I know that on January 18th, 1944 Rocky fractured his right thumb whilst building a bridge out on night manauveurs when he crushed it under a hammer. I know to that his sojourn to the French beaches was short lived for by June 19th he was back before a medical man once again. But this was no case of broken thumbs or, as was the case way back in 1943 whilst

Rocco was still stationed at Fort Devens, food poisoning. This time he was forcibly committed for evaluation by his commanding officer, and not to gage his physical health either, rather his mental state for Rocco Francis Marchegiano was facing court martial...

My source for the following wished to, understandably, remain nameless. Initially he, being involved in an aspect of historical military preservation, had been intent on working a small vignette on Rocky to be included in a roll call of famous former serving soldiers, however, on discovery of the material he decided that, "...not wanting to cause embarrassment to his (*Marciano's*) family and friends, I've given up any thought of a vignette."

That this contact wished anonymity is a prevailing feature of my research, as stated briefly above, there have been numerous individuals who are only too happy to talk about the subject of this biography, ranging from those who barely knew him but have heard from those absolutely in the know. Others also who befriended the fighter before he became a force through to those whose name they feel would be tarnished should they allow themselves to be associated with a truth. The problem seems to stem from the fact that many associate Marciano with a certain type, a type that was created and moulded by that brilliant manipulator Chick Wergeles (*who will appear later in this story*).

Rocky Marciano was an exaggeration of Rocco Marchegiano, those genuine traits in the fighter that were deemed archetypical of the famous personalities from the middle of the twentieth century, i.e. a generous, friendly and open nature, humility, love of family, etc, etc, all things that were in accord with the perceived image of the ideal American, were highlighted. The exact same happened to Joe Louis, an exaggeration of those qualities that were deemed desirable, and the repression of those that were not. Over the years the image birthed through this coupling of media relations and fan courting has become indelibly part of the man, vigorously defended by those who probably should know better [6].

As mentioned, many individuals have offered their stories, opinions, truths, half-truths, etc, yet the conundrum this caused is readily imaginable. I needed verifiable documentation, without this all was useless. Despite the fact that the picture that was emerging was one which not only seemed to sit comfortably with the character now coming into focus, but was the easiest to elicit, almost as though these contacts knew that with their anonymity they had nothing to lose. However, this latest piece of information is documented from one of the highest sources in America, namely the military themselves (7).

Reiterating above, scant records exist concerning Marchegiano's years in the service of his country, those that do, as mentioned, concern mainly his medical history whilst under the calling of his President for the protection of his country. These, as stated, are able to verify Rocco's whereabouts at a particular time through his admittance to some hospital or surgery on a specific date. And in June of 1944 they also showed incontrovertibly that the soldier was facing court martial. That my source discovered this material led him to remark (*and thus in essence validate the above*), "Rocky always seemed to be a decent person, and whatever he did could probably be charged up to his being an immature kid far from home."

It seems strange to me however that the source was unable to locate the exact nature of events leading to Marchegiano's court-martial for a scouring of the material he provided gives up the reason. On a medical card from the 94th General Hospital dated 19th June, 1944, under the heading 'Present Illness' we read: 'Pt. went to English civilians house, and while there states that he discovered he (*the civilian one presumes*) was "a queer". An altercation occurred, the man's pocketbook disappeared. During the rest of the evening he, according to the pt., was "grabbed by another civilian," and the pt. hit him.'

That Rocky was involved in several skirmishes as it were, inter-service, namely amongst other serving soldiers, during his time in the forces is attested above, however, here he seems to have overstepped the line. Sure, fights amongst themselves were turned a blind eye to, in some quarters they were positively encouraged. But an attack on a civilian, regardless of the defence that the civilian in question was "a queer" was unacceptable (8).

It seems Marchegiano's company officer was concerned for his soldiers' mental health and put him forward for evaluation. Was Rocco too punchy, too aggressive?

Results of his psychiatric evaluation were unspectacular yet revealing, he showed no neuropathic traits, as in nail biting, convulsions, sleepwalking, etc, he clashed occasionally with authority, "occasional arguments" in his own words. He admitted to finding work monotonous, being fired from one job because he simply failed to show up regularly. When his sexual proclivities were probed he admitted that he lost his virginity at the age of fifteen, thus dispelling the stories that he was girl shy *(and exonerating all those who said he wasn't)*. There was certainly no evidence in the report that would show this soldier was pathologically prone to violence. The remaining progress of his court-martial and exact events upon the day are lost completely at this time and the following months until his return to America on the 13th of November 1944 are unclear. Nevertheless, in early November he turned up in Rohen, France, which leads one to wonder as to whether he had been plucked from the beaches themselves and ensconced at or near the 94th General Hospital which was believed to be located in France around this time (9) before facing his superiors in military court. But this is speculation, and a dangerous pastime, however what is not speculation is the fact that on 7th December 1944 Rocco turns up at Fort Jay, New York. He is suffering once more from pneumonia, that illness which almost cost him so dear when but an infant. Yet what is telling here on the form headed; Report of Physical Examination of Enlisted Personnel prior to Discharge, Release from Active Duty or Retirement, Marchegiano, under his grade is no longer listed as part of the 348th Combat Engineers as previous, this time the legend 'Gen Pris' *(General Prisoner)* has been inserted.

December 1944 through until March of 1946 is again a blank. That Rocky received the Army of Occupation (*Germany*) Medal may infer that he saw service in Germany at this time, yet the fact that the next solid evidence of his time in the service of his country shows him to be in the Fort Benjamin Harrison infirmary, again suffering from Pneumonia, tends to negate this. For Rocco is listed as being transferred to the hospital from the Fort Benjamin Harrison Disciplinary Barracks where he is believed to be a prisoner, the terms 'DD Susp' on his medical forms of the time infers that he was not on active service but is instead serving a period of confinement, or at least is at the very end of one (10).

There is of course the possibility that this is his second period of imprisonment whilst in service, with his exact records being lost of course this is a possibility, yet with those who could help to entangle and de-jargon these years remaining quiet (11) we are left only with the rare abstract passages with which to chronicle his journey through what is a complicated, jumbled period of his life.

Rocco Marchegiano remained in the Fort Ben (*as the area was cordially termed*) infirmary for a little over a week, bed rest and penicillin were the nature of the days for him whilst resident there, until, at the tail end of March he was returned to duty finding himself at Fort Lewis, Tacoma, Washington.

Had he really spent all that time from June '44 until March '46 interred? His Discharge papers certainly show that he lost some 563 days from active service (*time for which he was not paid, which would no doubt have jarred him immensely*), this equates to approximately eighteen-and-a-half months. That he opted to remain in the forces longer than he initially intended, i.e., the terms of his calling up, 'for the duration of the war or other emergency, plus six months, subject to the discretion of the President or otherwise according to law,' may go some way to affirming that he wished to make up for lost time, and in so doing earn himself an honourable discharge (*the thought of carrying around the stigma of that a dishonourable discharge would bring to him and his family was not an option*). It seems this was a definite possibility for a former veteran acknowledged that it was not uncommon for service men who had, "ended up in the glass house (*military prison*) to have time added on to their terms of service in order to be spared the indignity of a dishonourable discharge, the fact that your guy (*I didn't mentioned that it was Rocky*) never got his Good Conduct Medal goes some way to proving your assumptions are pretty sound."

One can only speculate at the ways in which Marchegiano whiled away his monotonous hours during this possible period of confinement. Perhaps his mind wondered back to his time in Wales, the first time he had tasted any sort of real freedom away from the binds of family.

That Rocky felt a certain emotional attachment to his time in Swansea can be attested to by the fact that in his later years Marciano would frequently return to Wales, inconspicuous in grey ratting cap, worn to conceal his baldness which he viewed as an embarrassment, whilst dressed in battered corduroys which became almost his costume of choice.

"He had more money than I had ever seen yet he always dressed like a tramp, sometimes he would go for days without shaving," recalled his friend Izzy Gold, before continuing. "He'd have a big event coming up and I'd say to him, 'Rock you can't go out looking like that.' But he had it all planned out. When he got to where he was going the people would see him and he'd be kitted out with a whole new set of clothes, even get a suitcase to put them in."

In this rumpled guise Marciano would re-visit those places he had frequented as a soldier whilst munching happily on his particular delicacy, cockles and mussels, eased down with copious helpings of bread pudding and laver bread, a Welsh delicacy cooked out of seaweed, for desserts. Near the end of his life when he appeared lost Rocky seemed to be overcome with a sense of nostalgia, returning to those places where he had found contentment, wherever in the world they may have been.

It strikes me now as I compose this how strange it seems looking back that it was as a direct consequence of the indiscretions of one Rocco Marchegiano that we had Rocky Marciano at all. For had Rocco been a stand out soldier, a nose clean, head down sort of individual then he would have seen out his terms of enlistment and been in Civvy Street around February of 1946, the war having ended in August of '45. Instead he had time to make up and he used it well (12) for it was whilst at Fort Lewis, Washington that he joined both the camps baseball and, eventually, boxing team. It was with the latter that he took part in his first officially recognized bouts. Of course, had he walked in February none of this would have happened and the world would perhaps never have heard of Rocky Marciano.

In later years the then champion of the world would recall his first official boxing match for the base. "The guy I was fighting dressed in the same room with me. He was talking in a loud voice about how he was a pro and what he was going to do to me. He didn't scare me, because I knew I was in good enough condition so he couldn't hurt me. But I knew I could lose, and I wondered what it would feel like to lose in front of all those people.
"We got out into the ring and this other guy was warming up in his corner, shadow-boxing and everything. We boxed three rounds. I didn't knock the other guy out, but I won the decision. The post newspaper wrote it up, and for the first time in my life I saw my name in print as a boxer (13)."
This was the beginning for Marchegiano, for it was in these crucial extra months that Rocco started on the path that would eventually lead to the championship of the world and riches

and rewards beyond even his wildest dreams. However, as seemed to be the way with Marciano, it nearly all came tumbling down around him before the end of April was out...

Notes:

1. I quote Rocky's nephew Louis Marciano Jr. when he mentioned that his uncle; "always favored and protected the common man, especially an underdog, but when it came to the establishment and/or people of supposed higher social standing he could be quite cutting. He would be much more direct in how he voiced his opinion."

2. This was not the first time that Marciano had loaned out money for as childhood friend Izzy Gold would later recall that as a youth Rocco had once loaned out money to a neighborhood kid - when payment was late Rocky reacted in what would be a harbinger of future events and, "...broke the kid's jaw!"

3. It is rumored that Marchegiano's own felt under cap from this time turned up in one proud Welshman's home, no real evidence was ever produced so perhaps it was just someone wishing a connection to the former serviceman who remains a presence of sorts in Wales. Initially I believed that Marciano's connection to Wales was something that still resonated today, yet as good friend and Swansea resident Clare Benfield answered when asked as to whether there was still a real feeling for Rocky in her home Country she replied quite candidly as always. "Sadly, I have to be very honest, and say that no, I do not feel that Marciano is much known about in Wales (and not least in Swansea), or fully appreciated in terms of his historic links to the area." I enquired about The Adelphi the venue for the infamous bar brawl and where the upstairs had been turned into a bar named 'Marciano's' in honour of the former champ. "When I visited Marciano's in Wind Street," recalled Clare, "I must admit I had an overwhelming feeling of 'if only this was my place, I'd furnish and run it so differently', but then it's a very small venue and the Adelphi pub it's above is a drinkers' pub really, but nice enough. Having said that, I'm sure that a lot more could be done with the whole building if someone who was, at heart, keen about Marciano and also had a bit of flair, was in charge/ownership. I mean you could come up with something that had a Marciano 40s/50s theme, say, but not give the impression that it was wall to wall boxing."

4. The former GI wished to remain nameless for fear of reprisal, "It's got so Rocky's some kind of saint you know," he commented, "And the real stuff, the real guy, well you could get lynched for telling it!"

5. *The fact that this recollection was gleaned whilst Sheriff Moidel was in court giving evidence against a female who he accused of assaulting him may not lend an air of complete believability to the result.*

6. *Joe Louis was in essence the symbol of all that was good in a fighter, both in the ring and in personality, even today there are those who deem the great former champ as the ideal champion., Unfortunately for Rocky, where his possible shortcomings have been exposed they have been used against him by a certain sector of the public who seem to be almost envious of the fact that Rocky was able to overcome and achieve, Louis on the other hand is forgiven any foibles, after all he was Louis, the great icon, hell he looked the part of heavyweight king, but Marciano, 'man how the hell did he ascend the throne!!' such vehement defence, or refusal to accept that their hero was human, may possibly be a reason why some factions are so quick to seize on anything that can be used to denigrate the man and/or his achievements - Rocky is my hero, yet the revelations that have been uncovered throughout the research have been met with a certain sense of the obvious about them for at the end of the day the man was a fighter pure and simple, there was rarely science showed in his performances, he was displaying the pure aggression of a savage, every character is made up of various sides, akin to a prism, and it is this rainbow of selves that make the whole, for too long Rocky has lingered in darkness, it is my task to bring him into the light.*

7. *This material came to me whist the draft for this volume was sitting at its intended publishers awaiting finalization.*

8. *You must remember that at this time it was illegal in most countries to be a practising homosexual and many unscrupulous individuals used the often trumped up allegation that the person they had assaulted was attempting to seduce them in order to gain lenience, almost a case of self-defence, it being seen as their masculinity, if not their actual safety, being threatened.*

9. *That the quarters in France contained facilities for holding prisoners is attested by the letters of a former nurse from the time.*

10. *I, grasping at straws, and yes, wishing to believe the hype, muted that he may have been at the barracks in the form of a guard, but was informed that had this been the case his medical file relating to this period would have reflected that, and it did not.*

11. *Wishing to ensure that I had covered all bases, shared this material with Marciano's youngest brother Peter who had kept a rather distant eye on the project since helping to amend a very early draft of this first volume, I realized that this would be of interest to the family and besides had Peter not written me previous in the hope that I could '...come up with a new twist that has not already been written about... -which- ...would be great,'*

yet when presented with the 'new twist' Peter reacted strongly, 'I really don't know where you are going with this - this is one of the things that turns me off with so many writers who want to sensationalize Rocky Marciano's life - I am not aware of Rocky my brother ever doing anything that would put him in prison,' Peter then pulled his support for the project by announcing that he no longer wished me to 'correspond' with him again, he did however rather tellingly with his final line wish me good luck - Peter's withdrawal happened after the bulk of this manuscript had been completed thus there may remain references to his initial support throughout.

12. This extra time would later be glossed over by friends to infer that Marciano had opted to stay on for an extra year, ""You could see his point," reflected a confidant of Marciano's in the hope of validating the claim, "In the Army he had few worries and the allotment checks went home like clockwork. Without trying to belittle Rocky, you got to remember he had little schooling and he knew no trade outside of sports"""""""", but of course the problem was that Marchegiano, had he stayed on for a year would have left the following February, not December '46.

13. It was not the first time that he had read his name however for his exploits on both the High School football field and in the minor league baseball games had drawn the attention of the local Brockton press from as early as 1939.

part two   chapter two

The Smoker

"I would do anything to win, defeat is never an option."

Rocky Marciano

During the first half of the twentieth century when boxing was still on its rise to prominence before hitting her zenith in the turbulent troubled sixties, there had grown a sub-culture of its own that owed its roots to the very birth of the modern sport when most states in America had outlawed "this barbaric spectacle". Indeed boxing would not become universally accepted as an officially sanctioned pastime until the late nineteen-thirties. Thus in order to legitimize a bout between two opponents for the benefit of an audience the combatants would be offered an "exhibition" behind the closed doors of a gentleman's club. Here the self-appointed hierarchy of society could witness a match between two closely matched boxers without fear of the authorities becoming involved. It was such bouts as these that provided the financial means of support for some of the greatest early champions from John L. Sullivan through to James J. Jeffries.

As time eased the inhibitions placed on those involved in the fight-game, and the gentleman's clubs in particular made way for the more accessible members' only clubs, this tradition of matching two combatants against each other for the benefit of entertainment continued on, yet with a slight transformation. No longer was the match viewed purely as a spectacle of scientific self-defense, rather it became a slugfest where fighters were brought in simply to pound upon the other whilst the patrons in such national clubs as Knights of Columbus, Eagles, Elks and Hibernians, as well as the more established Legion posts and Catholic Youth clubs across America were wined and dined whilst the often hapless participants in the macabre theater played out their drama without the assistance of sanctions or regulations to impose some form of order on to the proceedings. However, these shows did provide some purpose to the fighters involved. For one they were paid for their trouble, although their purses were deemed training expenses only so as not to impinge on the participants amateur or professional record [1], secondly they gave the men in the ring experience in the machinations of the game they ordinarily never otherwise would have received.

Yet as the bouts grew more popular a larger number of less discerning members were finding themselves places in these clubs, turning the once socially graceful affair into a riotous night of binging and belligerence where even the fighters themselves would find themselves the brunt of audience jibes if they were felt to be not giving of their all; this once preserve of the dandies found itself fast becoming a microcosm of the boxing world in general. By the forties these events had garnered a name; "Smokers", a term loosely coined from the bilious tobacco smoke that clung about the ring from the readily consumed cigars of the patrons. In fact members even began to associate themselves with the cigar itself identifying themselves in a Masonic way as being members by the puffing, or chewing, of as large a cigar as possible, or, if they did not smoke, the wearing of a lapel pin bearing the image of this tobacco filled log. Thus it was into this carnivalesque atmosphere on the evening of April 15th 1946 that the boxer to be known later as Rocky Marciano would be unveiled upon the world outside of the

Army. It was to be an inauspicious beginning and one many there that night, including Marchegiano himself, would perhaps sooner forget.

That April the erstwhile private Rocco Marchegiano had found himself on a fifteen-day furlough; after spending precious time with his family he would venture out to catch up with members of his clique who were themselves either on leave or de-mobbed (2). Amongst one of the first old acquaintances he saw on his sojourn was the older Alisay "Allie" Colombo, elder brother of Vinnie with whom Rocco had that childish falling out over a ball some twelve-years earlier.

The two would reminisce about their youth (3) and swap tales of their careers in the service for at this time Allie was a master sergeant at the nearby Westover Air force base. He would be referred to later by Peter Marchegiano as someone who was, "…not particularly good at sports, but was a great organizer, he was the one you would go to in order to sort out roster's, for coaching, and to manage a team."

He also was a dreamer, and his dreams rested on his younger friend Marchegiano, especially when he learnt that Rocco was boxing for his base. The two set out, in Allie's mind at least, a failsafe plan to riches. When his friend left the service of Uncle Sam Allie envisaged that he would manage him as a fighter. For sure Alsack, as Rocco would call his old friend, could foresee them both scaling the summit and ruling the world. Later when this idle talk seemed on the verge of becoming a reality he would virtually inhabit the Brockton library. Here he ingested every piece of information he could find on the history and intrigues of the fight-game. For now however the pair parted with Colombo's head filled with optimism and dreams whilst to Rocco's mind the idea seemed nothing more than a relatively easy way to make money for he still balked at the idea of taking up the sport in earnest. Allie would have to be patient and wait at least another year before he could seriously begin to plan his world domination. Yet Rocco's plan for "relatively easy money" would happen far sooner than he could ever have envisaged.

Forever the family man, Rocco was visiting his uncle, Mike Piccento, an avid fight fan himself. Over a bottle of wine, and copious cigarettes, a less endearing habit picked up by the normally health conscious Marchegiano in the services, the elder man was regaled with tales of his nephews prowess in the ring which would lead to uncle Mike propositioning his nephew to the possibility of fighting whilst here home on leave. The soldier was keen. Wheels were set in motion quickly when the very next day Rocco was introduced to an acquaintance of his uncle's, a former fighter by the name of Generoso Caggiano, better known as 'Gene', a promoter of amateur bouts in Brockton. Gene would prove pivotal in the career of young Rocco in the very near future but for now he found himself running a series of "Smokers" at the local Ancient Order of Hibernian Hall and he desperately needed an extra heavyweight to fill the card. Thinking that a local fighter would draw more Brocktonians to the show he offered the bout to the eager Marchegiano. Added to this was the incentive of thirty-dollars (*his training expense*s) to be paid in cash straight into his eager hands at the end of the engagement.

Yet the smoothness of this arrangement was not to be continued, for on the very day of the fight things seemed to be transpiring against young Rocco.

"I had to be there at eight o'clock," recalled Marciano. "And mom picked that night to have a big family dinner for me. She didn't know I was boxing, so I had to eat everything and act like it was just another night going out with the guys. I got to the arena stuffed from all the food, and I was still full when I went into the ring."

"It was a scheduled four-rounder, and my opponent was a tough kid named Ted Lester. Allie found out later that he had been runner-up in the New England heavyweight championships two years in a row. Caggiano had promised somebody more in my class, but said he couldn't get anyone and had to fill out the card with Lester.(4)"

In fact Lester, whose real name was Hendrick Van Leesten, but more commonly known as Henry, had more than a decade's experience, both in and out of the ring, than his opponent this night, it would not be the last time that the embryonic Rock would be faced by such adversity, but now, as later, he would show little respect for such odds.

"I did pretty good in the first two rounds (5)," continued Marchegiano. "But in the third Lester starts working on my body. I backed against the ropes, which were loose, and they sagged. My feet went out from under me and as I stumbled, I kicked him accidentally. The referee disqualified me and gave the fight to Lester. This was my first home-town fight and I lost it."

The referee that night, one Sned McDonald, was nevertheless adamant that the foul had been intentional, later commenting that, as he saw it, "Rocky was leaning back against the ropes as Lester threw a right uppercut, before it connected the kid just plain kneed him in the balls. I knew it, the audience knew it, there was a huge groan from the crowd."

"Most had come to see their local boy fight," continued McDonald. "They went home steaming."

Rocco would slink back to his dressing room to the jeers of the crowd (6). "It was one of the worst feelings I've ever had in my life," admitted Rocky. "I knew I had to win, but I was exhausted. I couldn't even lift my arms, I'd never been so disgusted and embarrassed. I just sort of slipped home quietly that night."

On the following evening Louis 'Sonny' Marchegiano confronted his eldest brother about the incident, Rocco's reply was telling. "Sure I kicked that guy. What was I gonna do, let him beat me? When a man's in a fight, the only thing that matters is winning. Don't you ever forget that. I was disqualified, but I didn't lose the fight."

This was however to prove to be yet another turning point in the then seemingly directionless life of Marciano, for in those first rounds before fatigue had set in, he had fought with a controlled ferocity that had caught the eye of one of the judges at the bout, a former heavyweight by the name of Joe Monte who had, in his youth fought two men who had or would hold the heavyweight championship in James J. Braddock, and Max Schmeling.

Monte saw potential in the rough-house infighting of the Brockton boy, leading this former boxer to confide to Rocco's father Piereno that if the lad knuckled-down, got himself in shape then possibly, just possibly, he might have a future in the sport. On hearing this Rocco vowed to take this sport a little more seriously, give up smoking and be in the best condition he could for when he entered the ring again. It was a promise that stuck (7).

Notes:

1. *None of these bouts were ever undertaken in order to be recorded for posterity. One can only speculate at the exact number that many future champions took part in during their amatuer or early professional career. Famed trainer Lou Duva who was a close friend of Marciano's was adamant that Rocky had taken part in several "smokers" before he ascended to the heavyweight championship, in fact he maintained that these were against Rocky's own brother Peter. Clearly here Lou was mistaken however for Peter was some seventeen years younger than Rocky. However Duva was correct in a way for Marciano did face his brother Louis in exhibitions back in 1951, the result of these unsanctioned bouts would cause trouble for both of them as shall be covered later.*

2. *It would seem too that he would use this time to celebrate his freedom from his enforced captivity yet he seemed to celebrate a little too freely for when he returned to Fort Lewis he brought with him a dose of Gonorrhea.*

3. *Even though they did not generally hang out together for Allie, born December 5th 1919, was four years older than Marchegiano.*

4. *There are a couple of discrepancies in Rocky's memory here, firstly it is doubtful that his mother was unaware that her son was fighting that night, and secondly that Gene was unable to fill the card; I quote from the Brockton Enterprise itself on the morning of April 16th 'Marchegiano, former outstanding Brockton High athlete, playing in the line in football and catching in baseball, will make his ring debut outside of an army camp "squared circles." He is booked to face Art Courtney of Lynn, unless post entries alter the heavyweight class set up. Both tip the scales at 185 pounds'*

5. *According to the Brockton Enterprise Times the following morning however the bout had ended in the second: 'In the only heavyweight bout of the evening, Rocco Marchegiano, of this city, enjoying an Army furlough, lost to Henry Lester, New England championship tourney runner up, when he was disqualified by referee Sned McDonald. Lester was awarded the bout when Marchegiano forgot himself in the excitement in the second round and fouled his opponent…The main bout of the evening as far as the crowd was concerned was the Marchegiano-Lester affair, which made up in spirit what it lacked in finesse.'*

6. *Including no doubt from the one voice who was alleged to have shouted just moments before the incident, "You can't beat him so kick him in the nuts!"*

7. *The initial source for this bout was naturally, 'Rocky Marciano: Biography of a first son' by Everett M. Skeehan. In the biography Skeehan dedicates some fourteen pages to the bout –despite only allowing less than a paragraph from the time of Marchegiano's calling up to this point- giving in-depth conversations between the principle characters such as Louis "Sonny" Marciano, Mike Piccento, Rocky himself and Allie Colombo, et al. That these events occurred at all have to be taken with a pinch of salt for Peter Marciano, Rocky's youngest brother, remains adamant that Skeehan never met, let alone spoke, to either Marciano or Colombo. In fact there is a feeling about the entire book that a lot is fiction, the authors attempt to cover up his shortcomings in research by fattening up the book with alleged conversations that he would never have been privy to thus making the task of those who have followed all the more difficult as we have to sort out the genuine from the authors own musings. There was also an inference that Rocky was, "noticeably overweight" with, "flab that bulged at his…belt." Images of Marciano from just a few short months later –see above- however seem to show a conditioned fighter, so one presumes that by 'getting in shape' was a reference to his smoking habit. Yet there is of course the possibility that Rocco was somewhat puffy at this time coming so soon after his enforced idleness due to the time he had spent at Fort Ben for he was known to put on weight easily when not training continuously. Another inconsistency to Skeehan's account comes from the recollections of a former Brockton*

resident and hall of fame referee namely the late Arthur Mercante, Sr. who in his ghosted autobiography with Phil Guarnieri 'Inside the Ropes' recalled;

> *It seemed like yesterday when Rocky went to my uncle Joe Monte*
> *To see what uncle Joe thought of his prospects as a pro. My uncle*
> *Told him to forget it…*

part two   chapter three

Goodbye Uncle Sam

"Our generation - the ones who survived or were spared - have spent the rest of our lives trying to make every last minute count one way or another. It was the deal we struck privately to keep our sanity and honor those who didn't make it."

Dr. Jack Matthews

With his tail proverbially between his legs, at least on the outside, Marchegiano returned to Fort Lewis to serve out his remaining year, but even his journey back would not be without incident.

Using his influence at Westover where he was placed in command of flight scheduling, Allie Colombo had managed to wrangle his friend a free ride on a plane heading for Washington State. This not only allowed Rocco to spend an extra couple of days at home, but also allowed him to cash in his travel allowance when he arrived back at base. All though did not go to plan, for when the plane touched down on a stop-over in Kansas City, Rocco was uneremoniously bumped off his flight by an officer who needed the seat for himself, fortunately Marchegiano found himself another route to carry him back to Fort Lewis. Meanwhile, Allie, firmly ensconced back at Westover Air Force base was oblivious to the unfolding events when he discovered that the plane he believed his buddy to be on had begun to experience difficulty [1].

The incident thankfully passed with-out major incident and Allie was amazed when he contacted Rocco shortly afterwards only to be informed that he had been completely unaware of how proceedings in his absence unfolded; it was however to be a strange omen of future events.

Safely ensconced back at Fort Lewis, Marchegiano returned to the the amateur boxing and baseball programs, plus to add to his growing sporting resume he became the sometime sparring partner of an aspiring heavyweight from Washington; as journalist Dan Walton recounted to author John D. McCallum:

> Harold Bird, the local businessman who was a great booster of boxers in our area, had been talked into taking over a good-looking young giant named Big Bill Little. Big Bill had dreams of becoming the heavyweight champion.
>
> Bird was tutoring his protégé in Homer Amundsen's gym in Tacoma one day when in walked a stocky GI from Fort Lewis who says he's a fighter and is willing to work out with Big Bill.

When he gets his tights on and with those short arms, hairy chest and waddling style, he makes Harold think of a bear. Anyway, Big Bill stood 6-5 and weighed 225. He was pretty fast for a big guy and was in excellent condition. The soldier looked to be about 5-9 and weighed around 180.

Well, they worked a couple of rounds and Big Bill didn't even work up a dewy sweat. The GI from Fort Lewis didn't back up though, and he took some good cuts at his towering opponent, but with his stubby arms he didn't even come close to tagging the big guy.

After the workout, Bird handed the soldier $8 and he was happy. Bird told him to come back the next day, but for some reason or other he never showed up-and that was the last that Harold Bird saw of Rocky Marciano.

After he had ascended the heavyweight throne the then champion reflected back. "Yes, that's all true. I was in the Army out near Tacoma and one day a notice came to the camp that sparring partners were wanted at this Tacoma gym and anybody could reply. I was flat broke, so the next day I went in there, and they put me in against this giant who must have been seven-feet-tall. I don't think I even came close to hitting him. They asked me how much I wanted so I mentioned two-dollars a round would be OK, so they gave me four-dollars. I really was rich then.

"When I was out in Tacoma the last time I asked Harold Bird whatever happened to Big Bill, and I told him I thought he had a champion. Bird admitted he thought he had one too, and told me about his sad awakening. One day Big Bill got hit on the lug and it was curtains, and although he was big enough and game enough his chin just wasn't made to take punches. Bird made him quit fighting (2)."

'Big Bill' did indeed "quit fighting", yet he walked away with an impressive record of only two defeats in some forty-eight fights, all this was explained in an interview he gave in 1964 whilst appearing at the New York World's Fair in the guise of the giant mythical American archetype, Paul Bunyan. Whilst reminiscing about his past he took time to reflect on his brief meeting with Marchegiano some eighteen years earlier.

"Rocky was still fighting amateur at the time and no one really ever heard of him in the Northwest. But he impressed me immediately as soon as we climbed into the ring. Here was a man half my size by comparison, who showed absolutely no fear and gallons of guts. It was easy to see he came to fight."

Between May and early August Pt. Rocco Marchegiano would participate in five official inter-service bouts, winning four (*three by kayo*) and losing one, before being picked, under the tutelage of lieutenant George 'Bud' Hansen, and master sergeant Alexander Hendricks (*see image above they are in front and center to right and left respectively*), for the Amateur Athletic Union's Junior National finals in Portland, Oregon.

Rocco's inclusion in the tourney after such a seemingly inexperienced campaign was due in part to one Herman DeVault, then a member of the Oregon AAU boxing committee. He had made a trip to Fort Lewis to see the champion Joe Louis in yet another exhibition and happened upon this, in his own words, "...awkward kid, he won his fights with one-punch left-hand roundhouse knockout swings - after clowning on the ropes, sticking out his chin and letting the other fellow hit it."

Still he was impressed enough to recommend this "clown" be a representative of the impressive Fort Lewis squad. For Marchegiano, the only heavyweight from amongst some eleven fighters was, on paper at least, by far the least experienced in a team made up of former Golden Glove winners, plus one featherweight by the name of Sammy Buttera who had competed in no-less than 105 amateur bouts, losing only two.

The tournament itself was to be held over three days beginning Wednesday August 21st, and culminating on the 24th, this however would bring forth an unforeseen decision for Marchegiano, one that he never dreamt he would be forced to make. At the same time, his beloved baseball team upon which he had proved popular at first base, had qualified to play in the AAU finals held in Tacoma, Washington, he wrestled with the final verdict for a while before making his decision.

"I decided to go to Portland. It was the first time I'd ever picked boxing over baseball when I had a choice."

Many believe that the championships in Portland, held upon the sight of a former Chinese vegetable garden but by now transformed into the impressive oval shaped Multnomah Civic Stadium, an outdoor arena (*the first time such an event had been staged in the open air*) to be the best represented tournament in AAU history. There were to be well over one-hundred boxers representing both the services and private clubs from as far afield as Texas to Canada.

Marchegiano's first fight in the tournament would take place on the second day of competition against one Frederick L. Ross whom he disposed of inside the very first minute, "With," according to John Pincetich, lead sports writer for *The Oregonian* on the morning of Friday 23rd, August, "…an overhand right that would make a Mack truck stop and think again."

For decades afterwards the aforementioned Ross would never figure out how he lost. Whilst stationed in England with the American Air Force in 1963 the then captain Ross recalled vividly to British journalist John Krueger his encounter with the future heavyweight champion of the world:

> His ire was aroused against Marciano (*wrote Krueger*) when the future champ showed up in his corner wearing 'a silly little cap'. Ross resented this because to him 'boxing was a serious business.' He felt 'extremely confident' as he waited for the bell. With 'no sweat' his first jab 'landed good' followed by a 'testing right cross.' Then he 'went right in' and powered home his 'best punch' but, 'Rocky just grunted and came right back.' A shower of Ross blows drove Marciano 'clear across the ring.' 'I was dumbfounded when he didn't go down. With my last one I just teed off from the toes. It drove him into the ropes. Then I dropped both hands, I thought he was done. I dropped both hands to get the most power and knock his head out into the ringside.'
>
> ...However this last flurry at the outset was only leading to Ross' downfall, as other fighters were to later discover. 'You either became overconfident and off your guard when you found you could hit him so freely, or you completely lost your confidence when

you discovered your best punches weren't hurting him,' said Ross of Rocky. 'I hit him with everything I had and I was following up for what I thought would be the kill when I got it.

'I didn't come to my senses until two hours later when I was walking down the street with my dad...'

This demolition of the previously unbeaten Ross led young Rocco into the semi-final the following day. It is conjecture as to whether Marchegiano stayed to watch the remaining bouts that evening in the ring that had been erected in mid-field and flanked by chairs and bleachers, or if he returned to Swan Island barracks, the temporary berths for all competitors that week.

His opponent in this, for him, penultimate fight of the tournament, one Richard Jarvis, again folded within the very first stanza when Rocco landed a thunderous left hand to his opponents jaw after Jarvis had decided to trade blow for blow with Rocco in the middle of the ring. However, as that left punch landed a terrific pain laced through his clenched fist and shot straight up his arm.

As Marchegiano admitted later, "I didn't know how to punch right, and I broke the knuckle on the forefinger of my left hand. The bone was jammed almost up into my wrist." It was an horrific injury [3] but one that he was at first reticent to tell either Lt. Hansen, or M/Sgt. Hendricks at least until after the final for fear that they would pull him from the tournament.

The injury was soon discovered nevertheless when Hendricks prepared his hands for taping. Rocco pleaded with his trainer to allow him to fight, so confidant was he that he would win, in actuality, at least according to Herman DeVault again (*who was there throughout the proceedings following Fort Lewis' fortunes*), Rocky became so emotional over the thought that he may not get a chance to compete in the final that, "...he cried in the dressing room before he went into the ring. Ask Sam Jacobs of the Jacobs Furniture Co., who was his second. He wept like a baby (4)."

Despite his initial concerns Hendricks, perhaps inspired by Marchegiano's alleged display of despair, relented and thus in order to aid his fighter sprayed, "something that looked like Freezone on my hand. It turned all the hairs white and then the hand was frozen."

Thus Rocco entered the final bout later on that very same night crippled by the use of only one hand, his right. He was going against the six-foot-three Joe DeAngelis who had been crowned the New England Golden Gloves heavyweight champion in 1944. This nonetheless was not their first meeting, for as DeAngelis later recalled they had been informally introduced earlier in the tournament when he was with two of his team-mates.

"The first night there we were having supper in the cafeteria of the former Kaiser shipyards when the Army group came in and a blocky aggressive fellow came over, introduced himself as Rocky Marciano (*sic*), and asked if we were from Boston. We said we were. Rocky looked at me...and remarked: 'You must be Joe DeAngelis. I've been reading about you. You're good. You'll make the finals here, and when you do, I'm going to stiffen you'." DeAngelis continued, describing his bout with the untamed Marchegiano.

"When we received instructions in the middle of the ring, I got a chance to size Rocky up real close. He was the most solid, hard, muscular man I had ever seen, yet his hands were like lightening. When the bell rang, he charged at me, his head lowered like a bull, swinging those looping left and right hands, boring in all the time...I held him off with lefts, saw a good opening for a right, and belted him square on the jaw as hard as I've ever hit anyone. He didn't even shake his head!

"Later in the round I got him with a few more good shots which he ignored. I've knocked out a lot of men in my day, but never hit anyone so often and as hard as Rocky, but with no result, hitting him was like hitting the side of a god-damned rhino, I was afraid I would break my hand! Rocky kept coming and swinging with everything he had: I kept moving and trying to time his rush, let go a few punches, and then move again.

"Midway through the second round, after Rocky had missed a series of punches, someone at ringside razzed him. Rocky was enraged. He walked over to the edge of the ropes and yelled down: 'If you can do any better, come up here! The kid wont stand still.' Rocky was really mad. He had counted on a quick kayo. He was over-anxious and was making mistakes."

Those in the audience, who had at first been cheering for the destructive soldier, were now changing their allegiance to the flashier DeAngelis. "It was a helluva lousy feeling," Rocco would confide later, "I think they figured I was throwing the fight."

DeAngelis continued, "The third round was the wildest. Knowing how hard Rocky could punch, I was very careful. I knew I had the fight won, I just couldn't make a mistake. Then Mickey (*McGuire, DeAngelis' second*) yells, 'Fifteen seconds Joe, you won.' Then, Bam! Bam!"

That 'Bam! Bam!' was a last desperate combination left-right from the seemingly humbled Marchegiano which knocked DeAngelis cold. To the amazement and bewilderment of the crowd though, it was to be the unconscious mans' hand which would be raised in victory, for Rocco's last ditch attempt to rescue the fight had been futile by a mere second when the bell rang, thus ending both the bout and the count. Rocco was gob-smacked by the decision (*some believe that Marciano was in fact disqualified for hitting after the bell*).

As he sat disconsolate in his dressing room after the fight nursing his injured left hand he contemplated giving up the sport altogether then and there. "I told him not to do that,"

DeAngelis claimed. "Sure I beat him over three-rounds, there are a ton of fighters who could do that, but there's not many out there who could beat him over six, ten, or even fifteen (5)."

Herman Devault would continue with his recollections of the then clumsy amateur in an article from *The Oregonian* in 1951, "I talked with Marchegiano quite a bit through that tournament as he was waiting to go on or watching other fights, 'What do I care about the next fight?' he'd say. "I'll knock him out!' And he did."

"After the tournament he said he wanted to go pro and asked me to manage him. I have to laugh at how I kissed goodbye to the probable next champion, 'You'll never get anywhere, you're too awkward and too much of a clown.' I told him. So now I run a ranch house and someone else is the champs manager!"

This was however to be Rocco's last hurrah for Fort Lewis, he would never step inside the ropes for them again his injured hand saw to that, the dislocation to his knuckle saw to it too that he would spend the ensuing weeks undergoing a pioneering new treatment for his damaged hand that he would later credit for saving his career as a boxer (*the following are notes taken directly from Marchegiano's medical records*);

> Fracture, simple, complete, comminuted, with impaction, 2nd metacarpal, left hand, a.i. 23 Aug'46, Portland Oregon, while patient was engaged in an authorized boxing match - Application of elastic traction per kirschner wire (*stainless steel pins*) - 31 Aug 46; The left hand and wrist were propped and draped in the usual manner. A steady traction was applied to the left index finger for approximately three minutes in order to reduce the fracture and kirschner wire was driven

through the midshaft of the proximal phalanx (*bone at the base*) of the left index finger and looped about in order to apply elastic traction. The left short arm cast was applied with wrist in cocked position. A banjo wire splint was incorporated into the plaster of paris and elastic applied to the kirschner wire and the banjo splint - 1 Sept 46; Patient's left hand is markedly swollen and tender. The plaster of paris cast was applied and elastic traction released somewhat and the patient has been relieved moderately - 2 Sept 46; Swelling is still present but not marked. I believe that this patient's swelling will subside - 12 Sept46; This patient is comfortable. swelling has gone down in the fingers of the left hand. It is merely a matter of time for the fracture to heal

"So there I was with a busted knuckle," recalled Marciano in 1956. "And I had to go to the hospital (*Madigan General Hospital Tacoma, Washington*). An Army doctor who was a Japanese-American fixed up a special splint so my knuckle would heal right. He did a wonderful job. If he hadn't I'd never have been able to fight again. I wish I could think of his name so I could thank him."

Marciano never could recall that doctors name, often over the years he would attempt to contact this man he deemed his saviour, addressing him through interviews pleading with him to make contact. Never

It remained one of his biggest regrets that he couldn't thank him personally for saving, not just his hand, but his future as well.

Never however did that doctor come forward to claim his just credit for saving that private from the hum-drum existence that seemed destined to be his lot in life. To be fair it is hardly surprising that he did, for the man in question was one of the most humble human beings to ever carve for himself a career in a profession beset by attention seeking individuals, and his name, Shohiro Thomas 'Tom' Taketa.

Born in 1921 the future Dr. Taketa prided himself in being an American, educated in the Marysville, Ohio school system and attained regional prowess as a standout basketball star at Northern California's prestigious Yuba College, that fact that Tom made the team at all is remarkable as in his prime he stood little over five-feet-six-inches. However, as he was securing himself popularity in a fast growing particularly American sport, his own ethnicity and patriotism was called into question. With America now finally ensconced in the war with Germany and Japan Tom, being of Japanese origin, found himself under curfew and awaited removal to relocation camps, those prisoner of war centres that most modern Americans, referring to that time as "an unfortunate piece of our history", would rather forget ever existed on their own soil, in order to be spared the indignity of ending up in one of those basic detention camps the always patriotic Tom volunteered to serve his country during the second world war (*later he would himself play a leading role for the U.S. government in the conduct of hearings regarding World War II's relocation camp*).

That he became a distinguished practitioner of medicine in the forces is attested by his being singled out to escort General Eisenhower on a visit to service hospitals near the end of hostilities. It was perhaps his experiences during this time that led him after the war to pursue a career in the medical profession, studying for six long years to earn himself a degree from the prestigious Stanford University. The now Dr. Tom Taketa would base himself in Oxnard, California where he became a chief of staff at the St. John's Regional Medical Centre, gaining recognition too at the U.S. Naval Radiological Defence Laboratory in San Francisco, NASA's Ames Research Center, and U.C. Berkeley's Lawrence Radiation Laboratory. While serving in these roles the remarkable Dr. Taketa conducted research on the impact of x-ray technology that helped the medical profession understand the parameters within which x-rays could be used safely on the human body. Whilst at NASA he is credited with literally writing the book on life support specifications for conducting life science research in outer space.

Truly the one who saved Marchegiano's hand was a remarkable man. I guess in a career that ended with his death in September of 2006 aged 85, the fact that he is credited with giving the world its only as yet undefeated world heavyweight champion is pretty minor in comparison to his other more illustrious achievements, yet save the future for Marciano he certainly did and it was a future Rocky would soon have to face up to with a great deal of uncertainty, for on 27th December, 1946, private Rocco F. Marchegiano, serial number: 31-301-298, would become a private citizen once more when he was finally honorably discharged from the service of Uncle Sam. He would carry with him memories, some which he would share, some that would be forever locked away, whilst worn upon his chest, three silver medals as proof of his past three-and-a-half-years in the service of his country, namely the European African Middle-Eastern Service Medal, Army of Occupation (*Germany*) Medal, and the Victory Medal (*but of course no Good Conduct medal*), along with a strange sense of self-esteem mixed with melancholy brought about by his still heavily bandaged left hand. Before he finally was ready to come home though, he had a trip to make.

He stopped off in Chicago to visit the uncle of an army pal of his who also happened to be a trainer of professional boxers, Rocco went there believing the meeting would perhaps take place in a gymnasium of some description, instead he was dismayed to find himself in the back of a grocery store owned by another member of his pal's family, and even more disconcerting, upon meeting he was asked to strip to his underwear! After being asked his age the strange ritual was complete, and the prognosis from the uncle of a friend who merely appraised him with his eyes, "Forget it kid, you'd get killed in the pro's, your arms are too short, your legs too thick, your too old to start out now, forget boxing, go home, raise a family and be happy."

Later Rocky would be apoplectic when he recalled this bizarre meeting, "How dare this guy who's never seen me fight, who doesn't know me, tell me I'll be a failure in boxing." For the first time in his life he failed to take someone's advice, it was a wise move, for with-in five years Rocco Marchegiano would be standing on the brink of the heavyweight championship of the world.

Notes:

1 .Originally I had included the alleged explanatory quote from Allie Colombo; "The reports kept coming in that the plane was in trouble, I kept thinking, 'Holy Christ I've killed Rocky.' I couldn't believe it. They kept saying the plane was in big trouble and would probably have to try a forced landing." But to quote Peter Marciano, "Allie could not have quoted this directly to Everett because Everett never met Allie."

2. Rocky's youngest brother Peter Marciano, before he distanced himself from the project, as mentioned in earlier notes, penned in the margins of the earliest manuscript regarding this incident itself, 'Never heard this before – Not good.' It quickly became apparent that if he had not heard a particular story then to him it had never happened. I hope that this does not come across as an attack on anyone in particular, for some of Peter's notes and statements in particular have been invaluable, rather it is frustrating to the researcher attempting to dig into the truth that those who could tell us definitively are reticent to do so and when they do they tell us only

what they want us to hear, some drop hints, innuendoes and the like but then fall to silence when pushed. As I mentioned to certain individuals 'I can only do what I can with evidence presented not with evidence withheld.'

3. "Examination of the left hand shows an oblique fracture at the base of the 2nd metacarpal with lateral bowing at the fracture site" -so read Marchegiano's medical report stamped AUG 26 1946- from Marchegiano's extant military medical files.

4. I searched for said Sam Jacobs that I may ask him but was unable to track him down...

5. I am indebted to researcher Bobby Bearden for helping to piece together this particular chapter which he achieved through sharing with me an email he received from one Herbie "Rusty" Patzer back in 2003. Patzer had competed in the same tourney as Rocky and was able to lay to rest the story that Marchegiano had received two byes to aid him through to his bout with Jarvis. "As for the two opponents who refused to fight Rocco. This is untrue! There were only two other heavyweights entered in the tournament. Graham Bryant beat Pete Lampis on the 1st night and DeAngelo beat Bryant on the second night."

part two   **chapter four**

Barbara & Rocky Mack

"I had spent all those years in the Army, now I was home and faced with nothing…I knew I had to do something, but I still didn't know what."

Rocky Marciano

Firmly entrenched back in Brockton the future for the newly de-mobbed Marchegiano seemed at first as cold and bleak as the weather which consumed the city. Upon his return Rocco swiftly joined the local 50-20 club, a social union for former soldiers, it was a move which entitled him to collect the grand sum of twenty-dollars a week from the veteran's unemployment fund in order to keep him financially afloat over the short term. Plus in order to keep on top of his swiftly mending hand were weekly visits to a near-by Veterans Association hospital to continue treatment on that brittle hand, a hand that healed far swifter than I had originally thought (*a belief propagated in my mind at least by the writer Paul Savage who penned the first small screen adaptation of the life of Rocky Marciano namely*

'Marciano' in 1979 which showed the eponymous hero sporting a heavy cast for some time after his return to civilian life).

I had initially heard rumors that soon after returning to Brockton Rocky had taken part in an amateur tournament, in fact the Massachusetts State Championships held in the Mechanics building, Boston to be exact. Had this been correct then it would put to rest any idea that his hand had been an impediment to continuing to dabble in boxing. I had the name of an opponent, I even had an image (*see below*) but I could not find the definitive proof, I could not find the account, dated and signed by the press of the time which led me to believe that the event must have taken place a year later, that is until I was contacted by a Mr. Cecile W. Gardner of the Boston Library who found the proof which validated the bout and helped to add to our understanding of Marchegiano's evolution as a fighter.

On January 4th, 1947, Rocky did indeed find himself fighting in Boston, his opponent this night was believed to be a game but out-gunned Jim Connolly but whether this was as part of the Massachusetts championships is unclear, what is certain however is that on the evening of Saturday January 11th under the name of Rock Marciano (*the first known instance that the future champ would appear under the name that he would later make famous*) he again found himself in Boston where he blew away the previously unheard off Lew Trocher in the first round. Again the fact that this result was posted up under the title of 'Amateur Boxing at Mechanics Building' may indicate that this was not part of the championship tourney itself but perhaps a preliminary that led to the finals which took place the following week.

There is so little extant information regarding this tourney, even the local press gave but a cursory nod to the preliminaries making it, at this time, impossible to say for certainty as to how far Rocky progressed in it, perhaps his participation was the culmination of the previous bouts in Boston and his appearance on the night of Friday January 17th again in the

Mechanics Building was as a finalist. Perhaps this may have been the first stage of the competition (*it would have been unusual to have a final on a Friday night, unusual but not unheard of*). Yet in whatever capacity Rocky was there he was at least present, or to be exact Roscoe Marchigiano, as *The Boston Globe* hailed him, was present.

Under whichever constantly morphing name he appeared however one thing was certain and that was the plain fact that he would find himself on the receiving end of defeat. His conqueror was a hulking tannery worker from Lynn on Massachusetts' North Shore (*and not South Boston as reported in the results column of The Boston Globe, which also put 'Roscoe' down as from Boston*), who also happened to be defending the title he had won the previous year.

Robert 'Bob' Girard wasn't only big he was also smart, with fast pulverizing hands. His one drawback however was, like Rocco's, the very brittleness of those hands. If he failed to connect properly he would, in his own words, "…feel the pain right down to my toes," leading him to box on the offensive whenever this occurred and possibly costing him victory over several less-than-worthy opponents.

"How do you think I beat Rocky, I beat him because it was three rounds," said Girard in a magnanimous gesture towards the man he had defeated. "There were a hundred guys who might have stayed three rounds with the Rock. But no man in the world was gonna beat Rocky in fifteen rounds; not Dempsey, not Ali, not anybody…Every time he hit you, you saw a flash of light. You either grabbed him or you moved back, because if he hit you twice you're gone."

Perhaps however Girard's victory was aided by Rocco's raw power being hampered on this occasion thereby making him unable to land twice for as *The Brockton Enterprise*, in a small, almost overlooked paragraph mentioned, 'Rocco Marchegiano of this city, suffering an injured hand in a preliminary bout (*is this referencing the Trocher meeting from the week before or perhaps another bout that very night!)*' had fought and lost to Girard in the final heavyweight class bout, it appears that that hand of his was perhaps not quite healed after all.

Rocky never spoke openly of these early bouts, or at least his recollections were either never recorded or quickly lost, thus one can only speculate as to his feelings at tasting defeat, perhaps as we uncover facets of his character as we move along this loss may have been seen by him as a failure and perhaps sign to move on and away from boxing, possibly he remained in competition yet frustratingly those who are in the know are not saying.

What we do nevertheless know from around this time is that Rocco, in his free time, would often accompany his friends to dances at West Bridgewater, Holbrook or Brookville Grange, some four miles from Brockton. It would be here at the Grange one fateful evening that his eye was taken by a statuesque, dark-haired girl who, "seemed to float across the room." He was immediately entranced. This vision in question was the then eighteen-year-old daughter of a Brockton police-officer, her name was Barbara Cousins.

Born on August 30th, 1928, Barbara was the only daughter of Lester and Elizabeth Cousins'. She had been in her youth something of a water baby, her natural ability in the water would lead her to becoming a highly prized member of the Brockton High School swimming team where her prowess would gain her numerous junior national titles, plus laying claim to records that would remain for decades after her last competitive appearance. At the time of her first meeting with Rocco however she had left that competitive side behind her - there is no satisfactory explanation as to why - and was now employed as a telephone operator at a local switchboard. In the summer months she would again don her swim suit and take to the waters once more, albeit by merely moonlighting as a lifeguard at the local Campello-Montello lido, it was the only association that remained from the glories of her youth.

Rocco, if you were to believe the account of some, was a shy boy when it came to girls. Others nevertheless would vehemently dispute this. Yet according to his own account it would take him most of the night to finally strike up the courage to introduce himself to Barbara, and then only after, "I sent over five or six Cokes and right at the very end of the evening when they were shutting down the lights and you can phony it up a bit I approached her." Although admitting that he couldn't, "dance a lick," but, "gee, with her I almost could dance."

He would begin following her every week to various dances, "just to watch her move, I was fascinated by her athleticism." The pair would almost immediately grow inseparable (1).

This new blossoming relationship was to bring its own rewards in terms of Rocco's employment status for with his hand now at last responding well to the weekly diathermy treatment he was receiving Barbara's father, using his considerable connection's, secured his daughters beau a job with the Brockton gas company digging ditches and laying pipes. It was a job that Rocco longed for, at last he was again out working his unconditioned muscles, plus, more importantly, once more contributing to his family's meager income. Soon, much to Marchegiano's relish there would appear the opportunity to add a few extra dollars onto the table, and it would come from an old friend whose head was filled with dreams.

Allie Colombo was once more on leave from Westover Air Force base when he looked up his old friend Marchegiano. Still fresh in his mind had been the conversation from the previous year concerning them teaming up to conquer the world. Allie had never allowed this image to stray far from his thoughts; now with this in mind he approached his comrade with a serious proposition.

An idea had been fermenting in Colombo's mind since he had been introduced to a certain Richard J. O'Connell (*since misspelled as O'Connor*) at Westover a few months previously. The then fifty-six year old O'Connell was working under a civilian contract at the base as a custom's officer, a job he had held for over two-decades. Allie's interest in this individual was piqued by the fact that in his youth O'Connell had boxed professionally at bantamweight and never severed his ties with the sport. By early spring of 1947 he had become an unofficial scout for his friend, the Holyoke, Massachusetts, fight promoter Auriel Renault. Allie Colombo saw an opportunity and pounced upon it.

Initially he approached O'Connell about getting Rocco some fights, but the experienced O'Connell baulked at the suggestion, at least until he had seen the boy in the flesh, thus Colombo's proposition to 'The Rock' was a simple one. Join him on his trip back to Westover and spar a couple of rounds in their gym; let this O'Connell see for himself that Colombo wasn't over exuberant in praise of Marchegiano.

It took little to persuade Rocky to accompany Colombo to Westover, it was not for any ambitions of following a career in the prize ring though for at this stage in his life he still held out hopes of baseball stardom, it was more rather that he did not want to let down either Allie who had spent so much time and effort trying to put the whole deal together and himself. He needn't have worried for O'Connell liked what he saw that day, so much so that he promptly contacted promoter Renault in Holyoke.

Within a matter of days Rocco found himself booked to appear in the Valley Arena, Holyoke, where he would act as the first course in a bill headlined by Middleweights Saint Paul and Tee Hubert. This would be Rocco's first contest since the previous August, some six months before.

There was however one minor problem to overcome; after the disastrous Lester bout the previous year Rocco had decided to keep his boxing secret from his mother. If he was going to fight he knew that there was a chance that his name might appear in the local paper, Holyoke was so close, he couldn't take a chance of his beloved mother finding out. In an effort to prevent this the boys decided that a change of name was in order. After allegedly debating a wealth of possibilities finally a name was agreed upon, Rocky Mack.

It seemed an unlikely choice, but it was premeditated (*so the story goes*) by the day upon which the bout would take place, St. Patrick's Day, March 17th. The last name, so the pair argued, sounded vaguely Irish, with it they felt they may get some partisan support (2).

Rocco, who had been allowed a day off from his job at the gas company, arrived at the Valley Arena (*'the rambunctious, hand-clapping, foot-stomping' venue for the bout*) alone at two-thirty on that Monday afternoon where he was to meet both Allie and O'Connell. There he went through the pre-fight preliminaries, physical check-up, weigh-in, etc. Rocco tipped the scales at a trim 192lbs and for the first time came face to face with his opponent.

His adversary was an experienced (*at least by the then Marchegiano's standards*) professional by the name of Les Epperson who was taking part in his seventh paid bout, winning five from his previous six outings, and he was in no mood to lose again this night. Apart from seasoning he also had on his side the town he called home, none other than Holyoke itself. Here he had built up a firm fan base in the small communal city where he had settled after moving from Memphis, Tennessee in 1942 at the age of 18 just before being called up to serve his country (*he saw action in Burma as part of the 5307th Composite Unit which would find fame as the notorious 'Merrill's Marauders' named after their commander brigadier general Frank Merrill, every man in this unit was awarded a Bronze star for meritorious service, unflinching devotion to duty, and unyielding nature in the face of seemingly insurmountable odds*).

Epperson had carved out for himself an amateur career of some standing, indeed he was the proverbial all around sportsman, for aside from boxing he excelled in football and softball too representing Holyoke at a semi-professional level in all three disciplines. Many who had filed into the Arena that night were convinced that they were about to witness a remarkable potential fulfilled, and so they were, only not from whom they envisioned.

As was his way Rocco made no show of deference to his opponent, they simply shook hands and parted their own ways until that evening. Epperson returned to his home whilst Marchegiano accompanied Allie back to O'Connell's where he surprised his host by consuming a vast portion of steak before settling down for a few hours comfortable sleep [3]. Finally the moment arrived to leave for the Arena. As the three of them made their way across town for what was to be the professional debut of the fighter who would become known as Rocky Marciano neither 'The Rock', nor Colombo, could then have known where this inauspicious beginning would eventually end or the roads it would lead them down.

"We had a big crowd on hand," recalled Allie in Everett M. Skehan's biography, "(be)cause the local papers had played up this fight even bigger than the main event. You know, Holyoke against Brockton, that sort of a thing." - Sadly here Colombo (*perhaps, or the one to whom he is alleged to have said it*) seems to be guilty of exaggeration, or at best, simply fanciful recollection for previous to the battle there was no mention of Brockton, nor any overt publicity. In actuality there was merely a brief almost apologetic mention in the *Holyoke Transcript* which did not even credit Rocky as coming from Brockton at all: "A special heavyweight opening match will bring together Les Epperson of Holyoke and Rocky Mackjianno of Westover Field, a four rounder."

Yet for a while it seemed that Mack/Mackjianno/Marchegiano, from Westover Field, would not even be climbing between the ropes at all for before the bout had even begun there was a hurdle to overcome, as it would be in the future, the problem was caused by money.

O'Connell had promised Colombo $50 for the fight but Renault, who had taken over the Arena from his uncle in 1944 two years after the building, formerly known as the 'Gas House' had ironically burnt to the ground (4), threatened to baulk at the deal. "I went in to see Renault," continued Allie. " 'You're nuts,' says Renault. 'We never paid more than $35 for a four-rounder before and we ain't starting now.' 'Okay,' says I, turning to Rocky. 'Take off your trunks, we're going home.' Renault nearly choked when he saw Rocky getting dressed, and finally he gives in (*as stated before and so will be again and again the truth of these statements attributed to Colombo must be taken with a pinch of the proverbial salt but it has become the official version and so makes it into here by dint of that*)."

With the fight underway Rocco was mad at the alleged confusion over his fee, he went in slugging wildly, even more so than usual. Luckily for him it appeared that Epperson too was not the most accomplished of artisans in the ring either.

"Both were wild swingers but Mack was able to concentrate on Epperson's body in the first two rounds," reported the *Holyoke Transcript Telegram* on the morning of March 18th. The beginning of the end for the outgunned Epperson came towards the end of that second round when Marchegiano/Mack caught the local boy with three wicked rights in quick succession. To his credit Epperson stayed on his feet, but he was dazed and groggy at the bell. Then in the third, to allegedly paraphrase Allie again, "Rocky hits him with a right to the body that breaks a rib and the fights over."

The actual ending came just forty-two seconds into the third with Rocco throwing a right uppercut that seemed to start from his boots, the force of the impact was so great that it knocked the hapless Epperson straight out of the ring. The referee began his count, but realizing it was a fruitless endeavor, he waved it over.

"I didn't like it. It was a tough fight and seemed a tough way to make a buck," recalled Rocco. "But," added Colombo (*as I continue to paraphrase from Skeehan*), "Then the real fight starts. The fight to get the $50 that's agreed to."

"Renault's accountant at the box-office window hands me $20 and says, 'You get $35, but $15 is for the license.' 'No soap,' says I, starting to look for Renault, but along he comes with two cops saying, 'Throw these two bums out of here.'

"I try to explain what's happening to the two cops but they say I ought to take what I got and go. 'I aint got anything,' I scream and everybody starts talking at once. While they're gabbing I go back to the box-office to take the $20 and get out of there before somebody gets mad and somebody gets hurt.

"Renault follows me and when he sees the hullabaloo I'm raising in the box-office with the crowd streaming out after the final bout of the evening, he tells the accountant to give me $35 and we call it even. When I went back to get Rocky, he wanted to wait around to 'bust' the guy but I showed him the money and got him out of there."

Marciano himself would recall his feelings looking back in later years. "I walked away from that whole affair disgusted with the sport, if this was what it was like in the pros, I thought, then forget it."

"I had a heck of a time getting him ever to fight again," conceded Colombo. "And to make matters worse, his left hand blew up, giving him a lot of trouble."

After this defeat the career of Leslie V. Epperson, better known as 'Lester' is lost to us, the only fully confirmed reports that I have been able to uncover came from the obituary page of the *Springfield Union-News*, Tuesday, August 18, 1987 edition (*kindly forwarded by Margaret Humberston Head of Library & Archives Wood Museum of Springfield History*). The information is unfortunately brief but helpful. 'Lester' it notes, passed away Sunday the 16th in Holyoke Hospital at the relatively young age of 63 (*there is no mention of cause*), his professional life took him away from sport and into the printing business for he became a lithographer with Area Printers. His social achievements, outside of his early sporting endeavors which listed his bout with Marciano (*albeit with the wrong month, the obituary stated that the match took place in February not March*) as a highlight mentioned that he was general manager of the local Brian Boro Club a worldwide organization that celebrated Irish routes.

And this is where the Epperson story ends, save for the mention of those he left behind, a son and daughter respectively, who provided him with four grandchildren. One wonders whether those grandchildren knew of his meeting with Marciano and thus his place in the annals of boxing's' rich history, yet in retrospect when measured against his exploits during the second great war his defeat at the hands of the future world heavyweight champion is meaningful only as a footnote to his heroic life…

Notes:

1. *"I'll never forget the first night I met Rocky,"* recalled Barbara herself in a five-part article printed in The San Antonio Light, June 1956, as she reminisced on the beginning of a relationship that would last for the remainder of both their lives. Barbara however would remember the events with slight differences, *"He hates to dance-he is a good dancer but he is terribly shy -but one night some friends of his talked him into visiting a dance hall in Brockton. I was there with another fellow, but once Rocky asked me to dance I forgot all about who brought me. And Rocky took me home…He dated me the next night, and the next night, and the next…He didn't do anything terribly exciting. We saw every show in town and went to parties my girlfriends had but I knew he was the only guy for me."*

2. For a time however it seems his pseudonym and birth name became confused as attested by Holyoke Transcript Telegram who on the morning of the show, announcing the line up for that evenings card, morphed Rocco Mack/Marchegiano into Rocky Mackjianno.

3. This was to become an almost ritualistic act before all of Marciano's later bouts; it was perhaps a sign of his complete confidence in his own ability that he never worried about his opponent, thus allowing himself to relax completely.

4. It would burn down twice more in suspicious circumstances before closing for good in 1960.

Part two   **chapter five**

The Dream that Died

"I never wanted to be anything other than a ball player when I was growing up. Boxing then was just a distraction for me, nothing more"

Rocky Marciano

After the disappointment of the Epperson bout Rocco returned to Brockton even more determined than ever to carve out for himself a career in his first sporting love, baseball. Had it not after all been his mistress since childhood carrying him through his life thus far, and did it not seem that fate was once again intervening to give him a chance at fulfilling this dream, for he felt sure that he was destined to stand shoulder to shoulder with such legends of the sport as Joe DiMaggio and Ted Williams - indeed one day he would stand with his heroes as an equal, only not in the manner he believed at the time.

If it had not been for his damaged hand he felt then surely he would have won the Golden Gloves the previous year. Had it not also been for, as he saw it, the machinations of greedy unscrupulous promoters (*who would plague him in later years*) perhaps he would have settled on a career in the roped arena, yet instead he had constantly been denied, or fallen through some mystery into a stupefied approach to the sport.

The eager Marchegiano then, in order to give that fickle nature of fate a helping hand engaged in sand-lot baseball with earnest during the early months of the year. This also brought him and his beloved Barbara extra income as a means of supporting their fast paced courtship due to the small expenses paid to the players. Theirs was a courtship which would soon lead to thoughts of marriage, but first this respective suitor wished to make his own way in the world.

His chance seemed to have found its way to him in April of that year when the boys on the local Ward Two baseball team were informed by Allie Colombo's oldest brother, Eddie, that a reporter from the *Boston-Herald* by the name of Ralph Wheeler was in town to watch one of their games. Eddie himself had touted the boys on the team to Wheeler who was a friend of his and had assured him that there were many promising players amongst them. Besides being a scribe on the prestigious paper this Ralph Wheeler was also a scout in the Massachusetts area for one of the premier ball clubs in America, namely the Chicago Cubs. Thus there was great excitement amongst Rocco and his old childhood buddies, all of whom were now approaching their mid-twenties. For them this break represented the last chance they felt to secure for, not just themselves but their families as well, a better future. In turn they played harder than they had ever done before in their lives. Wheeler was suitably impressed.

Steadily letters began arriving announcing that certain individuals had been picked to try out for the Cub's farm team situated in Fayetteville, North Carolina. Amongst those chosen were Ritchie and Vinnie Colombo, Eugene Sylvester, and Red Gormley, yet nothing arrived on Rocco's stoop!

"I couldn't understand it at first," mused Marciano later. "There were all my pals getting their invites and I had nothing, then at last mine showed up, it wasn't until later that I discovered what had happened to get me the call."

Eugene was "what had happened". At the time Eugene Sylvester was considered the best prospect out of the small group of childhood friends and as such he held a certain sway over the decision process, it was a distinction that was to remain a highlight of his life. In as much he was astonished when his pal announced that he had not, as yet, received an invite to join the others in Carolina, so amazed was he that in fact he took the decision to contact Wheeler himself and explain quite categorically that, "if Rocco wasn't picked then I wouldn't be going either." It was a brave move on his part, but hadn't he and Rocco been friends for years, and had the Rock not spared him from a beating on more than one occasion; thus the deed was done, Ralph Wheeler's response initially was never documented, yet Eugene's ploy seemed to work, for soon the expectant Marchegiano received his own invite and believing that his dreams would finally be fulfilled made preparations to depart. His mother was ecstatic when she was greeted with the news from her eldest that he was going to become a baseball star, at last no more fighting; or so she thought.

Thus the motley band of wannabe big leaguers squashed themselves into the battered gray two-door sedan of Vinnie Colombo and headed off to the hoped for eternal sunshine of Fayetteville. Apart from a brief stop-over in New Jersey they had made the trip in one go, all the while fretting over whether they would impress. "It was the only time I ever knew Rocky to be worried about anything," commented Eugene. "Nothing ever fazed him. I guess he saw this like the rest of us, as his last chance to escape oblivion."

"I should have known from the start that all wasn't going to go to plan," narrated childhood friend Red Gormely when recalling his road trip with Rocco. "Firstly we mis-planned our journey and got there a day late; the manager didn't like it at all. It seemed like we got off on the wrong foot right away. Fayetteville itself was a small town but we didn't care…we were obsessed with making the teams, we both were confident. We figured we were as ready as we'd ever be for making it in baseball. We had a room at a boarding house owned by a Mrs. Brown… (*She*) served terrific home cooked meals for fifty cents. It was put out on platters and you could take all you wanted. Rocky and I ate and ate and ate."

After only a few days however Rocco began to experience pain in his right arm making it almost impossible for him to throw a ball to second base. All his dreams seemed to be tentatively hanging by a thread, panic began to set in. Remembered Vinnie, "The Rock was still getting his hits though; he belted one shot to deep center that really opened up the coach's eyes. But Rocky ran so slow he only got a double out of it."

The injury to his arm was not new; it in fact dated back to his time in the services. "A base hospital in Swansea had a good ball club, and I organized an outfit to play them at a buck a man. We had a good team except for a pitcher, so I took that chore (*be*)cause I had a good fast ball, a fair curve and good control. I pitched a heck of a game, allowing only three or four hits, and putting everything I had into it. But that night I had a sore arm. I guess that's what ruined me in 1947."

"Despite this we managed to hang around for a few weeks," continued Gormely. "Vinnie and Ritchie were the first to go, they moved on to another team which left Rocky, Gene and me, the competition was tough, far tougher than back home, I noticed after a bad practice Rocky'd light up a cigarette. I don't think anybody ever wanted something as much as we wanted to make the team.

"I remember at nights the Rock would do exercises on his bed, press-ups and the like, then one night the bed collapsed, 'I'll have to share with you,' he says, and I say, 'That's fine.' The next thing I know he's giving me a little jab, I said, 'Rock what's this?', 'Just a little jab.

Don't worry I won't hurt you.' He replies. The next thing I know we're going at it full steam, and the Rock knocks me right out of bed, 'Jeez, you're alright aint you?' Is all he says as I lay on the floor. He was practicing on me, and I don't even know he's a boxer yet.

"Finally after about three weeks the manager called us to one side and told us both that we'd been cut from the team, it happened after Rocky laid out one of the competing players. That happened like this as I recall.

"A Southern player had hit a grounder, the Rock bobbled the ball, and this rebel beat it out, the ball had skipped behind Rocky, but not far enough so the guy could advance. The next thing I knew, I heard this rebel say, 'Pick it up you nigger-loving Yankee.' Rocky hit him with a left that broke his nose, one punch and the kid went down. He was grabbing his nose, and the blood was spurting all over the place. They helped this kid from the field [1]."

The duo was dejected at their failure, only Eugene remained of the original quintuplet from Brockton, but he too would fall short just weeks later. In order to try to save face the pair moved on to try their luck elsewhere. "I went down there with big ideas I guess," reiterated Marchegiano, "I was awfully disappointed when I didn't make it. I was just ashamed to go home, everybody knew that I had gone down there for the tryout. When one of Allie's brothers got a spot over at the Goldsboro Bugs in Wilson, North Carolina, I went over and played there awhile. They kept me for my hitting but the arm got worse and the manager finally told me to go home."

This nevertheless was not quite the end of the dream, according to Red Gormely again, "I remember we tried out in Macon, Georgia, too, where they got you a job days and you played ball at night. But we were only there two or three days when the coach said, 'Forget it. Go back home'."

The realization finally dawned on Rocco that it was all over for him in terms of baseball stardom. At first this thought was hard to come to terms with, he had been so besotted with the idea since he first walked out into James J. Edgar park when he was a child, but now it was gone. "He took it real bad," Gormely went on, "…it was like someone had died, he kept mumbling about how was he going to show his face back home, I tried to tell him that we weren't the first to fail, but he had none of it, failure wasn't an option for him. Then he tells me about his fights and his eyes kinda light up, he begins to rant on about me fixing him up with some fights right there in Macon so's we don't have to go back with nothing. At first I thought he was grasping at straws, and then I realize this kid's serious, even on the train home he continued, so I talk him out of it, what a palooka!! There I was sitting next to half the money in the world and I didn't know it."

Years later in his role of local mailman, Red would find himself delivering letters from all over the world to the door of Rocky Marciano, world heavyweight champion. "I wasn't bitter though," he contended, "Why should I be, the Rock was my friend and I was proud of him, we all were."

Notes:

1. *This was not the first time Marchegiano had thrown punches on a baseball field, author Phil Guarnieri recalled a conversation he had with former sports caster Warner Wolf who had interviewed Rocco back in 1966: 'The Rock told him how he had a reputation as a guy you don't mess with even on the baseball diamond. Rock told him that when he was playing catcher and guys were coming in hard to score whether he had the ball or not he would administer the tag with the gloved hand in the form of a semi-punch and after a few of those none of the guys wanted to come sliding into the plate much less barrelling down the line. Rock told Warner that this was his personal message to the opposing team.'*

part two   **chapter six**

Crossroads

"I told him what a waste it would be if he never fought again, and if he didn't how he'd regret it for the rest of his life."

Allie Colombo

Failure to secure a place in the world of his dreams would come as a traumatic blow for Rocco. "I was running out of options and I knew it," he would confide. "After the Epperson bout I had turned my back on boxing, and now baseball had turned its back on me. I was so sure I was going to be a baseball star, I just hated going back home."

Despite his conversation with Gormely on that dejected journey home he was merely suggesting something of which he had lost heart, therefore now there seemed only one viable avenue left; football. In the 1950's this sport was still in its relative infancy in terms both of professionalism and fan support, sure the amateur leagues were thriving, but the paid ranks were still struggling to catch the attention of a nation. It would be another two decades before the emergence of the Super bowl which would cement the games popularity placing it second only to baseball in the heart of Americans. Still, it paid better than those menial 'blue collar' jobs which seemed to await him.

Thus for the remainder of the year this prospective sporting star would devote himself to the sandlot games that were regularly held in the Brockton parks. Although playing as an amateur he would receive a small allowance for his participation, yet as Barbara recalled, "He was a good tackler, but boy was he slow, Rocky was built for power not speed. Deep down I think he knew this wasn't going to lead him anywhere but he kept plugging away just in case."

All the while the now no longer youthful Marchegiano trained assiduously at his local YMCA, he was determined to get into the best possible condition he could in order to be ready should that call ever come from a scout for one of the big teams desperate to find themselves a star. It had happened, regardless of how tenuously, in baseball, why not in football too. To this end he had given up smoking, a residue from his service days, and begun to again work out aerobically, yet recalling the advice of earlier he would still refrain from lifting weights [1]. Perhaps his most unique, some would say bizarre, form of exercise however was his penchant for practicing moves underwater, first in the form of lunging tackles for his abortive football career, and later adapting this technique to the throwing of punches.

Charley Goldman, later to become the then Marciano's trainer would explain this practice to an incredulous New York reporter in 1950. "Rocky he just dives right into a pool [2] and practices punchin' underwater until he has to come up for air. He says punchin' underwater develops the muscles of his back because he has to punch without getting' set on his feet in the water.

"What's wrong about that? I've known guys who developed punch by throwin' rocks at rabbits, or shoein' horses, or working in a boiler factory."

Back in 1947 however when the idea of reporters converging to watch him train was still a fantasy, he would devote his weekends to football thus forgoing the luxury of time spent with Barbara. "She was very understanding," Rocky would say looking back. "Even then she understood what was needed to succeed." All the while, unbeknownst to Rocco he was being watched, but not by a studious scout for a pro football team, but by his friend, Allie Colombo, who still held the promises made the year before regarding him and his best friend making it big in boxing close to his heart.

"I would watch him play in O'Donnell Park," recalled Colombo. "I still get chills up and down my spine just thinking about how he was wasting his life playing ball. Everything he had done as a kid - the fight with Julie Durham, the time he was eight and I put him in the ring with a twelve-year-old kid, five inches taller and thirty pounds heavier, in my Uncles backyard…I just knew he had to be a champion."

For Allie too he saw in his friend a chance to make something out of life for the pair of them especially as he now had been released from his Air force duties and was struggling to find a path for himself in civilian life. There was nevertheless a rumour that Allie had put an end to a promising military career himself for as Marciano recalled in 1969, "He (*Colombo*) already had been in the army eight years and he was going to make a career out of it. He saw me fight one night. Everybody was laughing at me because I was awkward and crude. But Allie didn't." Rocky then continued to describe how his friend walked away from his service to his country and ploughed his savings of just under two-thousand dollars into helping launch Marciano's boxing career.

"He gave up his security because he believed in me. He never told anybody." If this is true it was one hell of a sacrifice on Colombo's part for at this stage Rocco really had no intentions of turning professional, let alone becoming a champion (*or perhaps he did, as his inclusion in the January tourney showed Rocky was involved with the sport far earlier than many people believed, there really is no way of knowing whether Rocky was competing around this time or not, perhaps he was for that sacrifice on Allie's part must have been based on something he saw or knew).*

Thus with, it seemed, everything riding on this big chance Allie chased him, chased him as hard and relentlessly as Rocco chased down opposing players on the field. Although there were many reasons why he pursued him so Colombo maintained that the first and biggest was concern for his friend. "I watched him go from being a kid full of ambition to a young man who seemed almost drained, this football thing was him clutching at straws, I knew it and he knew it, but he wasn't listening to me. So finally I approached his mom and pop, they were the only ones he ever truly trusted."

Eventually his father would heed Allie's advice and speak to his eldest son. "He was no' happy, I could see that, so I take him and I tell him, 'Rocco you a big strong boy, you go fight, you go be somebody'. He was worried about what his momma say, but I say, 'I speak to her, I the man of this house, she do what I say' (*sic*)." Finally his "momma" acquiesced, but on the condition that at the first injury he would quit the ring.

"I used to have to bare my chest to see that there were no bruises," said Rocky to author Harold Mayes. "When she saw (*a*) rope-burn I was very close to having to call the whole thing off." Also, under no circumstances was he ever to expect her to come to any of his fight.

"The Rock was like new man," said Allie. "He actually came to me and asked me to help him train; he was full of enthusiasm about it all. I think the main reason he turned away from boxing was because of his mom, he never liked hiding the fact he fought away from her, but when she said okay, it was on."

At first Allie knew his limitations. He was fully aware that in order to move Marchegiano into the professional sphere of boxing he was going to need assistance, with this in mind he at first considered approaching his old friend Richard (*Dick*) O'Connell in Holyoke, but Rocco balked at this suggestion, "Forget it, I don't want anything to do with that bum." He still felt sore at the fiasco of the Epperson match and believed, rightly or wrongly, that due to O'Connell being instrumental in setting up the bout that he was therefore one of the main instigators for the ensuing calumny. It would be the sign of a trait which would follow the then Marchegiano through-out his adult life. He would hold a grudge if he felt someone had steered him wrong, as Eugene Sylvester was quoted as saying after his friend had retired over a decade later. "If the Rock liked you, if you were his friend, you had it made, but if you crossed him, forget it, he was unmerciful." Rocco however already had someone in mind; re-enter Generosa "Gene" Caggiano.

Caggiano, who had promoted the Lester debacle the previous year, had himself been a professional fighter in his youth, though by no means old when Rocco approached him he was a mere thirty-six, yet the pinnacle of his career had allegedly come when he had fought eight rounds with a young Henry Armstrong who would go on to be the only pugilist to hold three world titles simultaneously. His glory days behind him now he had retained his connection with boxing through training and managing amateurs, occasionally promoting shows both in Brockton and near-by Buzzards Bay. None of these ventures had made him wealthy for at this stage in his life he was employed as a mechanic by the local Eastern Massachusetts Street Railway Company.

At first suggestion of managing Rocco however Gene was apprehensive. He would be taking a gamble in bringing this, as he saw it, raw novice under his wing. "I was aware of him, but only through his loss to Lester," he recalled. "And when I was told he had already fought as a pro I became even more nervous about the entire affair, but in the end I thought, 'What the hell have I got to lose?' "

Later it would emerge that this was not the first time Rocco had approached him about resuming a boxing career, he had in fact first made advancements towards Gene in early January of that year (*tying in nicely with the Boston tournament*) but the pair had not got beyond the talking stage only.

To Allie, who one presumes was unaware of this earlier contact, it appeared that a minor stroke of fortuity had arisen which would see all three Brocktonians together rise to great heights, Caggiano as manager, Colombo as trainer, and Rocco as champion. This association seemed a natural. Thus, for now at least, the future seemed bright for the first time since early spring, the Marchegiano roller-coaster moved on.

Between late October and early the following February the driving forces behind Rocco's fighting career would guide their boy through at least seven successful amateur bouts. "Kind of bootleg boxing," as Rocco would reflect, for although these bouts were technically amateur he did receive a purse for each outing averaging around thirty-dollars a time. Yet Caggiano, who would be offered a choice of four prospective opponents for each battle, would admit that during this early phase of Marchegiano's amateur showings he held an unusual uncertainty as to his charges ability. He would confide that he was, "nervous about over-matching the kid, each time he fought I thought I had put him in over his head."

He was not the only one who seemed perplexed by the future champion's success…

Notes:

1. *Marciano's reticence to train with weights intrigued me especially as today it is such an integral part of any athlete's preparation that it seems almost alien not to have utilized it at all. It has become almost second nature to argue that Rocky was too small to compete with the giants of the modern era yet I contest that had he been around in his prime and competing amongst the modern heavies he would have been physically larger possibly by at least as much as thirty-pounds. This belief that Rocky would have been bigger and the mind-set that kept him away from lifting the heavy iron is explained by author Phil Guarnieri; 'There is no doubt that if Rocky was fighting today he would be fighting at a much heavier weight. Back in the 40s and 50s it wasn't so much they didn't know how to maximize muscularity (although muscle building is far more scientific and sophisticated today --- as are the machines that build them) but they thought it was bad for you. A loss of flexibility, a muscle bound fighter, were inimical to the success of a fighter, and they were all the result of weight lifting. The famed trainers Ray Arcel, Gil Clancy as well as referee Arthur Mercante all preached against weight training for fighters. This mind set continued on to the 70s and even early 80s. When Ali saw the movie Rocky and watched Stallone doing weights he said to those around him that it is the worst thing a fighter could do. Joe & Marvis Frazier co-authored a book on how to train fighters. They agreed on everything until it came to weight lifting. Joe born in 1944 was adamantly opposed to it; Marvis born in 1960 was strongly in favor of it. A clear generational difference. Joe countered that he never lifted weights but that he was still plenty strong. And of course Joe was plenty strong --- but he would have been stronger still if he lifted weights. Muscle mass does add strength but it is a zero-sum game because it subtracts from endurance. You will never have heavyweights fight at the pace of a Marciano or a Frazier, who in his prime came closest to Marciano for sheer endurance, durability and guts, because either the huge muscles or huge bellies of today's heavyweights use up too much oxygen. And in Marciano's day it was endurance and not physical mass that was considered the more important attribute. But things changed, as they invariably do.'*

2. *There were times when Marciano would even jump from the second floor window, as his friend Nicky Sylvester recalled, adding that when Marciano threw punches under water the surface around him would be calm, but the water would be splashing violently over the sides of the pool several meters away.*

part two   chapter seven

Lowell

"When I fought there I was just another fighter…I guess I owe all that followed to that place."

Rocky Marciano

The championships in Lowell were extravagant affairs with preliminaries having begun on December 30th and due to reach their conclusion on February 9th, 1948. The main aim of this competition was to find the eight boxers who would represent Massachusetts in the New England finals later that same month.

The venue itself which had been chosen to house the bouts seemed a fitting site, for the building had been constructed in the thirties and was dedicated to the American Veterans who served their country, decorating the exterior walls are the names of famous generals and battles in which America made her mark, one can only imagine how the combatants in the almost insignificant by comparison skirmishes with-in felt as they entered the building surrounded by the carved names of such famous modern warriors. The shows organizers, wishing to cement the popularity of this event which was only in its second year, had pulled out all the stops in the hope of filling the 4,000 capacity auditorium, against them though this year they had the weather to contend with for the county was locked in a bitter winter resplendent with heavy snow and temperatures in the evening dipping well below freezing. To everyone's relief however the shows proved to be a roaring success.

On the 19th of January none other than Bob Girard found himself once again back in the Lowell ring; he had competed here the previous year making it all the way to the final where he had lost to one Joe Browne, now this year high expectations were laid upon his broad shoulders. Perhaps this proved to be too much for him for, surprisingly, he was unceremoniously knocked out of the competition by Dan Solomont in the opening stages. Whilst Girard slunk home his conqueror, by a strange quirk, would have to get past Marchegiano himself if he wished to progress any further.

Rocco's inclusion in the tournament was entirely down to one man, Jim McMullen, who in his role as the director of boxing for the Lowell Sun [1] Charities Golden Gloves was the key voice in who did, and conversely did not, make it into the championship.

There was one fighter though who definitely would make it, his name was Charlie Mortimer, and he was the protégé of none other than McMullen himself, however, through the practice of a form of nepotism, Mortimer would not be amongst those in the preliminaries but instead would be entered straight into the last four, it would be up to the rest of the boys to earn their shot at him, yet this brought about its own problem.

Due to the complexities of the competition there would be only three heavyweights who could make it through to the finals, McMullen needed a fourth or his fighter would be excluded. To this end the director of the Sun Charities show found himself in Bob Girard's neck of the woods, Lynn, Mass, sometime in January to watch an unnamed yet, at least at the time, heralded heavyweight compete with the singular intention of getting this unknown fighter to take part in the closing stages of the Gloves. This entire episode is rather shady however, for it was not just the name of the boxer which has been lost, the exact venue, and even date have also vanished from memory, or at least are unavailable to this archivist, had it not been but for the brief recollections of McMullen himself published in *The Lowell Sun* itself in 1966 when he recalled to journalist Frank Dyer his reasons for being in Lynn, the whole affair would have been lost.

"This heavyweight, a big redhead, had a pretty good reputation and the word was that he was knocking guys into the parquet seats. So I went down to Lynn to get a look at him," McMullen recalled. "He ends up fighting a tough looking kid from Brockton and for about two rounds this redhead caught more bombs than you could imagine. Finally, the kid from Brockton caught him with a right and lifted him about a foot off the canvas. Knocked him cold. After the fight I got the kid from Brockton to box in the Golden Gloves."

Thus it was that on the wintry evening of Monday, February 2nd, Rocco made his debut in Lowell. The late Frank Sargent who covered the show for the local *Lowell Sun,* described his initial appearance thus. "Up from Brockton came Rocco Marckegiano (*sic*), a heavyweight with a lot of dynamite in his right glove. This boy slugged it out with Dan Solomont of Seekonk, R.I. (*see above*), in the first two minutes of the initial chapter and then caught his foe with a right to the jaw which caused the Rhode Islander to go into a lengthy slumber." The compelling photograph which accompanied the article shows the hapless Solomont falling forward with arms spread wide as if attempting flight, all around him is a cloak of dark emptiness, Rocco had already walked away as if he knew his foe was never going to rise before the count reached ten.

Yet despite this conclusive victory, Rocco was not the star of the show for that honour belonged to the aforementioned Charlie "Chuck" Mortimer, a clean shaven, nineteen year old from Lowell who looked more like a movie star or model than a fighter.

McMullen's protégé seemed, at least on the surface, to have the potential to win the tourney, especially with Girard out of the way. There were some whispers however that all was not strictly above board in the Girard decision, but there is little proof of this, yet the publicity machine turned quick for Mortimer now thanks in no small part to his victory that self-same evening when he scored his own first round victory over an unfortunate Joe West, therefore being hailed as the "hitter" of the tournament.

"Chuck Mortimer who simply can't wait for the call to come out fighting will finally get his chance. He'll positively appear against…Rocco Markegiano (*sic*)…when the heavyweight open contenders close the card. Practically every sports fan in greater-Lowell is anxious to ascertain how hard this highly-touted boy can hit."

So far the script had run to plan ensuring a local boy was in the final the following Monday, so for McMullen, the local press, and the almost 4,000 spectators who crammed into the Memorial Auditorium, they would have to wait just a little while longer to see if their "highly-touted boy" could blast out this unknown Brockton fighter, who was also able, they had to at least acknowledge, hit a bit himself.

The night of February 9th was buzzing, a palpable sense of excitement surrounded the entire venue as a capacity crowd were on hand to witness an enthralling bout between their home-town boy and the upstart who was trying to deny him a place in the forthcoming Tournament of Champions, a regional tournament due to take place a mere fortnight later in which the winners of this nights bouts would take on the corresponding holders from New Hampshire and Maine in order to find the overall champions of New England who would then, with much fanfare, move on to the National finals to be held in New York the following month.

For the first two round the southpaw style of Mortimer ruled the day as he peppered the slightly heavier Marchegiano with shots from every angle [2], but to the surprise of the crowd this Brockton boy would not go down, either Charlie had lost his fabled power or his opponent was far tougher than they had initially given him credit for. At least, most agreed, they were getting their money's worth this evening; they were going to witness their boy crowned champion, sure Marchegiano had fought back aggressively in the first two stanza's but all felt that the sharper shots had come from Mortimer.

Their initial feelings that Charlie was the superior fighter seemed confirmed in the opening stages of the closing third round when the Brocktonian appeared to wilt and was forced back against the ropes. Then, to the astonishment of all present, as recorded in the *Lowell Sun*, he, "…came to life with startling suddenness in 1.20 of the third, stepping inside Mortimer's guard whilst coming off the ropes to deliver a roof-raising right uppercut that put Mortimer face down until his seconds hustled in to roll him over." The swiftness of Rocco's destructive power could no longer be denied. Those observers that evening would one day rate his right uppercut as the hardest punch ever thrown in a Lowell ring. "In recognition of his win," recorded *The Brockton Enterprise*, "Marchegiano was awarded a golden glove with a ruby (*which he promptly gave to Barbara upon his return home as an engagement gift*), a gold medal appropriately inscribed, and a gold colored bathrobe proclaiming himself the heavyweight king of the tourney."

Thus it was this Brockton heavyweight who carried the hopes of Massachusetts into the New England finals and not the original now abandoned prospect who lay prostrate on the canvas, unusually though Mortimer's adoring crowd did not switch their allegiance, as it should be, to his conqueror. In fact Marchegiano was viewed as a detestable character who had broken every rule in the ring and, in the words of columnist Frank Sargent, "…used everything but his teeth on his foes, for he has appeared in two fights and both times his opponent has wound up on the horizontal end of a haymaker. The crowd boo's his apparent use of elbows, thumbs and head."

This would be a charge that would follow Rocco into the professional ranks whence he would defend his seemingly rough-house tactics thus, "You can't lose a decision if your opponent is flat on his face." This disparaging of the victor again seemed to stem from McMullen who was left with a bitter taste in his mouth over the defeat of his boy leading him to comment later, "I didn't think too much of him. He seemed a little too cute. You'd hit him and he'd fake getting hurt. Then you'd relax and he'd slam you [3]."

The vitriol continued, as recorded by Sergent again, "Although Rocco, whose name sounds more like an Opera stars than a pugilist, will carry the colors of the state into battle against Vermont, Maine and New Hampshire…next week, there will be a lot of Lowell fans rooting for his opponent - any opponent." It would only be a matter of time however before the vagaries of both the boxing public and those who reported it would be changed in his favour, (*McMullen's opinion would take far longer*) now though Rocco would leave his thoughts on it all to himself and concentrate on the upcoming New England Golden Gloves tourney that his victory had ensured.

For the deposed Mortimer however this was to be his last bout, he would be quoted in later years as saying, "I had come off twelve straight wins, after the loss I figured if you can't win them all what the hell's the point."

With-in weeks the fighter with an Opera stars name found himself back in Lowell this time in an attempt to lay claim to the New England title, and with it a place in New York. It is a matter of conjecture as to what permeated through his mind as he stood once again in the magnificent Memorial Auditorium and gazed at the two tier seating that seemed to stretch forever upwards, dissected as it was at this time by a vast banner which read 'Lowell Sun Charities New England Golden Gloves Tournament of Champions' which stretched half way around the interior of that imposing venue. Or indeed his mindset as he stepped foot again in that roped arena which he would later describe as, "the best ring I ever fought in." Especially as he knew that the majority of those there present had come to see him lose.

It was only really Lowell's own sports columnist John F. Kenney who would voice his opinion in Rocco's favour recognizing that he was more puncher than boxer, indeed he would become one of Marchegiano's most vociferous supporters in the early years.

On that first night of competition, February 17th, the crowd would not get their wish, indeed they would not even get the chance to see their nemesis so much as climb between the ropes, nor even leave his dressing room which he shared with the seven remaining members of the Massachusetts team. For prior to the scheduled bout it was announced that his drawn opponent in the initial semi-final, a certain Ralph Piscope, winner of the Maine heavyweight championship, had forfeited the bout, leading Marchegiano to be declared the winner by default. Thus a bemused Rocco, wishing to believe that it was fear which directed his opponent to abandon the fight, dressed and ventured into the crowd to watch the remaining bouts in order to see who he would be pitted against in the final scheduled for the following day.

The reason for Piscope's withdrawal would be explained by *The Brockton Enterprise* as due to the "brand new addition to his family which required his stay at home." Was there perhaps a hint of reticence about his withdrawal however as Rocky believed? There are those who knew him in life nevertheless who will adamantly claim that he was not a coward, of that they are right, he was not, no man who served his country whilst at the same time juggling a young family and attempting to better his lot in life by studying law as Piscope did, in fact no man who steps between the ropes to fight could ever be called a coward. There was however perhaps some flaw in his fighting character that would show itself the very next year when he once again made it to the New England finals, this time he would fight, and it would be against the much hyped Pete Fuller.

Frank Sargent of *The Lowell Sun* recorded it thus: "Pete Fuller...faced a fellow named Ralph Piscope of Maine who seemed all the world like he had gotten into the ring by mistake and was looking for a path out. Fuller scored with a series of rights to the bread basket (*stomach*) and had his bigger foe in agony as early as the first round, although (*Fuller*) didn't put out the lights until the third round." Sure Ralph was no coward, but the evidence seems to point to a distaste for taking punishment, or at least folding when the odds seemed stacked in favor of his opponent. Perhaps against the Brockton boy he knew the odds were absurdly on the side of his competition, discretion it seemed may definitely have been the better part of valour.

Meanwhile the heat to find Rocky's opposite number back in '48 was fought between Dave Hinkley, the champion of Vermont, and pre-tournament favorite who moved with the speed of a light-heavyweight, against the slower moving New Hampshire champion George McGinnis. The bout was a huge anti-climax, it lasted a little over a minute with Hinkley being counted out after seemingly stepping into a right hook. Once again it set up a mouthwatering prospect with two punchers squaring off in a final within the Lowell ring.

Again the Auditorium rang to the voices of a capacity crowd ranging from the working man eager to witness a good bout, to civic dignitaries eager only to be seen. The applause meted out to both McGinnis and Marchegiano was equally respectable, everyone believed this one would not go the distance, yet none could, or would, lay it on the line and choose a winner. However most were in accord when they agreed that the man they felt had the easiest job that evening was the referee Joe Zapustas. "As long as he could count to ten he would do okay," said McMullen with a nod at the power both fighters carried into the ring.

At the outset they tore into each other with savage abandon, McGinnis because he was fuelled by his earlier stoppage victory, Rocco because he knew no other way. For full two-minutes the carnage reigned and then suddenly a big left hook from Marchegiano landed on the right side of George's face, in an instant his eyebrow seemed to explode sending a shower of blood geysering out onto spectators seated at ringside. Referee Zapustas had no option but to stop the action and inspect the injury, it was horrific, not needing a second opinion from the ringside physician he did not hesitate but called a halt to the fight then and there; no one in the crowd complained - particularly those in the front row.

Now the boy from Brockton had added the New England heavyweight championship to his Massachusetts and Rhode Island title, for his efforts he was presented with a resplendent sash belt complete with, according to *The Brockton Enterprise again,* "suitably engraved Golden gloves belt buckle, also more new ring equipment including boxing shoes and a new silk robe."

Rocco Francis Marchegiano had announced to the world beyond his beloved Brockton that finally he was on his way, but oddly, for now, the world wasn't listening. Caggiano however wasn't so much listening as watching, and what he was seeing moved him to the thought that he finally had someone with potential, no matter how limited. Indeed he was ebullient over his boys victory, I refer to *The Brockton Enterprise* once again who quoted him as saying, "Rocco did very well, smart in following up and taking advantage of that first important blow, and his opponent didn't have a chance for a comeback, not laying a glove on our champion." Caggiano knew he was on to something now and he wanted to protect his investment, thus he decided to put his charge under an informal contract which would read as follows:

> Agreement made this twenty-seventh day of February, 1948, between Rocco Marchegiano, 168 Dover Street, Brockton Massachusetts, and Generoso Caggiano, also known as Gene Caggiano, 797 Warren Avenue, Brockton, Massachusetts, as follows: In consideration of the time, efforts and teachings of Gene Caggiano to Rocco Marchegiano in the art of boxing, the said Rocco Marchegiano agrees with Gene Caggiano that in the event of the said Rocco Marchegiano should turn professional and enter the professional field within the next five years, the said Rocco Marchegiano will enter into a contract with Gene Caggiano to retain Gene Caggiano as manager.

The above was witnessed by those named, and by Rocco's brother-in-law, Vincent Pereira, it was an agreement nevertheless which Marchegiano would soon conveniently forget. To his chagrin however Caggiano would not forget, and this innocuous piece of paper would come back to haunt them both in the not too distant future.

Notes:

1. *The Lowell Sun newspaper lent its name to the tournament, sponsors of the tournament then and remaining proudly associated to this day.*

2. Rocco weighed in at close to his heaviest official weight for this bout, 192lbs.

3. McMullen made this statement before he had seen Marciano rise to the championship and his impression inevitably changed.

part two **chapter eight**

Brooklyn

"You gotta knock out a New York fighter to be sure of a win."

Tommy Rawson

Marchegiano's crushing victories in Lowell opened up to him a celebrated whole new world as the week ahead would give him a taste of success that would fuel his desire for more.

First the entire team representing *The Lowell Sun* charities in New York would be feted at a gala victory dinner held at the prestigious Parker House hotel in Boston, there they rested before their journey the following day onboard the fabled Yankee Clipper, one of the fastest trains in America. Here the team were presented with their royal purple and gold silk robes and trunks emblazoned with sponsors logo, these items would remain a source of great pride to Rocco as early photos from his professional career would attest as he is captured adorned in those very trunks.

"Upon arriving at Grand Central (*station*)," proudly reported *The Lowell Sun,* "...the entourage will proceed to the Park Central hotel one of the finest in New York, where they'll establish headquarters and a training table. The team will partake of only the best steaks, chops, green vegetables and other foods which grace the tables of boxing greats.

"When time permit's the huskies will go on a rubber-neck tour of the town, drinking in the millions of interesting sights to be seen in Manhattan. Special buses will transport the fighters to and from the arena(s), with the final celebrations to take place after Wednesday nights finals. Win or lose, the team will be guests of the N.Y Daily News at a banquet at the Belvedere hotel...In between times the lads will be signing autographs for the many enthusiastic fight fans, meeting radio, stage and screen celebrities and enjoying themselves as they've never enjoyed themselves before."

Yet despite being part of these celebrated times, the man himself barely registered on the Richter scale of the American boxing scene, indeed they caused only a minor ripple in his home state of Massachusetts with the local press at the time. Although devoting almost entire papers to the New England tournament, gushing over the brilliance of the show and the skill of those boxers involved, they merely gave this "...kid from the shoe city..." a cursory nod towards his punching prowess. As George McGuire would write of Marciano in *The Lowell Sun* retrospectively as late as February 1969, "he was a burly, bruising, awkward fighter when he won the Greater-Lowell and New England heavyweight crowns here in 1948." McGuire, seemingly in order to emphasize his point continued. "He was a lousy boxer. All he possessed was a sneaky right-handed uppercut."

It would then be only in hindsight that many would reflect back on Rocco with fond memories as he scaled the professional rungs to greatness, for such is the fickle nature of a public. When this occurred they would take him unquestionably to their hearts, a feeling which would be reciprocated by the man himself, with those from Lowell in particular claiming his ascendancy began with them in their very ring.

In a way they were right, for had this raw fighter not walked away with the titles from *The Lowell Sun* sponsored tournaments it is doubtful he would have continued on for much longer. Not one to live by the, "It is better to have tried and failed" route, an inability to succeed was seen as an embarrassment that he would do his all to avoid, something which had been drummed into him by his father who felt his own life had not been all that it could have been. This feeling would instill in his son an almost morbid fear of failure. Yet ironically it was his having to come to terms with, that which on the surface at least appeared to be a failure which would convince Rocco that his future may indeed lay with boxing.

It was on the morning of Monday, March 1st, that the New England amateur boxing team would rise early in the Park Central Hotel, their Brooklyn, New York base for the forthcoming Golden Gloves tournament. All eight boxers, ranging from featherweight Francis Collins through to Rocco at heavy quietly crept into the room of coaches Tommy Rawson and Frank Cabral who, slightly startled at being awoken, informed the boys that they didn't need to rise this early. Yet it was not for extra-curricular training, nor through the sheer nervous excitement of what was for many their first trip to New York which had caused them to arise at the crack of dawn, more it was an innocent and almost naïve need to vent their collective faith through prayer. In this regard it was arranged that later that very morning, and for the subsequent three thereafter, the entire team could be found amassed about the altar at the small St. Francis of Assisi church which was situated but a short walk from their accommodation. This was seen by many as an edifying incident which illustrated that despite the stereotypical image that had been harnessed by both the press and public alike of the time as portraying boxers as soulless thugs who fought in back-street saloons many, indeed most were in fact just your typical boy-next-door type.

However there was nothing typical about Rocco Marchegiano, and that evening the paying customers at Ridgewood Grove Arena who had come to see these initial stages of the National Golden Gloves finals being played out would find out just how atypical he truly was.

This tournament in New York was viewed by both competitors and public alike as the pinnacle of amateur boxing, success in New York almost guaranteed you a path into the professional ranks and an undoubtedly glorious future. It was here that boxing buzzed, anyone who was anyone could be found amongst the many whom had lost their way, from the top managers to top fighters. Champions of the world walked these streets by day and night taking in the bright lights that even the most gifted knew would one day fade. The city was also home to Madison Square Garden, the most prestigious venue in all of sports, to step between the ropes of this palace of pugilism was to have ascended the summit.

Everything rested in the gloved and bandaged hands of Rocco now and he knew it, here at last, after all his ups and downs, his moment to truly make something of his life, both for himself and his family. These thoughts undoubtedly permeated through his mind as he walked through the dazzling, daunting streets of Brooklyn with his team-mates wending their way to the offices of the *New York Daily News,* sponsors of that evening's entertainment. Accompanying Rocco were his erstwhile manager Gene Caggiano and the ever present Allie Colombo, who was now firmly established as his trusted second and conditioner, even though, as New England coach Tommy Rawson would reflect, "…he was no more than his training buddy, running with him and carrying his spit bucket, but he broke up the monotony of the grind and I guess in that way he was invaluable. [1]"

The almost countrified boys awestruck by this metropolitan city had made their ways to the offices of this sponsoring paper in order that they may be appraised as to the order of that evening's bouts. Most seemed quietly pleased with their opponents, but when those there gathered discovered Rocco's first round pick they were stunned almost to a man, I say almost, the only one who seemed blasé about it all was Rocco himself. The reason for the, to most, groans of disbelief was that the name thrown into the ring with the New Englander seemed an almost insurmountable obstacle to overcome, that name was Coley Wallace.

Wallace was big, standing at an impressive six-foot-three and, according to his officially recorded weight at the time, scaling some 221-pounds. Rocco, although blockier than he would be in later years, still only pushed the scales to the 190 mark. Also to add to his burgeoning task this Wallace was considered by many to be a truly outstanding fighter, in fact, the local New York papers, so convinced were they that this man was going to walk away with the title that they were advertising in big bold letters how you could sit back and watch his coronation from the comfort of your own living room. "Fight Fans see the local favorite Coley Wallace in action…as he wins the Golden Gloves tournament." Faith indeed in the fighters ability for this advert was placed on Monday, the tourney not concluding until Wednesday, their "local favorite" still had three prospective opponents to maneuver past first.

Wallace's reputation however was not built on sand, there was definite substance there. On the eve of his opening bout against Marchegiano he was coming off an unbeaten streak of seventeen straight wins, sixteen of them by knock-out. Included in his resume was the previously untouchable amateur Paul Simpson whom he took apart in three clinical rounds, it was through this bout that he would gain the almost unique distinction of being compared to the legendary Joe Louis. Previous comparison had already been made due to a clear similarity in looks, particularly profile, but now his skills led to a belief that he would be a future world champion, no doubt about it. It had become not a case of if he could beat his opponent but how quickly, the public, especially in New York, expected him to win and win big. This unknown kid wouldn't stand a chance.

It would appear that the omens leading up to the headline bout between Marchegiano and Wallace did not bode well for the Brockton fighter (2), of the three previous contests featuring members of the New England team all had ended in defeat. Coach Tommy Rawson put it down to the fact that under the New York rules each match was run over the three rounds of only two-minutes duration meaning that the boys from that state were already conditioned to fight with-in the allotted time frame which leant towards them being quicker, both in movement and punching. Whereas, Rawson argued, those from other areas where the three-minute rounds were in affect had allowed themselves to become accustomed to, as Rawson termed it, the "three-minute instinct" meaning they did not fight with the same tempo. The losses of all three by decision that night seemed to validate this theory. Next to be served up would be Marchegiano, would he too carry this 'instinct' into the ring, or would some other force be driving him on, it mattered little to the crowd who gave him perfunctory applause as he entered the ring, they saved their throats for Wallace.

The ensuing bout has become an almost mythic match-up not just in the life of Rocky Marciano, but in the history of boxing itself. There have been so many versions of the events which unfolded in the ring that night that it has become almost impossible to separate actuality from the Chinese whispers which have led to its convoluted reality over the ensuing sixty-years. Even now it remains an enigmatic, yet still most commented upon amateur bout in the history of the sport. The reasons for this are two-fold, first the account which Wallace himself would give, and take to his grave in 2005, the second is the account which would pass through the hands of those Marciano biographers who have gone before. The constant truth of it however is that, officially at least, Coley won, but it is the manner of his victory that has become elaborated upon.

"It was an easy fight, I had him down twice," Wallace would recall, adding. "Marciano was like a street fighter, a good beginner. He was swinging wild, never hit me solid, and didn't hit that hard. I found Rocky to be a strong determined fighter. After I floored him in the second round, Marciano came up swinging. Although I won the decision I had to admire his grim determination." This account has since been taken as fact for generations leading the Pulitzer Prize winning commentator, sometime boxing writer, and friend of Marciano's, Jimmy Breslin, to concur with Wallace. He felt that those who did not believe that Coley won the fight in the manner he maintained were taking part in a sort of, "…revisionist history. Were they there or were they making it up?"

Marciano on the other hand remembered the bout rather differently; as did his team coach Tommy Rawson, although with a slightly altered account to his famous charge. As late as 1965 the pair would reflect back to the bout in question. "I got underneath his punches and hit him in the rib cage and clubbed him on the back of the head. He stood tall like Ezzard Charles but he couldn't box me because of my awkward maneuvers, I had a little bob and weave even then. So I did fairly well in the first round," remembered Rocky. Rawson however stated quite categorically that he did not have such a good start, Wallace roughed his fighter up with forearms and elbows, hitting him at will with solid shots. "He threw Rocky all over the place," he declared. In the second Rocky conceded that he was soundly beaten for the full two-minutes, nevertheless Rawson again disagreed. "Rocky took the bull by the horns, he just lifted Coley Wallace like a sack of flour and shoved him around, and Wallace began retreating."

In the third however both were in accord with Marciano tearing into the taller fighter, stubbornly attempting to pin him to the ropes, with 45-seconds left he succeeded and teed off on his foe with abandon. Added Marciano "Then the bell rang and I'll never forget what happened next, because I was standing there watching Wallace's corner and saw it. One of his handlers threw a towel at Wallace in disgust, as if to say, 'You big bum, you blew the fight!' " Yet still the New York fighter got the decision leading Marciano to comment, "I don't like to put a rap on boxing, but even in the amateurs there was maybe some skullduggery."

It was Allie Colombo who on another occasion would add the reaction of the crowd to his friend's denial of victory, "They booed so loudly, I couldn't hear myself talking to the Rock as we left the ring. Everybody in the place wanted to pound Rocky on the back. We could hardly get through the crowd to the dressing room."

Each retelling nonetheless is subject to the human frailty of memory and perceived reflection, neither wishing to deny for him that which he felt was rightfully his. In Rocco's case this meant a victory, and in Wallace's it would be a vindication of his legacy, for, despite his initial brilliance, he would never fulfill that enormous potential which had been hoisted upon his broad shoulders. Sure he would go on to win this tournament on a decision over the highly regarded Bob Baker, he would even carry himself through three more victorious Golden Gloves competitions at regional level before finally coming unstuck in 1949 against the same Bob Baker, he would also fall short in his attempt to win a place on the '48 Olympic team on which many felt he was assured. In 1950 Wallace would turn professional and began what many felt was a guaranteed path to greatness, but it never happened.

Initially Coley would remain unbeaten as a professional that is until he met an unassuming and unremarkable heavyweight in June of 1951 by the name of Elkin Brothers who literally blew Wallace away inside of two-rounds, his career would never recover, retiring in 1956 with a less than impressive record of seven losses in twenty-seven fights. He would forever blame his inability to make an impression in the paid ranks to the intervention of his manager

Frank "Blinky" Palermo who was a fully paid up member of the Mob, that gangster element who unofficially ran boxing after the war. However in reality, the plain fact was that he just wasn't good enough.

Coley did however find a modicum of fame through his unnerving similarity to Joe Louis by portraying the man no less than three times on both the big screen and small, before retiring into the background and ending his career as a liquor salesman. Thus his victory over the then Marchegiano would forever remain, in hindsight, his greatest moment, a triumph over the man who was destined never to lose a bout in the prize ring, what harm would it do to embellish it.

It seemed however that the more he told his side of the story the more it became both added too and entrenched as an established truth, he was such a sincere individual in his advancing years that many were to fall under his spell, and, as the bout fell further and further back through time, its echo's became distorted and unimpeachable. Who would be able to refute it? Well there was one man who could, one amongst many who was there that night and who would not wait years to recount it's unfolding, that man was the late John F. Kenney, sports editor for the Lowell sun, and on Tuesday March 2nd, he would scribe the following for the edification of his readers:

> A tree grows in Brooklyn, and for all of the boxing fans packed in Ridgewood Grove for the first round of the All-Eastern Golden Gloves championship yesterday afternoon certain of the so-called authorities associated with the judging of relative ring merits of amateur boxing boys could well be lashed to the trunk and left to the vultures, or even suspended by the neck from one of its

spreading branches. In one of the most putrid decisions ever handed down from a Golden Gloves tournament anywhere…Rocco Markegiano (*sic*) of Brockton was penciled into the limbo of eliminated contenders after glorifying The Sun Charities' New England team in the hearts of 3000 fans by administering Coley Wallace, New York metropolitan champion, the pasting of that…goliath's career. In a word it was a stinkeroo.

…The fans from Brooklyn, Manhattan, Bronx and Queens who up to bell time didn't know Markegiano from a hole in the wall, milled their way from the back of the arena down to the very ropes after the final bout's decision was rendered. They raged for fully 15 minutes in fruitless protest, button holing anybody who looked like an official, and at times even threatening violence. Said a reporter from the Puerto Rican newspaper, El Mundo, 'How can New York expect various zones of the United States which have district tournaments, to return after a decision like that?' He was talking as fans picked up Markegiano as a baby and smothered him with pats on the back,…finally setting his feet on the Grove floor at coach Tommy Rawson's insistence. All the way up to the far dressing room the bewildered Rocco was pounded enthusiastically, his way impeded by fans who just wanted to shake hands with him. Hundreds of throats gave volume to the one yell, 'You won that fight son,' or another, 'The decision is only two blind men's not ours boy!'

...Rocco came out of his corner at the first bell and swished one of those uppercuts right at the giant's jowls. He missed. Wallace closed in to devour this presumptive New Englander, where-upon Markegiano slammed one into Wallace's stomach and threw a right to the...face that you could hear as far as Beaver brook in Dracut. Mister Wallace's expression changed. The fans began to take off their overcoats. If there has been any thoughts in the minds of the Lowell fans that Rocco acquired his Lowell victories too easily, or that he went to New York actually untested by reason of the fact that he never had to take it, well, they should have been here. Wallace beat Rocco back to the ropes by sheer power in that first round, but Markegiano wheeled quickly and put Wallace into the same spot, trying desperately to connect with that uppercut. Momentarily, the...behemoth put both gloves to his face for self-protection. The fans loved it. Apparently they had not seen this before from Wallace. They adopted Rocco, heart, glove and trunks from that moment. Markegiano bore right in. Belting Wallace to a point where it was reckless. Having only attack in his instincts, he was wide open. But here's where Wallace lost the fight in this man's book. Wallace swung back…again and again, but missed by the margin of home plate to outfield. They were tied in at close quarters at the first round's end. Markegiano couldn't knock Wallace out. That was evident in the first round. It was that kind of a fight. As the second canto started however, Rocco pitched everything he had into an aggressive, always moving offense. The bigger man backed up, circled, wheeled away and never counter-punched. Wallace always covered, then fought his way out with ungainly punches that only landed without aim. Wallace apparently had figured at this stage that if he swung often enough he might catch Rocco with something wild. Markegiano was driving rights and lefts to Wallace's head in a neutral corner when the bell rang. Markegiano didn't win the third and final round. Nor did he lose it. Wearied to a point where only self-gumption carried him through, the Brockton…hope kept on whirling them in there, but his Sunday punch was ineffective. It wasn't because he wasn't connecting, but because Wallace was too tall for the smaller Rocco's whameroo. His big poke to the jaw connected often enough, but by the time it reached its objective it had passed the radius of effectiveness. To hit Wallace with that sleeper Markegiano had to hoist it upwards as a hod-carrier carries up the bricks. The stronger Wallace kept on weathering a terrific attack, but when he threw a fresher set of punches at Rocco in the third round he always found more gloves in his face…these were mostly exhausted punches, but they were there. Just before the bell sounded, Markegiano rallied all he had left and was fighting only with his heart as Wallace awkwardly stumbled with what appeared to be puzzlement and panic. They were all in at close quarters when the last bell sounded. By that time the joint was going crazy. Gene Caggiano, who handles Rocco back in the Bay State, leaped into the ring with wild delirium. So did Rawson and Cabral. The fans were applauding the happy Markegiano to a point where the announcer could hardly be heard. The loudspeaker finally got its request for quiet. The announcer looked over the slips in the traditional manner then spoke: 'The winner,' he said, 'Wallace.' Ridgewood Grove became pandemonium. A roar went up first and it was of one word: 'No.' It continued for a quarter-hour. Reporters demanded explanation. These were from Jacksonville and Buffalo and other spots unacquainted with Markegiano. All they knew was that they had seen a fight won and lost and they wished to record it that way.

Thus Rocco, who had to all appearances won the day, did not, according to the officials marking the scorecard for the bout, emerge triumphant from this match. It was Wallace, so they agreed, who had won the fight. "But scoring sheets are not as articulate as thousands of fans," continued Kenney. A demand for the scoring of the bout brought out the objective facts, Judge Rudy Keppler voted for Marchegiano, while Judges Delaney and Referee Barney Smith voted for Wallace.

In the immediate aftermath there was talk, in an attempt to pacify the growing feeling of chaos with-in the arena, that Rocco would be named alternate on the All-Eastern team to meet Chicago's standouts in a later tournament. Whilst all this turmoil bubbled over meanwhile, Rocco had eventually made his way through frantic applause and congratulatory abandon to his dressing room where he was to entertain for the first time an enthusiastic press eager to get his reaction to the universally condemned decision. "Why can't I go in as a number one heavyweight?" he enquired on hearing of the ruling regarding his possible inclusion into the all-eastern team. "I think I could lick Wallace again." Yet to the incredulity of those present he refused to talk down about his alleged conqueror, "Wallace is a good boy. He gave me the hardest fight of my experience." Yet in private the vanquished Marchegiano would resent his erstwhile victors glory as down through the years Coley's lavish reworking grew more and more improbable.

Whilst still in the dressing room immediately after the bout the then unknown fighter's turbulent emotions, at one time somber, at another ecstatic, were alleviated when he met face to face with the former heavyweight champion Gene Tunney who entered his dressing room in order to congratulate the amateur on his fight. Tunney also reiterated the opinion of the majority that he was robbed out of victory. He would add to this his complements on Marchegiano's unique style of infighting which Caggiano had been attempting to add to his fighters limited arsenal just prior to the bout. "It was this fight and the comments of Tunney that convinced Rocky that he could go places in the sport," remarked Rawson later. "He wanted another shot at Wallace, and with the AAU tournament to be held in Boston just a month away we both knew that victory there would seal for him another crack at Coley."

Rocco himself would later admit that this setback again left him disillusioned with the sport to the point that he was almost on the brink of walking away once more. That is until he read the above article whilst sat in New York's famous Times Square the following day. "When I read that article in the morning I knew I had a future." Many years later, by which time having ascended to the heavyweight championship the then Rocky Marciano discovered that the author of the piece lay ill in Lowell's Meadowcrest hospital, he saw this as his chance to thank the writer for his inspirational words, thus he sat down to pen a few of his own to the stricken Kenney:

> I wonder, Jack, if you ever realized how much your wonderful story on the fight I had when I represented your Lowell Sun team in '48 in New York meant to me. It was the inspiration I needed to continue fighting. First of all your Lowell Sun Tournament gave me the opportunity to get started in boxing again after being away from it for two years after being out of the Army. Then when I did so well and qualified to make the trip to N. Y., I wanted to win that tournament very much, and then to lose in the first bout of the N.Y tournament was a disappointment, but then I got your wonderful story for me. Jack I still have that story and it is on the first page

of my wife's scrapbook. That was the real beginning for me.

Your Friend
Rocky Marciano

Eventually, in 1954, Marciano would get to visit Kenney in person whilst appearing as a guest referee at the very same Lowell Sun Charities tournament that had launched him on his path to the championship some six-years earlier. Upon meeting the afflicted writer he would produce the fading and well-thumbed article.

"I can't emphasize enough how those words affected me," said Marciano. "I owe John everything; I have a debt of gratitude that can never be repaid." At the meeting Kenney vowed that when he had regained his strength he would come to see Rocky defend his championship in person, alas it was an oath he would not be able to keep for he was to languish in ill health for the next six-years before passing away in 1960. Marciano, despite his fondness for the man who had been the first to see the spark of genius in this raw uncultured lump of granite over a decade before never attended the funeral; it would not be the last time he failed to pay his final respects to someone who had helped to shape him.

For now though Marchegiano had returned to Brockton and this time his homecoming allowed him to greet his family and friends with his head held high, he was the toast of the city, at least in terms of sporting achievements, his name, albeit spelt wrong, was in every major paper in the United States, he had tasted his first bite of fame and he liked it...

Notes:

1. .Allie Colombo remains at the time of writing this (Feb. 2012) an enigma. I am confused as to his actual role in the life of Rocky Marciano for there are those who are adamant that Allie was crucial in Marciano's rise, that without him Rocky would never have climbed to the pinnacle of his chosen sport, "I'd never have gotten where I did without him," commented the former champion after his old friends tragic death in 1969. So it seems that Allie was central to Rocky, but in what capacity? Some maintain that the man who appeared in the corner for every one of his friends fights from 1947 through to 1955 was a great trainer in his own right, others that he was nothing more than a hanger on, still others that he was crucial in keeping Rocky grounded and focused. The latter seems to be possibly the nearest to the truth for as Marciano himself stated, "Allie was a real buddy. He kept my interest in boxing alive through all the difficult moments. Prize fighting is a very serious business, but Allie was very witty and when we got too serious he'd use his sense of humor to relax the atmosphere." Colombo's humor is attested to by all who knew him as was his sincerity and honesty. Remembered the late Mike Pusateri a fighter who came under Allie's influence after Marciano had retired, "I've never known a better guy in the whole world. He was like a big brother to me." As the Marciano story unfolds hopefully we will get a chance to understand a little better the role of this decent, honest family man for right now he continues to remain a slightly mysterious influence.

2. Marchagiano was announced as representing Lowell for this evening's festivities, it was not the first time that he would not be credited with hailing from Brockton (see part 2 chap. 4 - 'Barbara and Rocky Mack'.

part two   chapter nine

Goodbye Gene

"I'll show this bum just how good I am, I'll turn pro and make a million-dollars."

Rocky Marciano

In the immediate aftermath of the Wallace bout, Eugene Caggiano, with his eye on a quick buck, hastily arranged for an "amateur" bout at Canton Hall in their home town of Brockton, pitching the now nationally acclaimed Marchegiano against the rugged, yet relatively unknown Vic Sidlauskas. At the time it seemed a shrewd move on the promoters part, however it would have unforeseen consequences which would lead Caggiano inexorably towards losing his grip on the future heavyweight champion of the world.

"He hired a hall and promised $100 for my share if we'd sell tickets," recalled Rocco, continuing, "…we sold enough to fill up the place, and we helped put up the ring. Allie and a couple of other guys even installed the seats." Added Colombo, "We put in a full week and sold $700-dollars' worth of tickets."

The pair, along with the erstwhile promoter, would even go so far as to appear on WBET, Brockton's local radio station which occupied the second floor of the Brockton Enterprise building on Main street. The interviewer was one Fred Cusick who himself would later go on to find a modicum of fame as a ice hockey announcer, most associated as 'The voice of the Boston Bruins'. His memory of the meeting with Marchegiano was, nevertheless, of a, "…rather brief and not memorable chat. I don't even recall the date or events they were there to discuss."

The fight itself was a thriller whilst it lasted, Rocco eventually dispatched his foe in the third of a scheduled five, yet despite all their hard efforts in publicizing the bout it remained one of Marciano's least remembered matches, even in Brockton. Yet its postscript would haunt the pair of Marchegiano and Caggiano for many years to come when, on the following day Rocco went to collect his share of the proceeds. Once again, in an almost exact duplicate of the Epperson debacle a year earlier, he was, he felt, short changed.

"Caggiano offered me forty bucks. When I refused it he put it in an envelope and posted it to my mother," recalled Rocco. For months the pair would argue over who was right in their assumption over the exact amount that had been agreed upon, "I even offered Rocky my watch in order to pacify him, but he just yelled me down and kept threatening me over owing him $60, but I knew I never did," recalled Gene. Nonetheless by the end of March there appeared to be enough amicability between them for Caggiano to accompany his sometime protégé to the New England heavyweight championships held at the Boston Arena on the evening of the 22nd.

Marchegiano had chosen to participate in this one day tournament over the more prestigious Chicago Golden Gloves being held concurrently, for he had, as promised in the aftermath of

Even in his beloved Brockton he was not immune to occasional jeering as he was seen running with his faithful companion, Allie Colombo, by his side through the streets as dawn broke over the city, wrapped heavily in layers of sweat clothes in order to burn off his mothers' copious meals, his right hand covered in a heavy cast which would remain as an impediment for several months. "I didn't realize it at the time but the injury was a blessing in disguise. Now we could concentrate full-time on getting him ready for boxing," stated Allie. But still there seemed to be no-one willing to invest in his friends future.

Finally a conference was convened in the Marchegiano's family parlor, present were the two boys, uncles Mike Piccento, and Dominic Prosper, along with Barbara's father Lester Cousins, and of course Rocco's father Piereno. Also joining them was Gene Caggiano who found himself accosted at every opportunity over the alleged sixty-dollar shortfall he was believed to still owe. It was here that Rocco announced openly his intention to turn professional, Caggiano was aghast at the suggestion, "I told him to forget it, there was no way at that time that he was ready to turn pro, I thought he wouldn't make it, he needed more time, but what the hell did I know."

This was the last straw for the budding champion, not only had Gene, he believed, conned him out of money, but now he had the affront to denigrate him in front of his own family. Caggiano, on sensing that he had perhaps spoken out of turn, even if he felt it to be the truth which was shared by others than just him, quickly made his excuses and left the room, it was to be the last time that he would be directly involved in the career of his one time charge.

There were others however who believed in Rocco's ambition to the extent that many of his friends gathered together to raise funds to the sum of more than $125 in order to assist in paying his mounting medical bills that accrued as he sought to fix his hands. Rocco would forever remain grateful for their generosity. But of course his staunchest supporter, and the

The pair, along with the erstwhile promoter, would even go so far as to appear on WBET, Brockton's local radio station which occupied the second floor of the Brockton Enterprise building on Main street. The interviewer was one Fred Cusick who himself would later go on to find a modicum of fame as a ice hockey announcer, most associated as 'The voice of the Boston Bruins'. His memory of the meeting with Marchegiano was, nevertheless, of a, "…rather brief and not memorable chat. I don't even recall the date or events they were there to discuss."

The fight itself was a thriller whilst it lasted, Rocco eventually dispatched his foe in the third of a scheduled five, yet despite all their hard efforts in publicizing the bout it remained one of Marciano's least remembered matches, even in Brockton. Yet its postscript would haunt the pair of Marchegiano and Caggiano for many years to come when, on the following day Rocco went to collect his share of the proceeds. Once again, in an almost exact duplicate of the Epperson debacle a year earlier, he was, he felt, short changed.

"Caggiano offered me forty bucks. When I refused it he put it in an envelope and posted it to my mother," recalled Rocco. For months the pair would argue over who was right in their assumption over the exact amount that had been agreed upon, "I even offered Rocky my watch in order to pacify him, but he just yelled me down and kept threatening me over owing him $60, but I knew I never did," recalled Gene. Nonetheless by the end of March there appeared to be enough amicability between them for Caggiano to accompany his sometime protégé to the New England heavyweight championships held at the Boston Arena on the evening of the 22nd.

Marchegiano had chosen to participate in this one day tournament over the more prestigious Chicago Golden Gloves being held concurrently, for he had, as promised in the aftermath of the Wallace debacle, been named as a member of the All-Eastern team (*the only New England fighter to be awarded a place that year*), yet he declined, preferring a chance to claim local honors. It was, it appeared, a wise choice.

"The performer who scored highest in the 'color' department perhaps, was Rocco Markegiano (*sic*), the Brockton heavyweight who somehow last night proved that he was robbed of the decision in his New York Golden Gloves test with Gotham's AAU champion Coley Wallace," reported journalist John F. Kenney in the following mornings addition of *The Lowell Sun*.

Kenney continued, "Markegiano fairly battered Sol Fischera of Lawrence in his first test, then in the final bout of the evening emerged the better man in a gargantuan slugging match with George McGinnis of Belmont."

This was his second encounter with McGinnis, the first, as recounted above, was felt by many to have been stopped too soon by the referee after that cut above George's eye which had refused to stem its flow of blood. This time though the critics would get their chance to see a bout over the full allocated three-rounds. Kenney again, "Moving in all the time and holding his right uppercut back through most of the early going, Markegiano belted McGinnis to the canvas near the end of the second round for a count of nine, and had the Belmont gamester on the floor twice in the third round to win decisively."

It seemed, for a while at least, that all was going just right for Rocco, he had added the New England Amateur heavyweight championship to his swiftly impressive resume due to this victory over this, "...short, fat, dumpy looking kid..." as McGinnis was unflatteringly described by New England promoter Sam Silverman, who would soon play his own part in the rise of Marchegiano.

This was however to be Marchegiano's final amateur bout. Soon after emerging victorious his hands had begun to swell once more, upon inspection it was discovered that he had fractured his right thumb. Swiftly he was placed in a cast and sorrowfully bid farewell to any hopes of entering the Olympic tryouts due to begin in April and with them a chance to have a return with Wallace. To add insult to genuine injury, his job at the gas company was also placed in jeopardy due to his inability to work now that he had sustained damage to those hands yet again.

This time though, instead of brooding on what too many would be seen as a failure as he had done before, he would now gird himself towards a future in the paid ranks of boxing. "I was earning sixty-five or seventy bucks a week at the gas company but I couldn't work until my hand healed, they had cost me so much money that I thought it was about time they started making me some," he said retrospectively in 1962. Colombo though saw it rather as a last ditch effort to save him from anonymity before time ran out. "The Rock was worried," Colombo stated, adding, "He chose to turn pro when he did because he was afraid that soon he would be in too much pain to punch, then it would be all over, so he wanted to get as much money as he could as soon as he could."

Thus he returned to Boston in order to trawl the fight clubs which dotted Friend Street and neighboring Canal Street that flanked the Boston Garden and housed the menagerie of fight managers who frequented this hub of boxing. His main aim was to track down Johnny Buckley, now the owner of his own bar yet who had once been the manager of former heavyweight champion Jack Sharkey, but, as legend would maintain, as the Brockton boy walked into Buckley's Tavern through the front door, the proprietor was walking out through the back. No one, it appeared, was interested, not in this elderly amateur who was advancing rapidly towards his twenty-fifth birthday and was approaching them with the added handicap of his hand now in plaster. "Everywhere I went I was laughed at," remembered a dejected Rocco. "But I kept thinking I would show them, I knew I would make it."

Even in his beloved Brockton he was not immune to occasional jeering as he was seen running with his faithful companion, Allie Colombo, by his side through the streets as dawn broke over the city, wrapped heavily in layers of sweat clothes in order to burn off his mothers' copious meals, his right hand covered in a heavy cast which would remain as an impediment for several months. "I didn't realize it at the time but the injury was a blessing in disguise. Now we could concentrate full-time on getting him ready for boxing," stated Allie. But still there seemed to be no-one willing to invest in his friends future.

Finally a conference was convened in the Marchegiano's family parlor, present were the two boys, uncles Mike Piccento, and Dominic Prosper, along with Barbara's father Lester Cousins, and of course Rocco's father Piereno. Also joining them was Gene Caggiano who found himself accosted at every opportunity over the alleged sixty-dollar shortfall he was believed to still owe. It was here that Rocco announced openly his intention to turn professional, Caggiano was aghast at the suggestion, "I told him to forget it, there was no way at that time that he was ready to turn pro, I thought he wouldn't make it, he needed more time, but what the hell did I know."

This was the last straw for the budding champion, not only had Gene, he believed, conned him out of money, but now he had the affront to denigrate him in front of his own family. Caggiano, on sensing that he had perhaps spoken out of turn, even if he felt it to be the truth which was shared by others than just him, quickly made his excuses and left the room, it was to be the last time that he would be directly involved in the career of his one time charge.

There were others however who believed in Rocco's ambition to the extent that many of his friends gathered together to raise funds to the sum of more than $125 in order to assist in paying his mounting medical bills that accrued as he sought to fix his hands. Rocco would forever remain grateful for their generosity. But of course his staunchest supporter, and the one who showed the most faith in this aspiring boxer, was his now closest friend, Allie Colombo, it was his belief that all would come to them one day soon which seemed to fuel Marchegiano's desire to succeed. Both boys knew however that they would need a little help from someone involved in the world of boxing and in order to facilitate this it was Colombo who suggested to Rocco that they would do well to speak with a former professional fighter by the name of Joe Monte. This man who had lost one of his eyes due to an injury sustained in the ring, was heavily involved in the fight scene in Brockton both in his capacity as a judge and sometime trainer of aspiring pugilists. His advice was encouraging, as Marciano would reflect in The Saturday Evening Post of September 1956:

"You're a good fighter, Rocky," he says. "You got a good punch and could go a long ways. Get yourself a good manager and give all your time to this thing. Give it everything you got. Don't make the same mistake I did. I got a Boston manager, and he didn't have the right connections. You got to get away from Boston. You want to hit the big time. And there's only one way to do it. You and Allie, both of you, you got to get out of town. Go to New York and get one of them big-time managers. It's the only way."

Rocco took this advice onboard and thus made the bold move of taking his career into his own hands, hands incidentally which by late May had healed sufficiently to allow Rocco to spar again without pain. It wasn't that he did not appreciate the work that Allie was doing on his behalf, in the main it allowed him to concentrate on his training, but he hated not being in control of his own destiny. Nevertheless unbeknownst to him he would soon have to give up all control of his entire life to another, and, despite his best efforts he would never truly get it back again.

The move he made was a simple phone call to New England coach Tommy Rawson. "Rocky phoned me in late May 1948 and asked if I wanted to manage him, I told him that I was honored that he thought of me but I was strictly amateur, and besides, I felt I didn't have the connections to move him far. He seemed disappointed, but then I told him about Al Weill who had approached me after the Wallace fight and was interested in handling him, he left me an address so I passed it on."

Rawson was not the only one to recommend Weill, another was Eddie Boland. Boland, a veteran fight manager from Boston urged Marchegiano towards Weill, he was, he felt, the only one with the right connections to move Rocco forward at the pace he needed. "If he had stayed in Boston he never would have been champion, not even a contender, by the time he started getting the big fights he would have been too old to make the best of them," stated Boland emphatically. "I offered to write Weill on their behalf, for years he (*Weill*) went around telling everyone I'd sent this kid to him, but I really only sent him a letter."

Thus with all this in mind the pairing of Rocco and Allie sat down to compose a letter of their own to the formidable New York manager which they hoped would place them on a path towards sealing their fortunes:

> Dear Mr. Weill;
>
> Your name was recommended to me and I'm therefore writing on behalf of a young heavyweight fighter who I think has the potential to become the world's heavyweight champion. He is five-feet-eleven and weighs about 190, and one of the greatest prospects in the country, he finished competing in the Golden Gloves where he was robbed in a fight with Coley Wallace, who I'm sure you heard of. Rocco Marchegiano is his name and I've known him all my life. He has been a football star and a good

athlete. He is very strong and durable with plenty of ambition. I'm sure with proper handling he can win the title. Although we are close to Boston we are dissatisfied with a Boston contact and would much prefer New York handling. If you are interested please let me hear from you.

Sincerely

Al Colombo.

The boys sat back in eager anticipation of a reply. They would not have to wait for long.

Part Three: June 1948 -- December 1949

Providence

part three   **chapter one**

Enter 'The Vest'...

"(Weill)…is of the build referred to in ready-made-clothing stores as portly, which means not quite a stout. There is an implication of at least one kind of recklessness about a fat man; he lets himself go when he eats. A portly man on the other hand, is a man who would like to be fat but restrains himself -a calculator."

A.J. Leibling

Armand Alphonse Weill, also known as 'Weskit' or more commonly 'The Vest' because, 'he got all the gravy (*more often than not in the literal sense for it was said of his slovenly eating habits that you could tell the contents of the menu at the Stage Deli just by looking at his vest)*." But to most he was known simply as 'Al'.

Regarded as manipulative, shrewd, deceitful, and, to a greater extent inextricably linked to the more nefarious characters in the shadowy world of the sport of which he was a major player. Most disliked him, yet the one thing that was agreed by all, albeit reluctantly, was that he was thee driving force behind one of the most remarkable heavyweight's in history [1].

Born December 28th 1893 in Guebweiller, France, he first set foot in America at the age of thirteen when he came to stay with relatives in Yorkville, New York in 1907, and never left. With-in two decades he had become one of the preeminent managers and promoters in America. His rise to this position was one which now has become lost to history, never did he, nor indeed was he, inclined towards his own biographical tale; this is a shame for we have lost a great story of triumph over adversity, immigrant child made good in the land of opportunity. A small hint at his almost meteoric rise was suggested by Boston Promoter Manny Almeida however who would soon, along with Sam Silverman, become pivotal in Weill's plan for, "this Marchegiano kid."

"How do you think he got where he did," Almeida mused to a reporter after Al Weill's death in 1969. "He got there by greasing the right poles."

There is little doubt that this is a thinly veiled reference to the underworld elements who controlled boxing during the prohibition days of the young Weill's ascendancy, and who would tighten their miasmic grip once the law had been lifted and new outlets for power were needed. For boxing, with its element of outsiders both in and out of the ring, was a perfect breeding ground for corruption. Everyone wanted to be a champion when that title, regardless of division, still held an almost mythic quality and people were prepared to pay to achieve even the smallest piece of it so for Al to bed down with those who controlled the sport was no disgrace. As Almeida added to his own statement, "…then everyone was in their pockets, if they weren't then they never got anywhere."

The man who would emerge as undisputed underworld czar of the sport and for whom, it is alleged Weill himself served as a kind of shadow manager, was the notorious Frankie Carbo. Known by the sobriquet of Mr. Fury or Mr. Gray he had in his own past been a former Mafia hit man for the legendary firm of Murder Inc. Carbo's ascension to the pinnacle of boxing, albeit in the shadows, was forged through his association with the almost naïve James Norris, owner of the International Sporting Club, the official face of boxing in the late 1940's. Indeed there was not a major bout made nor champion crowned without the sanction of Carbo (*see chap; Mr. Gray & Octopus Inc.*). His was a reign that would not be challenged until the Kefauver hearings some three decades later.

For Weill by the late 1920's the moniker of 'The Vest' had already indelibly stuck to the man who was arranging matches at the soon to be defunct Harlem Olympic Arena in New York, he would go on from there to promote at the famed Ebbets field in Brooklyn, then on to the Boston Gardens. Here his association with both Almeida and Silverman was forged. Before, in 1931, being invited to promote solely for Mike Jacob's Twentieth Century Sporting Club which was the zenith of professional boxing for over a decade.

Nevertheless it would not be until 1936 that this top-tier promoter found his first world champion. He came in the form of Lightweight Lou Ambers whose career Weill himself bank rolled leading Al and his family into almost financial disaster sending him grey into the bargain.

Eventually Weill would take two more fighters to world honors in Joey Archibald at feather, and Marty Servo at welter. Yet despite these successes what he really craved was that cash cow which was wrapped up in the heavyweight championship. He had sniffed it with Johnny Risko in the late twenties and early thirties, and tasted it with Arturo Godoy in the forties, but he had yet to hold it. There is little doubt that as he sat in his office situated amidst the neon decadence and fakery of Broadway as he spoke on the phone that afternoon with Charley Goldman, thoughts of having at last found his champion were farthest from his calculating mind.

Yet he was moved enough by his recollection of Marchegiano from his New York appearance in March plus the letters he had received from both Boland and Colombo to give the latter "a bang" as he would refer to conversations on the phone. As Marciano related to Al Hirshberg and Milton Gross of The Saturday Evening Post of September 1956:

> We were playing a ball game for the Ward Two memorial club at Edgars Playground when Allie's sister running out of the house yelling, 'Hey Allie, there's a long-distance call for you - somebody named Al Weill!'…So Allie who was the catcher that day, ran all the way home with his shin guards and chest protector still on, and we held up the ball game. When he came back he acted like nothing unusual happened. He put his mask back on and we started the game again. When the innings was over, he says to me on the bench, 'Hey Rock that was Weill calling from Washington, he wants to see us first chance we get to go into New York. When you want to go Rock?'

If Rocco was excited about the news however he held it back commendably, for he informed Allie that his main concern at that time was winning the ball game they were involved in. A victory in this game would seal for them a make or break clash with arch-rivals Plymouth in the next series. Thus he opted to wait until after that game before making a move on New York. It would be over a week later after the pivotal game, which they lost, that Colombo called Weill back to arrange a visit.

Money was tight for the pair, they fretted over how they would be able to make the trip. Initially, to Colombo's horror, Rocco suggested they should walk it, if they left two days early they could rough it on the roads. Thankfully for Colombo another means was found when a Brockton truck driver, and frustrated fighter, by the name of Bill O'Malley heard about the boy's plight and offered to help them out. Every other night at eight o'clock he and another driver left Brockton for New York to deliver fresh vegetables, Rocco could travel with him, Colombo could hitch with the other.

They arrived in the Yonkers district of New York at the ungodly hour of three in the morning whence they took a subway to Manhattan, alighting at Times Square. Their appointment with the indomitable Weill was not until ten-thirty, thus they walked the streets of Broadway killing time pending 'The Vest's' arrival at his 1585 Broadway office.

Eventually the meeting was convened in Weill's small cluttered office on the third floor of the Strand Theatre building, an office he had inhabited since the early twenties. The man himself sat snugly behind his cluttered desk, ever present trunk of cigar protruding from between his lips, behind him a modest window bearing the stenciled legend: **Al Weill Promotions**.

Marchegiano was nervous standing before the inscrutable eyes of this big time manager, indeed he barely said a word allowing Colombo to talk for him. This was to be the last time his friend would directly influence his career.

Despite Colombo's immersion into all that was boxing since Rocco had first muted interest in the sport Allie would nevertheless display a naivety that would cause friction between him and Weill later. When asked for Rocco's weight Colombo replied, "one-ninety." His answer should have been simply "ninety" the hundred would have been assumed. Still, Weill was intrigued enough to pick up the phone that was almost hidden amidst the disarray of his desk and make a call.

As Rocky recalled, "We hear him say, 'I'm bringing down a new kid, a heavyweight. Get somebody ready for him. I want to see him work a couple of rounds'." With that the three men who would swiftly ascend the summit of the boxing world quickly made their way from Weill's office and down and out onto the teeming streets. From there they hailed a cab, negotiating the rush hour traffic to the CYO gymnasium on 17th street where they ascended the dingy steps to the second floor of the brownstone unassuming building, there to be met by the fourth and possibly most vital piece of the puzzle, Weill's trainer of choice, Charley (*sometimes spelt Charlie*) Goldman.

Notes:

1. *Initially I had been under the impression that Weill was a character who was universally despised, someone who would step over his own mother in order to forge for himself a career, yet as I delved deeper niggling doubts began to surface about the veracity of certain reports. After Rocky's retirement for instance when his impressions of Weill became forged even his own wife and others would maintain that Al was not as bad as he was being depicted by Rocky. There would be too contradictory stories for instance of his benevolence to his*

fighters, former boxers from his various stables reported that he was a genuine manager, Hank Cisco, a middleweight contender who fell under Weill's influence prior to the emergence of Marciano regarded Al as a missionary aid trainer, Hank explained, 'Foreign aid a check is sent and you don't know who it helps, missionary aid the people who give are there to help with their hands and stay till the mission is complete.' It seemed that my initial feeling towards Al stemmed from Marciano's own perception of his manager, was it that Al took as complete a control of those who fell under his guidance as possible which rankled Rocky: remembered Cisco again, 'Al treated me like a rookie in the army talking to me like a man in charge that knew what he was talking about.' This was Al's way, he could come across as dictatorial at times, as overly exertive, treating his fighters with what appeared to be almost contempt, yet for Weill I am left in little doubt now that he genuinely cared for his fighters, his episodes where his authority was meted out were more as he saw himself as a father figure putting his children in line for their own good; according to Cisco again, 'Al cared about his fighters both in the ring and outside the ring.' And as if to reinforce the now prevailing view of the role that Weill saw himself taking once a boxer had signed with him I refer to a statement his step son Marty Weill made reflecting back on Al:

'The boxers listened because they knew he was something more than a manager to them. He was a father...Al Weill took his fighters in and adopted them as sons. He supported them financially, even to giving them money to send home to their folks. Al saw to it that new boys were given a place to stay, money for clothes, weekly expenses and a meal ticket to a neighbourhood restaurant. Al would pay the trainer, gym expenses, cornermen and transportation out of his own pocket and let the fighter keep the purse. He didn't want the youngsters to get discouraged.'

So it seems that Weill was not the ogre that had been perceived through the reflections of Marciano himself, perhaps his resentment of his manager stemmed from a misunderstanding of his ways, the fact that Rocky was so much older than most who came under Weill's wing may have made their relationship untenable, Rocky already had his own personality. Marty again, 'Al Weill, had to be a psychologist as well as tougher and stronger than any of the fighters he managed...making not just men, but champions. He not only saw to it that they learned a skill but an entire new way of life.' For Rocky it seemed that Weill's way was uncomfortable and demeaning to this man, he was not a child to be manipulated, to be shaped, his animosity was aroused by age. Weill treated him no different than any other fighter he had managed and perhaps this is what Marciano found difficulty in accepting...

part three **chapter two**

...and Charley too

"...he was a quiet kid and seemed sincere. I could see he wanted to be a fighter and was willing to work. He didn't seem afraid in the ring. I knew he was hungry...I could see he had strong arms and could punch, which is the big thing. I figured maybe he had a chance to do something, not as a champion, mind you, but just as a good pro maybe."

Charley Goldman

Goldman was a short bespectacled little svengali with gnarled hands and nose flattened by, he would claim, over four-hundred fights as a bantamweight dating back to the early 1900's when he was but fourteen. He had learned his trade from the taverns and streets of the Red

Hook district of Brooklyn where he had landed at the end of the nineteenth-century from his native Poland where he was born under the biblical sounding name of Israel in the mostly Jewish province of Warsaw on 22nd of December 1887.

He took his first steps into the sport under the aegis of 'Terrible' Terry McGovern, a formidable bantam, and later featherweight champion from the turn of the twentieth century. It was from him that the diminutive Goldman would take his trademark black derby which was rarely far removed from his balding pate.

The pinnacle of his own career inside the ring came in 1912 when he fought the then bantamweight world champion, Johnny Coulon. That bout ended in a no-decision, although most papers from the time who claimed to be the arbiters of such decisions in an era when boxing was still illegal in many states judged that the victory should have gone to him. Charley was never bitter even though he would never get another chance to scale the summit himself for just two short years later he had been forced to terminate his own career due to the brittleness of his two small, yet powerful hands.

Yet in order that he should never sever his ties with the sport that this lifelong bachelor saw as his wife, his mistress, and his mother all rolled into one, he turned his attention to training and managing fighters himself. Over the ensuing forty-years he became one of the most respected and beloved figures in a business that was brimming with self-centered, down right malicious characters. The great journalist Jimmy Cannon once famously penned, "To call Goldman a mere trainer was like calling Rodin a stone mason. He was one of the great artists of sport."

It helped too that he had also, long before his association with Marciano, reached the heights of forging no-less than four men into the envious position of champions at their respective weights. These were Al McCoy (*middleweight*), Joey Archibald (*featherweight*), Lou Ambers (*lightweight*), and Marty Servo (*welterweight*). These last three having all at the time of their triumphs, been managed by Al Weill. Thus leading Charley to become his most trusted aid, the one he turned to when someone approached on the horizon who might, just might, have that extra something special.

The pairing of Weill and Goldman was one of the un-likeliest marriages in boxing, yet they worked perfectly together. They had met when Goldman was running his own concession stand at an amusement park in Carnasie, Brooklyn during the twenties. "He was just as smart then as he was later on when he was running big people," he recalled of Weill. "All you had to do was watch how he took over anybody who came around to see he was smart; so, we became partners in running a stable of fighters." The partnership dissolved however during the great depression of the thirties with Goldman finding employment managing a roadhouse bar in Orange Lake, New York.

His relationship with his erstwhile partner would soon re-ignite when, in 1936, his former partner approached him in the hope that he would train his fighters for him once again, starting with Ambers. This time though Weill would be indisputably the boss.

Like his sometime associate (*and lifelong friend*) Goldman also as yet had failed to produce a heavyweight champion, although he played a hand in guiding Chilean heavyweight Arturo Godoy to no less than two attempts at then champion, Joe Louis, in 1940, although Weill would later put this down more to political engineering on his part rather than genuine talent. Thus each was just as hungry for that prized possession, therefore when Weill received the letter from Colombo citing Rocco's credentials he had handed it straight over to Charley who eagerly anticipated preparing the fighter for a possible shot at the big time. However, not even he would have been prepared for the monumental task that lay ahead.

Goldman had not, unlike Weill, seen this Brockton heavy fight in the ring before so his impressions would be based purely on the perceptions of Weill; he was in for a shock. "The first time I saw Rocky, (*was*) the day the two of them came into the CYO gym (*he*) looked like he had come to sweep the place up."

Rocco himself summed up his first meeting with Goldman, "Frankly I was a little afraid of him. I know I was a little timid when I walked into the gym that day. When I first saw Charlie (*sic*) I couldn't get the words out and Allie did all the talking for both of us. Charlie had a white sweater on and was smiling a little the first time he talked to me. 'So you're the fighter,' he said, and I told him I was which was pretty close to a lie in those days because I was pretty terrible. He sighed a little and said, 'If you're a fighter, let's see you fight. Go in and put your duds on and come back here - we'll see how much of a fighter you are.' "

Thus Rocco changed into his Lowell Sun trunks and briskly, without even being allowed the benefit to warm to the task he was ushered into the thread bare antiquated ring in the corner of the sparse gym. Goldman, Colombo, and Weill perched themselves on the outer apron as inside the ropes Rocco stood, gloved up and nervously prepared to spar with a professional who had come there that day merely to train. That professionals name was Wade Chancey, a blonde, blue-eyed heavyweight from Staten Island who with a dozen professional bouts under his belt was deemed to be experienced enough to test this novice to the limit.

Goldman remembered that day well. "He was off balance every time he swung. And what a jab, his left arm was turned palm up and was bent over to his left [1]."

The pair Of Marchegiano and Chancey went at each other with as much ferocity as they could muster under the confines of sparring etiquette which demands that neither man is in there to really hurt the other. The real chance of this occurring were lessened by the padded, almost gladiatorial head guards that each were sporting, added to this the oversized gloves which negated power from punches aimed at each combatant. Even so Chancey was proving the superior of the rugged New Englander, deftly evading his bull like charges and wild swings, countering effectively and handling Rocco with ease.

"And then," continued Goldman, "he was backed into the ropes by Chancey. Rocky put both his hands up over his head and leaned back while the other guy walloped him a mile a minute. Naturally, Chancey went for the exposed belly, hitting Rocky some real shots. I stopped the action and asked Rock what he was doing. 'The fellows who taught me to fight told me that when I got against the ropes I should put my hands over my face and let him hit me in the belly until he got tired and then I could clout him on top of the head and knock him out.' So help me those were Rock's exact words. I had to walk to the other end of the gym and back when I heard that [2].

"Anyway when I called time again, Rocky hit the other guy, Chancey, with a right hand which nearly put a hole in the guys head and I knew that something could be done with this boy. If I hadn't called time straight away he might have hurt Chancey seriously."

Marciano takes up the story; "I throw the looper and I catch him on the chin. He goes against the ropes, Weill is yelling, 'Kill him! Kill him! Let's see you Kill him!' "

An incredulous Marchegiano made his way to the locker room after leaving the ring to shower off when he was approached by Weill's own Arturo Godoy who had happened to be in the gym that day and seen Rocky's punch. "Boy, you got it," he said, before continuing, as if sensing the Brockton boys' apprehension over the seemingly callous nature of Weill's remarks moments earlier. "Weill's O.K, you stick with him." Then he walked away muttering over and over, "Boy, you got it."

"While Rock was showering," Goldman added on his soon to be charges showing in the ring, "I talked it over with one of the CYO trainers who had watched the proceedings. When I asked the guy for his opinion, he says, 'Any truck driver can knock a guy out if he gets in a lucky shot. This fellow will never amount to anything.' "

On an enquiry from Rocco as to how he had done Goldman offered an honest assessment. "You got what nature gave you; if you're willing to work maybe I can do something for you." Al Weill on the other hand was at first reluctant to take a gamble on this raw fighter who had failed to impress, he felt that Rocco's showing against Wallace back in March had perhaps just been a fluke after all. "He's got no chance, I got enough broken down fighters. This guy ain't even broken down yet. He ain't got enough talent to be broken down."

Yet Charley admitted he saw something that day which made him believe this kid at least deserved a chance. "While he was dressing, I took stock of what we had here. In my fifty-years in the fight game, I never knew another fighter who started with so many things against him. That day I saw him he was 23, going on 24 (3) which by our usual standards is way too old to start a boy in four-rounder's. I like to get them when they're 15 or 16 so's I can keep them in the gym for a couple of years. By the time he's 20, a fighter should be well on his way in the business.

"The guy didn't even know how to face the bag, his feet were wide apart, his head away up in the air and his arms spread out - he didn't even punch the bag, he swooped down on it. But even through that I could see he had a strong right hand.

"But Rocky had three things in his favor right from the start. First, he had the body of a fighter - a strong chin, but not too big; a solid neck, a good chest, and a real broad back; nicely developed arms and wrists, though the arms were awfully short. Rock's reach is only 67 inches and I've known light heavies and even middleweight's with a longer reach.

"Second, he'd had a lot of all-round athletic background, I found out that in the football and baseball he'd play, he never once had to be taken out - a real iron man, you know. To fight you've got to have stamina. And then I found out about his Army fighting record where he'd been beaten only once or twice and always by decisions that could have gone either way.

"Third, and most important, here was a boy who wanted to be a fighter and wasn't afraid of the work that we both knew would be rugged to make up for lost time. Adding all this up I told him to come back…and we might be able to work something out."

Al Weill had little choice but to concede to Goldman, in most matter's Weill's word was the be-all-and-end-all yet when it came to fighter's he begrudgingly had to admit that Charley knew when he saw someone with potential, thus he went for the big gamble, but not at his own expense; at least not yet.

Notes:

1. *There is a parallel here with another heavyweight of the Marciano era who also threw his left in such a way, his name was Tommy Jackson and when asked why he threw such an unorthodox punch he claimed it was in case he changed his mind half way through and decided to throw an uppercut!*

2. *Later Rocky would give another explanation of his unorthodox defense to journalist Red Smith: "When I was in the amateurs," he said, "I boxed like this." He lifted hands and forearms high in front of his face, leaving his belly exposed. "When I first went with Weill, Charley Goldman asked me what I thought I was doing, 'I don't want to get busted up in the face,' I told him, 'or my mother won't let me fight'."*

3. *Rocky had shaved a year off his age, this would not be rectified until much later in his career.*

part three   chapter three

The Offer

"I had never been anything more than an ordinary laborer. I guess I realized that the fight game was my last chance to better myself."

Rocky Marciano

Marchegiano and Colombo accompanied Weill back to his office where the almost dowdy big time promoter was willing to take Goldman's advice and give Rocco a break, of sorts. Thus he put forward his proposal in as brief and succinct a way as possible. He would manage the fighter, at least unofficially at first, at this stage there was to be no formal contract offered; no free ride into the big time. Weill needed to see some proof that this so-called fighter from Brockton had something before he would commit himself any further.
"I want you to stick to stick around here," he told Rocky. "Charley will train you, you'll do everything that Charley says, then we'll get you a couple of four-rounder's." The offer was a

promising one, yet Rocco showed a stubborn side and was unwilling at this stage to leave everything he knew behind. Or perhaps it was the almost belligerent, some would say suicidal, streak that ran through Rocky, a streak that convinced him of his potential.

He had shown this side of his character when in the amateurs where he knew he couldn't, or at least shouldn't, lose. And it was this belief that followed him and served him well, albeit controlled, in the professional ranks. It followed him into retirement also when he once more felt untouchable. Eventually this streak that had served him so well would lead to his decline.

"I don't want to stay here, Al," came Rocky's alleged reply. "I want to go home for a couple of months'. I want to get in top condition, do some roadwork, practice, and in a couple of month's I'll be ready." Weill was taken aback, yet he had no ties to this kid thus, as Al himself recalled with an air of destiny over his find, "I sent him up to Manny Almeida, a friend of mine promotes in Providence, which is near where he (*was*) in Brockton, but Brockton is too small to have fights. And I asked Manny to put him in with the same kind he was, but no set-ups. Because you got a guy knocking over set-ups you don't know what you got."

Goldman, for his part, was still keen to work with the roughhewn fighter whenever he was able to get into town for he had seen the spark and was determined to bring it to life.

All was not wine and roses however, as Rocky would attest after his career had come to a close. "He (*Weill*) wanted me to get rid of my pal, Allie Colombo…Allie grew up next door to me and encouraged me and worked with me, I couldn't have managed without him, but Weill didn't want him around. Allie and me were both mad when we left [1]." Yet not mad enough it would appear to turn away a twenty-dollar bill from the seemingly ogreish Weill who called them back from the elevator as they were leaving to present them with the prize[2]. The pair quickly converted most of the currency into a meal at a nearby restaurant; it was here that fate almost intervened which if she had her way would have undoubtedly have cost Rocco Marchegiano the heavyweight championship of the world.

"While we were eating dinner," reflected Marciano in some detail, "in walks a guy from Boston who we knew from the amateurs, a guy named Jackie Martin. He was a fight manager and trainer, and (*his*) big claim to fame at that time was Pete Fuller, son a millionaire ex-governor of Massachusetts. Pete Fuller was a good amateur fighter, and this guy Martin trained and managed him. Martin asked me what we were doing in town, and we told him, and asked us if we signed anything. We said no, and he says, 'Look, how much do you guys want to sign with me?' "

Colombo mentioned the sum of a thousand dollars to which Martin announced that he had a call to make.

"I went out to call Fuller," declared Martin when broached on the subject. "But I got no reply, I went back to the Café and told 'The Rock' that I would phone him the next day, his buddy said they'd be back in Brockton, so we left it at that. I didn't speak to him again until he was champion of the world. If only Pete would have just been in I would have got Rocky Marciano for a measly thousand-bucks!"

Later Pete Fuller would confess that he had in fact indeed been in that day, and had taken the call but, "I turned the offer down point blank, I was still fighting then and I thought why should I turn over good money for someone I believed I could beat myself. Dumb, dumb, dumb…"

Rocco and his sidekick were oblivious to this fact at the time thus they used the remaining money from Weill to catch a bus home. There they began to focus on getting the fighter into shape whilst awaiting the call from Martin.

"We started a program of our own in Brockton, Allie and me," mused Marciano. "Seven days a week we woke up at seven and did roadwork, we took a different route every day so we wouldn't get tired of looking at the same scenery all the time. After a while I guess everyone in Brockton saw us running along the street."

Nevertheless it soon began to dawn on the prospective professional that the call from Martin was never going to come, so, with reservation, the pair returned to New York and into the arms of Goldman.

Notes:

1. *I asked Hank Cisco his thoughts on Allie, Hank, who spent a great deal of time in Marciano's training camp after his ascension to the throne got to know all those who surrounded the champ, including Allie: 'Rocky's greatest inspiration and guiding light was Allie Colombo…He reminded me of my brother, Joe, a friendly guy, always cutting up, smiling, joking…I think Allie served as a liaison between Al (Weill) and Rocky, that Al used Allie, who was a good person who Rocky respected. Eventually Al realized he could utilize Allie to get messages to Rocky. Naturally there was always tension when Al was in the room because he was always in command, took control and was domineering.'*

2. *It is these small little acts of generosity by Weill that initially led me to question Marciano's perception of Weill (see chapter: Enter 'the Vest' footnote).*

part three   **chapter four**

The Birth of a Fighter

"Charlie (sic), if I don't want to get hit, how do I get out of the way?"

Rocky Marciano

The lodging house of Mrs. Rosa Braune, a large matriarchal woman with Austro-Hungarian roots, was to be found on ninety-second street in the Central Park area of New York. Here in this brownstone building Al Weill had worked out a deal in which his fighters would get preferential treatment. Such was his feeling for this location that he would refer to the place rather grandly as "The house of Destiny" a title he bestowed due in part to his former champion Lou Ambers who resided there in the late 1930's and remained unbeaten whilst lodged at the address, including winning the lightweight championship of the world.

Indeed, from this auspicious beginning every boxer who came under the portly shadow of Weill would, at one time or another, find themselves in Mrs. Braune's care. And she was, by all accounts, a good house-mistress, darning the boys socks, collecting their mail, being the mother they missed, even ensuring all her boys were in their rooms by ten each evening; with

Weill calling just to be sure. In fact, in the words of Goldman, who himself inhabited the front parlor with its expansive window allowing him to keep an eye on his pupils as they came and went, walls covered with fight charts and photo's, including prominent above a fireplace one of himself in his youth and another of his greatest pupil, Al McCoy. "She is just like a mother to them boys', she even presses their trunks for them so they will look nice before going into the ring…Mrs. Braune is a restraining influence on them kids."

She was not even averse at times to prepare for her favorite boys her own specialty chicken rich meal if she felt they needed feeding up. Otherwise the fighters would eat at a Greek lunchroom in nearby Colombus Avenue paying for their food with a voucher allocated to them by the ever frugal Weill who had purchased the ticket for five-dollars; it had a five-dollar-fifty value at the lunchroom. Every time you ate the ticket got clipped and the only way a hungry fighter could expect another would be if he were able to produce the last voucher punched out to its entirety.

It was into this environment that the eager Rocco Marchegiano would find himself upon his frequent journeys back to New York over the ensuing weeks with the ever loyal Allie Colombo in tow. Their bills were paid by Weill but this was no mere charity however, Weill paid the rent for all his fighters who were based at Mrs. Braune's taking back what he felt was owed out of their earnings in the ring, even if it meant he had to first wrack up a bill before reimbursing himself [1].

Each morning in the big city Rocco and Allie ran around Central Park reservoir, its pastoral setting reminded the boys of home, before heading to the CYO gym to work with Goldman in the hope that this diminutive magician would go to work and create a masterpiece out of this malleable, ever willing, piece of human clay.

"We had to start from scratch," mused Goldman, as he pointed out the most obvious and pivotal weaknesses in Marciano's style.

"His stance and stride were way too long, throwing him way off balance. He threw his punches way too long, telegraphing them. He punched with his arms. He didn't get his shoulders or body into his punches. He didn't even know how to hold his hands, he was wide open…He didn't punch hard with his left. He threw one punch at a time." Slowly, but surely, the sculpture set to work creating his fighter.

"I started him off on defensive boxing, when I'd seen Rocky with his hands in the air, taking those body smashes, I knew how stupid that was, but I didn't say so to Rocky. I used a little psychology and told him that referees didn't give no points for standing up under the other guy's punches…then began work on the basics, I brought his right foot up about a dozen inches, and tied his ankles together with a piece of string that gave him just 24 inches of leeway. Once he was in this tighter stance which automatically gave him better balance and body control, I taught him how to put punches together, combinations, you know. The jab with his chin tucked behind the left shoulder, the right in front of the face and the left brought back to guard as the right is crossed and a left again, to the body this time, as the right resumed blocking.

"Frankly, Rocky wasn't able to do it when he first tried. I wasn't too disappointed though because I had figured right from the first that it was going to be a tough haul. Rock didn't have the knack of picking things right up the way some fighters do - things only become part of him after work and work and more work. But Rocky learned fast the first rule - when you make your move, think of what the other fellow will be doing next and what you should do after he has made that move.

"I had to teach Rocky more than I ordinarily did to a novice boxer - the jab, for example. I told you he 'jabbed' with his palm up, that's how green he was. Well, I showed him the right way, palm down, knuckle straight, the arm driven all the way from the shoulder. And I told him to turn his head to the right as he jabbed with his left. It's a little trick - but an important one - to add a few inches to the length of a jab. With Rocky's short reach it was a vital one for him.

"But," confessed Goldman, "I never showed him that Susie-Q knockout punch of his, That was all natural. Anything I did, I always told Rocky to ignore it if he thought that it was interfering with the way he threw that right hand. That was his number one asset - that and a steel chin and body. What I did do was show him how to use it to better advantage, digging his right into the belly and then doubling up by bringing it up to the face in an uppercut and dropping his own right under a jab and following it up with an over hander.

"One thing that bothered me right away was that he was punching only with his arm. I wanted to get the combined efforts of his knee, hip and shoulder behind his punches. So, first I had him snap the hip in exercises, right to left, left to right. Then I had him practice a shoulder snap too. When he had learned both real good, I had him combine the two at once. Finally, I got Rocky to put his knee into it too, like a shot-putter. With a bent arm like I showed him and hip, shoulder and knee action, he had a short, sharp punch, but with everything he had behind it. It was a killer [2]."

Whilst in the 'Big Apple' Rocco and Allie, when they were not training, would trawl the streets amazed at their change in fortune, two almost small town boys in the most vibrant city in America. Once they spotted the featherweight champion Willie Pep, all attired in his finery, with a beautiful woman on his arm, so they, like star struck children, followed him to see, they said, "…what life was like for a champion." Pep stopped to buy his girl a flower at a street vendors and pinned it ever so daintily onto her dress before kissing her gently on the forehead, then venturing into Leone's, a famous Italian restaurant, Marchegiano and Colombo tried to follow them in but were politely turned away for being improperly dressed. Years later when Rocco was himself a champion he would dine their frequently, then it would make no difference how he dressed!

That finances were tight for the pair is well attested, however this was especially true in New York. Once they plucked up the courage to ask Al Weill for a fifteen-dollar loan, they were refused with the (*alleged*) off-handed comment, "You haven't earnt it yet, go and have some fights then come back to me for money." It is reported that Goldman subbed them the $15 thus allowing the boys to stay on for a few days longer, it was good that they did, for it allowed them to show a true heavyweight legend just what was coming to town in the almost unimposing guise of Rocco Marchegiano.

One morning the former heavyweight champion Jack Dempsey came into the CYO accompanied by a heavyweight he was toying with the idea of managing. Despite being retired for over twenty-years he still yearned for the glory days of his youth even if it meant living it vicariously through someone else. Over the years since his official retirement in 1927 he had been openly searching for a prospect he could nurture and guide to the title, and in this fighter he thought he had found him. The man's name was Joe Weider, not to be confused with the same Joe Weider who would become synonymous with Body Building in the fifties and beyond, yet this guy was also by all accounts big and powerful. The old champ wanted to test him out, so he was put in with Rocco, Charley wanted to see just how his own pupil was responding to his teachings.

"Kid," said Dempsey to an awed Marciano, "I want you to hit him on the chin as hard as you can, I need to know if he can take a punch." So Rocco did as he was asked, the result was that

Weider could not take what this raw heavy could dish out, ending up in hospital with a broken cheekbone; after his discharge Dempsey promptly dropped him and he fell, like so many others who met Marciano on the way up, into obscurity. It was a shame for the hopeful Weider, had he sparred with anybody else that day the result may have been different, perhaps he would have gone on to secure for himself a lucrative career under the aegis of the formidable Dempsey. He was not the first man to succumb to the power of Marchegiano's fists, and he certainly would not be the last.

In-between his frequent trips to New York Rocco worked assiduously at everything he had been shown whilst back in his hometown, he even took on the dreaded speed-bag, which Rocco hated because he felt he was clumsy at it, footage of Rocky even in his title years sometimes would show him awkwardly popping this small leather bag, a look of intense concentration on his face, yet Goldman insisted for it helped to keep the fighters hands high.
Rocky's training regime had now begun to take over his life. Six mornings a week he ran, often as much as twenty-miles, he truly felt that stamina in his legs would prove crucial. He also became a frequent visitor to the local Y.M.C.A where he continued with his bizarre practice of wading shoulder deep into the pool throwing punches. "When Rocky got into the pool all the kids would get out 'cos they knew he was training," remembered Nicky Sylvester. "He'd go all the way in up to his neck and start throwin' punches and the water around him would ripple, but at the other end of the pool it was splashing over the sides, and the pool was sixty, seventy feet long! That was his power!"
Here he would perpetually break the punching bags of his friend Bob Galante who graciously continued to give him lifts to meet Barbara after his workout was completed, and where he displayed another of his sometime bizarre quirks. Remembered Galante, "Every time he would take a shower, he would put his clothes on when he was soaking wet without even

drying himself off! The seat of my car would be soaked when he got out!! No one could believe he would do that! No one does that!"

Despite his almost obsessive regime however Rocco tried to meet Barbara as often as he could, either at her house or several times a week he would meet her in Dunnington Apothecary's where he would indulge in a chocolate frappe whilst awaiting her arrival. However these moments were to become less and less as Marciano began to ascend the heavyweight ladder. "I have always been amazed by her," mused Rocky later in life. "She could have walked whenever she wanted, but she didn't, she stuck by me all the way."

Barbara herself would admit, "At first, to be honest, I didn't want him to be a fighter, I thought he ought to be a policeman like my father. But I could see it was what he wanted. What type of a girl would I have been if I had of walked out on him then when he needed me most." Her father however was pleased that his prospective son-in-law had chosen to be a fighter. "My father had always been interested in sports," remembered Barbara in 1956, "(*he*) promoted wrestling and boxing matches on the side (3). Lester Cousins support extended as far as arraigning for Rocco to gain private access to a gym located in South Easton some twelve miles from Brockton and owned by a friend of his, Ross Murray, sole proprietor of the Raynham dog track (4).

"We loved the solitude of this beautiful country estate," reflected Colombo. "Because of Russ, we had our own private training camp. It was a setup usually only enjoyed by champions and contenders." Murray had initially erected the fully equipped gymnasium for his own friend and professional boxer, Johnny Shkoor. Ironically, in the not too distant future, Marchegiano would face this very fighter in the ring, from then on Russ would become indefatigably one of Rocco's biggest supporters.

Financially also things would remain tight for the duo, due to the injury to his hand Rocco had finally been forced to quit his job with the Brockton gas company, however, Allie

Colombo, in a moment of extraordinary bravado, approached none other than Joseph Downey, the mayor of Brockton himself with the story of his and Rocco's plight. Said Mayor, sympathetic to their predicament, secured for them both some laboring duties for the city highway department, it was easy work, and well paid. For the pair it would serve the purpose for which it was intended, something to tide them over until Rocco made it into the professional ranks and could support himself.

It was a job they would sorely need.

Notes:

1. *However Marciano himself would later recall these earliest days in New York very differently, "Money was so tight back when I first met Al and Charley...you have to remember that Allie had drawn out every penny out of his savings account to pay for hotel rooms, meals and transportation and anything else we may need. Weil (sic) was such a hard ass he wouldn't pay for a thing. Things were so tough that when me and Allie got to the rooming house that Charley told us to go to, there was only one vacant bed for me and Allie had to sleep on a couch in Charley's room the whole time we were there."*

2. *Charie Norkus, a prominent heavyweight during the fifties recalled sparring Marciano and was amazed by the mans' power, he related to friend and auther Phil Guarnieri where he thought this came from: 'leverage --- the guy was able to get great leverage when he delivered punches. A lot of very strong guys can't get leverage when they throw punches but uncannily Marciano could get every ounce of strength in his blows.' Did this come directly from Goldman's tutelage? As we saw from Rocky's amateur career he possessed that raw power from the start, probably, at least , Goldman helped refine the technique and focus that natural power.*

3. *It seems he moonlighted a lot, for officer Cousins also worked shifts as a taxi driver, little wonder then that his daughter was spoilt - "I was the only girl in my high school to have my own convertible."*

4. *In the beginning both of Barbara's parents were enamored of their daughters beau, "We did think a lot of him when he first came to the house," said a 90 year Elizabeth Cousins in 1994, "He was humble and polite." Later however the feelings of Marciano's mother-in-law would change dramatically.*

part three **chapter five**

First Steps

"Giving Rocky money to fight was like feeding a bowl of blood to a tiger."

Al Weill

There had been a time when Manny Almeida was the king of boxing in Rhode Island's capital city of Providence. And as every king needs a palace for his he had the now sadly defunct Rhode Island Auditorium which once was located at 111, North Main Street, deep in the cities Mount Hope district which is a mere stone's throw from the Providence River that serves to dissect the populace industrial municipality.

The Auditorium itself was a mecca for sports, most notably acting as a home for the Rhode Island Reds Ice Hockey team who camped there until 1972. Yet eventually, despite being host to the growing sport of basketball after the hockey teams' defection, the building would quickly fall from favor. Its final event would be her razing in 1989. The remains of this once subtly magnificent temple of sport now lie dormant beneath a tarmac blanket which covers the spot today.

Back in the impressive buildings heyday however, when Almeida regularly filled the 5300 capacity horse shoe interior, this palace buzzed, especially on fight night.

Almeida had built his reputation in the nineteen-thirties primarily on the back of Providence's very own fight sensation Joey Archibald who had briefly held the world's featherweight championship in 1939. Archibald in turn had been manipulated into title contention by the formidable pairing of none other than Charley Goldman and Al Weill, thus beginning the tentative partnership that would launch Rocco Marchegiano into the professional ring nearly a full decade later.

Yet during the war years of the early forties Manny had given up control of his precious Auditorium and all but turned his back on the sport that he had been involved with since he himself first stepped between the ropes as a raw sixteen year old way back in 1919, preferring instead to devote his time to running the bar which bore his name on Mathewson Street [1]. Nevertheless, despite this period of self-imposed exile, by 1948 he had been persuaded back into the heady mire of the sport once again. Thus it was only natural, with his return, that Al Weill should turn to him once again when he sought someone to steer Marchegiano through his first tentative steps in the fight game, for, unusually in the world of boxing, Al trusted Almeida. At least he trusted him to the extent that Weill knew Manny would not attempt to poach the fighter from him should he turn out to show something that could be bartered into cold hard cash.

"Weill called me up and told me he had a husky heavyweight he wanted me to take care of, so as a favor to an old friend I threw him some fights," recalled Almeida. He admitted though that at first he didn't recognize potential in the boy that Weill sent, "I just looked at him as someone to fill my shows, he was convenient."

In fact the situation was convenient for all. Weill would have a free ticket waiting to be traded in, should he show potential, in Rocco, whilst Marchegiano in turn could learn his trade almost on his own doorstep, Brockton being a mere thirty-miles from Providence.

The first fight that Almeida organized for the "husky heavyweight" would take place on the cool, balmy evening of Monday July 12th (*a mere ten-weeks since his last appearance as an amateur*) but no-one who mattered really noticed, including Weill and Goldman who both remained in New York, they had more important fighters to worry about.

For Marchegiano though it represented a starting anew, not towards any aspirations towards becoming a champion, but simply as a chance to escape from his lot in life. "I never was really ambitious as a kid, sure I had my baseball, and I dreamt of that, but really I just wanted to earn more money than my dad and take care of everyone," Rocco would later confess. Therefore the first forty-dollars he was paid for this bout represented this step, albeit a minor one, into a fresh beginning.

Rocco's opponent on this night was, with all due respect, not the most devastating of propositions that Rocco would ever face. When Weill had asked Manny not to feed his boy "Set-ups" the man facing him this night would be viewed in hindsight by some as almost a perfect description for same. This allegation however is perhaps, to be truthful, a little unfair. Harry (*Haroutne*) Bilazarian was out of Boylston, Mass and had shown great aptitude for sport whilst at Worcester Boys Trade School where he stood out as a star athlete particularly on the football field. At the tail end of the second great war he found himself serving for the U.S Army at Fort Monmouth in New Jersey where he gravitated towards the boxing team, he was immediately successful when he won both the local light-heavy and heavyweight titles before being posted to Sapporo, Japan where he secured for himself the services light-heavyweight championship in 1948.

Despite his undoubted talent however Bilazarian's lean light-heavy frame barely allowed him to make the then heavy limit of 175-pounds which meant he just didn't have the bulk to tangle with the big boys since he had himself first tried his hand in the paid ranks back in February of that same year, before this meeting Harry had racked up nine previous bouts, winning just three. Of his six losses, no less than five had been by clean knock-out. He simply did not have the chin to compete with natural heavies. He was going to be no test for the power of Marchegiano.

Rocco arrived in Providence at two on that Monday afternoon for the initial weigh-in. His friend Tony 'Snap' Tartaglia had driven both he and Allie there ostensibly in order to assist in the corner during the bout, yet neither Tartaglia nor Colombo really knew what they were doing. Thankfully that very afternoon they had managed to secure the services of Frank Travers, an experienced corner man and friend of Almeida's, he was working with another fighter on the bill, a lightweight who was also making his professional debut, and he agreed to work with Marchegiano.

After the ceremony of the weigh-in and brief medical the boys went back to Tony Tartaglia's sister, Alvina, who resided in the Renaissance city. Whilst there, Rocco, ever the genial guest, fell into a deep sleep prior to his bout, a habit that would follow him throughout his career. When he eventually awoke he sat and ate a large rare steak that had been prepared for him. Later he would comment that, "Alvina's steaks were one of the highlights of my early days in boxing, I wish I had her cook for me in camp."

Such was his taste for this delicacy that later he would bring his own steaks, wrapped in wax paper and provided by his mother. When he was not visiting Alvina these lumps of meat would be broiled by Eddie Beck, owner of a diner not far from the auditorium, for as was his way it would not take him long to ingratiate himself into any society he entered. As remembered Nicky Sylvester, "He had this incredible knack of getting people to like him, you know so's they would do anything for him. Even when he was just a bum, working his way up, people still wanted to be near him, and everything they did, it was all for free."

The Marchegiano - Bilazarian match was the closing feature on a card that was headlined by an international lightweight tussle between Miguel Acevdo of Cuba and local boy Teddy 'Red Top' Davis. The Cuban barely managed to force out a split-decision victory in what appeared to be a thrilling battle of skill between two very well matched fighters. Due in no small part to the exhaustive effect of this battle the auditorium was almost completely empty when Marchegiano stepped into the ring. Apart from a small contingent of Rocco's followers from Brockton, including his brother 'Sonny', fewer than a hundred spectators had hung-on to catch the remaining matches, thus only a sparse crowd were privileged to have witnessed the Brockton boys official pro debut (2).

Those who had already left the building that evening would probably not curse their misfortune in the immediate aftermath of the verdict being announced, for the bout was not spectacular, at least not in the connoisseurs meaning. There was no battle of skill here, just a display of sheer brutal savagery from the new boy; as witnessed by *The Brockton Enterprise-Times* who covered their local amateur sensations first forays into the paid arena on the following morning:

'Heavyweight Rocco Marchegiano of this city launched his professional boxing career with a smashing forst round knockout of Worcester's Harry Bilzarian (*sic*)...The scheduled four-round fray was ended at 1:32 of the opening session when "The Rock" crashed a right-hander to the head of his adversary, sending Balzerian to the canvass, thoroughly chilled.'

Such was the power of the punch that Bilazarian made little effort to rise; even the referee saw no point in counting and made his exit leaving the hapless fighter where he lay.

Marchegiano had the fight in the bag from the first bell despite his opponent firing everything he had at the Brockton boy from the beginning, Rocco began banging away at the body and swiftly slowed down the charge before dropping Harry for a nine-count before the round was a minute old.

"The first time he knocked me down he broke my tooth, when I got up I was afraid I had swallowed it," recalled Bilazarian. "Then he knocked me down again, then I don't remember anything." Later he would add that he could, "…remember going back to the dressing room." The first knockdown was followed with hooks and jabs before leveling the helpless Bilazarian for keeps. It had taken Rocco just 92-seconds from the opening bell to notch up his first of no-less than twenty-nine victories in Providence. For an overwhelmed Bilazarian this was to be his seventh loss. He would however go on to hit a rich vein [3] by notching up no less than eleven consecutive victories following his bout with Marchegiano before his streak was ended by the anonymous Gordon Ifill, again by knock-out. Harry then went downhill quick, of his final six fights he would win only one, ending his career in 1950 with a draw against an opponent who was himself making his own professional debut.

When his career had finally wound down Harry would access his time in the professional ring with journalist Ziggy Sienuc, he admitted that he felt he could have done better and achieved more but he, "…made some awful mistakes." Bilazarian was a strong guy, despite his slim stature, and he tried to always come forward in a give and take style that was popular with the crowd but he just couldn't take a punch. He had advice too for those who were thinking of taking up a career in the sport based on his own experience; "It's all right to try, but actually there are so many opportunities for a young man today to take up a trade or go into business, that I think it is foolish to take up boxing."

As for the man himself, he went off to work for a gas company in his home town of Worcester where he remained for 37 years, in his spare time he immersed himself into the history of his Armenian heritage becoming a member of his local Armenian church where he had song in the choir as a child. Those who knew this generous, caring, deeply family orientated man, admired him, respected him and loved him. He died whilst this project was being put together on the morning of April 25th 2012.

There were no wild victorious celebrations for Rocco although his family and friends chests nevertheless swelled with pride that one of their own had become a professional athlete, albeit in the barbarous world of the prize-ring.

His mother however did not share everyone else's delight; she had spent the fight ensconced in St. Patrick's Church lighting candles accompanied by close friend and neighbor, a Mrs. Mangifesti. It would be a ritualistic act which she would continue for the remainder of her son's career. Never did she see, nor even listen, to any of his forthcoming bouts.

Later during her sons tenure as heavyweight champion of the world she would explain her visits to the church during Rocco's fights; "I go just to get it out of my mind. But once in a while we look at the clock and I pray…I pray neither of them get hurt. After all, the other boy has a mother too."

It would be but a mere seven days before Marchegiano again found himself back in Providence, this time before a crowd of 961 who had come to see the main event between New England welterweight champion Johnny Cesario and challenger Henry Jordan. Rocco's opponent on this occasion would be John (*aka Jack*) Edwards from New Haven, Connecticut, who was himself no more than a light-heavyweight scaling a little over 173 pounds compared to Rocco's 186.

John had earned himself the sobriquet of "Big Jack" due to lanky stature, he was renowned for having especially long legs and he used those legs to almost literally run from Rocco whilst the fight lasted, but in a roped off arena he had little room to use before it ran out and Marchegiano chased and inevitably caught him. The fight was almost farcical in its chase sequence and then its ending was the slapstick finale for it was a swooping left hook which landed flush on Edwards jaw at approximately the one-minute-nineteen mark of the opening salvo which aided Rocco into swiftly etching win number two into his record. The first punch to land was a looping overhand right which reportedly spun Edwards around before the left hook immediately followed it and put an end to the matter. "Edwards caved to the floor and sprawled full length", commented the Brockton press the following day.

This was as conclusive a victory as could be gained against someone who had fought just twice before, losing one by clean knock-out in his first outing against an anonymous fighter with the rather sinister sounding name of Dick Schreck before his own hometown crowd back in early May. Edwards it seems would consequently never fight again after his demolition at the hands of this, in the words of Boston Promoter, Sam Silverman, "clumsy, one-dimensional fighter."

It was this somewhat derogatory, but perhaps understandable view of the Brockton boy by Silverman that would lead to Rocco's next two bouts; in a way they were, perhaps, the most important fights of his career.

Notes:

1. *Later Almeida would relocate his bar to Wickenden Street in the Fox point district of Providence, this waterfront location was the congregational point for many of the Portuguese and Hispanic immigrants and their descendants who had settled in this diverse multi-cultural city. Almeida himself was a last generation Portuguese having been born in that country in 1903 and moving with his family to America when still a child.*
2. *His bout with Epperson would remain off the record for many years.*
3. *Thus putting paid to the legend that no one who faced Marciano was ever as good again.*

part three   **chapter six**

The Tank Job

"This Marchegiano kid's got nothing. He can punch all right, but I've never seen a fighter as clumsy. The kid doesn't know what he's doing out there."

Sam Silverman

It may be fair to say that Boston promoter Sam Silverman had very little faith in Rocco Marchegiano, at least at the outset. Yet Sam just may have been the most important man in Rocco's life, for without Silverman's almost lackluster attitude to his fighting ability Marchegiano may well have been fed those ubiquitous 'tank jobs', that term euphemistically given to those fighters used merely to pad a promising professionals record without ever truly testing his potential. Instead Rocco himself was, to all intents and purposes being used for that very purpose himself.

"Rocky's fights were all legitimate, good, hard fights. A lot of people were talking about how he was being fed setups. Marciano could have lost any number of times in his early fights," reflected Silverman himself in 1971.

The man described by journalists as the, "The real article fight promoter…big cigars, gray fedora's, ample belly. (*Who*) talked out of the side of his mouth, but dealt from the top of the deck," was in appearance the very twin of Al Weill (*see above*). But that is where the comparison would end, for Silverman, who never boxed a round in his life and yet became the most successful promoter in New England, would sometimes forget that fighters were human too.

Silverman began his career way back in the nineteen-twenties in South Grafton, Massachusetts, where he was tentatively employed by the then promoter, and former amateur bantamweight champion, Jimmy Deforest. "I gave him $2 a fight to carry water buckets," remembered Deforest in 1977. "I do feel that I was instrumental in starting his career."

It was a career which was destined to span five-decades beginning in earnest at New Bedford, Mass, where his comparative success allowed him to swiftly branch out into nearby Lynn. It was here he formed a partnership with the eminent Jimmie Mede. Before this association was forged, Sam, who was beginning to pick up the various monikers of 'Subway Sam', 'Suitcase Sam', or just plain 'Sad Sam', had been forced to travel as far as New York and New Jersey to give his fighters bouts. Yet the pairing with Mede allowed him access to a larger number of small fight clubs to house his growing menagerie of tigers.

None of these fighters who were completely under Silverman were world beaters however, yet, in the words of Michael Marley, former publicist for Muhammad Ali, "He used to build these phenomenal records for local white guys, all of whom would eventually get beat when they went on the road."

It was due in no small part to this ability to create a fighter that top tier managers would begin sending their boys to Silverman including of course Al Weill with whom Silverman struck up a rapport when the latter moved himself into The Mechanics Building in Boston where he would rub shoulders with Weill who was promoting there himself on an almost daily basis. Yet it was his move into Providence in 1944 that would lead directly to his influence over the career of the emerging Rocco Marchegiano some four years later.

Silverman had his eyes set on the prestigious Rhode Island Auditorium, then controlled by a consortium of managers who were slowly strangling the former palace of pugilism. In order to achieve his aims he pulled a coup of stunning magnitude when he managed to persuade the now semi-retired Manny Almeida to return to the fray. As soon as Almeida announced his imminent return the old Auditorium quickly released herself into his arms once again, only this time those arms were supported by another, Almeida's new partner, Sam Silverman.

Marchegiano, it is alleged, first came under the wing of Silverman when he approached Sam himself in the hope of getting some fights. He was hungry to climb back into the ring especially after the disappointment of an opponent pulling out of a scheduled appearance at Providence (*the Brockton press jumped on this as a sign of their local fighters growing reputation and labeled the no-show as, 'an intelligent use of common sense' by the foe's non-appearance*). Rocco needed to fight and he desperately needed the money.
"Me and Alsack were dead broke at the time," said Rocco. "We had to beg for money from relatives just to pay for food in New York. I hated the situation, but everyone was good to me, they showed faith so I pushed and pushed in those early days for fights so I could pay them back."

It seemed to Silverman that his prayers had been answered, for only a short while before an old friend of his, Jimmy O'Keefe, had made contact in the hope that Sam could find an opponent for his own fighter at short notice. For O'Keefe, a restaurant owner from Boston, was having problems finding bouts for his heavyweight who was undefeated in eight outings, seven wins coming by way of stoppage, including a first round knock-out of former Marchegiano victim Harry Bilzarian. But that success had come at a price, for now his opposition had dried up, indeed his last bout had been almost a month previously on July 15th when he had been held to a decision over six rounds by Johnny Melko. O'Keefe knew he just did not have the contacts to push his boy further up the ladder at this time, so he needed soft fighters to pad his boys' record. Not so soft though that they fell over at the first whisper of a punch, but not tough enough that they damaged the merchandise, just good honest matches that would be a level above sparring for his prospect, and earn a little money into the bargain. So sure was Silverman that he was doing his friend a favor that he made the match immediately, he called Rocco up with the news that he had made a bout for him again in Providence, and his opponent would be the Boston boy; Bobby Quinn.

According to some reports news that Rocco would be facing up to the Boston fighter was met with incredulity by most in the Marchegiano household, they had heard of Quinn and rated his skills highly (*as did The Brockton Enterprise-Times calling Quinn Rocky's, 'severest test to date'*), almost to a soul they believed their boy was rushing in over his head. The Rock nonetheless seemed belligerent to the supposed talent of the other guy, to him it was just another fight, a chance to earn some much needed cash. It was this blasé approach to reputations and supposed danger which Rocco would continue to carry throughout his life, often this would serve him well, alas, however, ultimately it would not.

Allie Colombo had recently married (*Marciano served as his best man*), as a gift he had received a car, a 1935 sedan, from his father-in-Law. As Rocco recalled, "It was a good car, only the radiator leaked. We always just made it to Hanford (*California*) before we had to put more water in, and then we could go the rest of the way to New York without boiling over." It was in this that he now began to ferry his friend to New York, and more importantly, to bouts.

There would also be a new face in the corner for the pair now on the night of Monday August 9th (*originally the bout was due to be held the previous Monday the 2nd*). Tony Tartaglia had work commitments and was unable to attend instead Al Weill himself, ever the opportunist, had set him up with someone to ostensibly work in their corner, that man went by the name of Chick Wergeles.

It at first seemed a strange choice, for Wergeles (*left - whose last name rhymed with Hercules*) was not the most competent of corner men, yet for the Brockton duo it was a sign that Weill was taking an interest, of sorts, in Rocco's career, for Chick, a shifty, enigmatic character in the story of Marciano's rise to the title, was a major player, and not just in boxing, indeed you could find his fingerprints in every high profile sport of the era. This proud Brooklynite who spoke with the broad inner-city New York accent as recognizably American as the archetypical Cockney brogue of London, had been born in 1891, and had, by his own admission, "First begun promoting fighters when I was eighteen." Yet Wergeles knew nothing really about sport at all, in fact Charley Goldman would later, in his own indomitable way describe the man as, "The biggest leach in boxing, he knew nothing about the sport at all. Hell, he thought a hooker was a dame of low morals (*instead of a fighter who specialized in throwing hooks*)."

He had begun his professional life as a printmaker, apprenticed to a New York printing firm at three-dollars a week. There he labored for three-and-a-half-years creating information pamphlets during the First World War. Ostensibly he hated the job, yet it would pay dividends and path the way to his future for it was here that he absorbed and mastered the ability to spin a truth, to create a fiction as it were and sell it to the masses. It was this adeptness and almost unique talent which would eventually lead him into his career as public relations officer for the old *New York Morning World*. Here he would build up a fighter's resume with expanded truths, half-truths, and downright lies in order to generate for them a greater presence in the media. It worked, and soon this unassuming kid had branched out into every area of sport, most notably horse racing and the emerging sport of pro-football, plus, perhaps most importantly of all, that pseudo-athletic world of wrestling where sporting endeavor and mass entertainment clashed in an often chaotic fusion. It was here that he formed an association with noted wrestling promoter Toots Mondt which would pay off handsomely down the road.

During the early thirties Wergeles was hired by Ned Irish, a promoter of basketball, to help popularize the game, especially those held in Madison Square Garden where Irish was currently holding station as chairman. Here Chick met Al Weill who was then serving his first term as match maker at the Garden under the auspices of Mike Jacobs and the Twentieth Century Sporting Club. Immediately the pair would make a mental note of each other's attributes and file them away for future use.

Although having steered himself away from boxing at this stage in his life Wergeles had not completely lost interest in the sport. From time to time he would be called upon by some manager keen to have his boy ballyhooed by the best. Indeed as early as 1932 Wergeles was regarded as being at the top of the heap when it came to publicizing a fighter, so much so that his name appeared in the hugely popular comic strip, Joe Palooka, a series of syndicated cartoons which featured the ongoing exploits of a genial fictitious heavyweight boxer.

It was this tentative hold on boxing which led Wergeles onto his biggest break when, in 1939, a group of professional golfers had invested money in the boxing career of their clubs very own shoe shine boy, this syndicate needed a front man, thus they approached Wergeles. Chick agreed to be the manager of record for the then unknown seventeen year old. It was an incredibly fortuitous move for that boy was Beau Jack, one of the most dynamic fighters of all-time. By 1944 Jack had served two terms as the lightweight champion of the world.

As 1948 came into view Jack's career was winding down and Wergeles was merely toying with boxing once again, however Al Weill recalled his old Garden comrade when he was figuring the angles on his new boy Marchegiano.

Always one to see the bigger picture Weill was tentatively planning Rocco's future and he knew he would need to sell this guy to the press one day, however his target was at least a year away, yet when Marchegiano called to ask Weill if he could recommend someone to work his corner, Weill immediately thought of Wergeles.

"Rocky was nothing when I first met him," confided Chick after Marchegiano's death some twenty-one years later. "Weill asked me to kinda take him under my wing, just to look him over. I was pretty shrewd in most of my dealings but I thought this guy (*Marchegiano*) was a bum, I thought, 'how the hell am I going to sell this guy!' After a while though he began to sell himself."

And the job of selling himself would begin that very night against Bobby Quinn.

For the first time in his professional career Rocco was squaring off with someone of comparable size in Quinn. Both fighters weighed in at the same weight, 183-even, as they prepared to face each other before an almost capacity crowd of 1,321 in the Auditorium. Neither was the main draw that night however, this honor was reserved for two welterweights, Roger Whynott and Benny Delgado. It would be Rocco though who would cause the biggest buzz.

Over the opening rounds Quinn indeed seemed too much for the still comparably novice Marchegiano, winning a close cautious opening round and taking the second stanza by a wide margin as he steamed into his opponent and pushed him back against the ropes, Marchegiano had to fight with all of his reserves to stave off the attack. Both were trading blow for blow in a corner as the bell ended the savage round. It is easy to picture Silverman smugly chewing on his ever present cigar as he watched in contentment at his friend's boy doing what he thought was a given, that is handing that, "Brockton boy a licking."

Then with all the suddenness of a steam train smashing through a wall Quinn was down. It had happened at the 22-second mark of the third and penultimate round, the punch that had put him there had been a right uppercut which had started from Rocco's knee and driven itself hard seemingly through Quinn's very jaw itself tearing him off his feet. The referee went through the formality of counting over the prostrate form but everyone in the audience knew this was a fruitless exercise; Quinn was out cold.

An almost apoplectic Silverman stormed into Bobby Quinn's dressing room after he had recovered from the shock of witnessing such a total capitulation to raw power. He stormed over the bind that he had been placed in regarding his promise to O'Keefe that he had nothing to fear from Marchegiano. An apologetic, dejected Quinn could only meekly mutter that he wasn't in shape.

Quinn nevertheless seemed to have pulled himself together immediately following what was potentially a career shattering defeat, rolling over four opponents in quick succession before losing a close decision to the vastly more experienced Anthony Jones. He would continue on until 1949 before losing interest in the sport, amassing for himself a record of twenty-bouts with just the two losses. Only Rocco had managed to take him out inside the distance. However, in 1955 he attempted to make a comeback with two fights against Roger Wiley who had won just one bout in nine previous. An older Quinn won the first bout, but disaster struck in the second when Wiley, the seemingly perennial loser, scored an upset stoppage victory. Quinn quickly retired again before once more changing his mind some two-years later when he struggled to a four-round points win over Jimmy Gillis. This was his last fight, some nine-years after his bout with Rocco he finally called it quits.

For Rocco this was win number three. Initially he was outraged by his close friends concern over the outcome of the bout, he roared at them after the conflict had been decided that never again should they tell him their thoughts on someone he was due to fight. Rocco did not care what others thought nor did he wish to fill his head with doubt as to his own ability.
If his companions were genuinely concerned about Quinn however, then the next opponent would, on paper at least, seem to truly deserve their unease, but they dared not share these feelings with Rocco.

part three   **chapter seven**

Deliverance

"I threw Rocky in to give this kid (Ross) another win...but when he flattened this boy, I knew!"

Sam Silverman

With his decisive victory over Quinn, Rocco at last believed he had found something which could possibly save him from the blue collar life that seemed his destiny after so many failures. Now he vowed to devote himself entirely to the sport. Thus with a mixture of optimism and apprehension that he had at last found himself, he returned to New York in Colombo's sedan in order to work with Charley Goldman.

There were those who would not have been surprised to hear that Rocco had walked to the big city however, for it was around this time that he had begun those long marches, usually comprising some ten to fifteen miles, which made up his daily routine. Indeed it was not unusual for him to hike more than twenty-miles to watch a ball-game, or even wander all the way to Providence to visit Manny Almeida at his bar, a haul of some thirty-three miles, and when he got there he would stay for only an hour before making his way home again!

On these sojourns he would often be accompanied by Nicky Sylvester whose company he found to be relaxing. Sylvester would play the fool while he and Alsack (*a pet name for his closest friend Allie*) tossed a football between themselves. Rocco would concentrate on throwing the ball with his left hand only in order to improve on what he thought was a weakness.

"Rocky was always training," Sylvester reflected. "Even when he was doing things like walking, he couldn't just walk, he had to be doing something else like throwing a ball, or shadowboxing, or something, anything to keep him sharp."

Now back in New York having won his last three bouts, and won easily, Rocky's confidence was mounting. In fact so confident was he that for the first time he plucked up the temerity to visit Weill in his office to ask merely if his invisible manager, for at this time there was still no contract between the two, would consider coming down to Providence to watch him fight.

"I've really improved, I think," he said almost bashfully, Weill's initial response was allegedly explosive but unsubstantiated yet soon however someone else would be advising Weill to see this Brockton heavyweight fight in the flesh, and this time Al would have little option but to listen.

Sam Silverman was still smarting over Rocco's humiliating victory against Quinn that had, he believed, cost him his hard earned esteem in the eyes of his associate for whom he had set up the match; he therefore hatched a plan to avenge this loss of respect by placing Marchegiano against one Eddie Ross.

"Ross was classy. He had twenty-six wins and twenty-three knockouts," Silverman would tell author Everett M. Skeehan. "He was fighting for me in New Bedford, and I was looking to keep him around for the summer. I figured Rocky was bound to get beat, and Ross was the kid to do it."

The match was made for the 23rd of August, and to the layman it seemed that Rocco was indeed being thrown to the proverbial wolves for Ross was being groomed as a possible top-ten heavyweight, previous to meeting 'The Rock' Eddie had won twenty-seven fights, all but four inside the distance.

Closer inspection of Eddie's record though would paint a slightly different picture for it was padded with names of perennial losers, including one Roy Williams who had the temerity to hold the great Ross to a draw over six miserable rounds. An immediate rematch was convened with Ross stopping his opponent in two. It did appear however that Ross owed more to the master manipulator Silverman than to his own talent, for as former promoter Jimmy Deforest recalled, "He (*Silverman*) had this gift for building a fighter, he would take them from scratch, and create them, yet along the way he was not adverse to knocking them back as well, let them lose a couple, then get a bigger gate for the rematch. Let's not forget, Sam was a businessman first, and a damn good one."

Whichever way the fighter had earned his reputation this slim, balding, innocuous looking fighter had developed quite a following throughout Massachusetts. It was a reputation based primarily on his two previous outings when his stock had risen dramatically through successive knock outs of the vastly more experienced Wilfie Shanks and Bobby Jones who between them had racked up almost eighty victories [1].

Eddie's appeal in Providence was made all the more remarkable when you realize that Ross actually hailed from Montreal in Canada where the majority of his early bouts had taken place. Nevertheless due to his previous victories a large crowd was expected to attend the Auditorium once again. The building was beginning to shape itself like a cloak about Rocco's broad sloping shoulders now, so often would he be venturing into her shadows over the ensuing years.

Nevertheless, despite expectations it would soon become apparent from the moment both contestants entered the ring that there was only going to be one winner, and it would not be Ross.

The crowd was initially astonished to see that Marchegiano was actually the bigger man (*a true rarity in his career*), he outweighed their favorite by some ten-pounds and looked by far the more intimidating of the two. Within the opening seconds it soon became obvious that Ross was overpowered as Rocco waded in with both fists.

Despite his Kamikaze style Rocco was beginning to show feint traces of Goldman's genius as he was sharper in this bout than he had ever been before (2). Now Marchegiano began to crowd his adversary forcing him onto his back foot, it was a premeditated act on Rocco's part, this tactic meant that his opponent had to stand and fight or back away to find room to box. And when he did make a move Rocky would leap in with his own wide looping powerful punches (3). The inevitable had to happen, and it happened sooner rather than later when after just over a minute of the first round the aggressive Brocktonite caught the hapless Canadian with a booming right to the jaw which sent gum shield flying from gaping jaw. Eddie Ross was unconscious before he even hit the floor.

It was not only the fallen Ross' jaw that was forced open by that punch, Silverman's also dropped, yet this time he was not overcome with the feeling that he had been made to look foolish once again, rather it suddenly dawned on him that Rocco might, just might, be something special.

Manny Almeida who had co-promoted the show that night, and who was already becoming subordinate to Silverman would comment, "This bout really opened up everyone's eyes, it was this fight where it all started for Rocky, here Providence fell in love with him."

Almeida it was who also took the bull by the horns and rushed to the phone to give Weill "a bang" and relate to him the tale of victory. Yet 'The Vest' seemed to take the news in his stride. He was due to enter hospital soon for surgery on complications brought on by his diabetes, he thus refused to allow himself to get excited, but he did bend to pressure and agreed to send no less a personage than Charley Goldman himself to act in Rocco's corner for his very next bout.

Marchegiano's future seemed to lay just ahead of him now bright and clear, for his opponent though the future, at least in the ring, would not be quite so glittering. Ross fought only four times after this defeat. Two victories over quickly forgotten names to round off the year and then just two more in the entire twelve months of 1949, once in January when he was out pointed by a relative novice and not again until November when that right hand from Rocco seemed to catch up with him once more as he succumbed in three lackluster rounds to Ian McNeil who himself had won just one of a mere seven previous engagements. Maybe it was the manner of this loss to an unknown, or perhaps the fact that it happened so openly before his home fans in Montreal that persuaded Eddie Ross to quit the ring for good as after that night he would never fight again.

Notes:

1. *The veracity of these victories can only be conjectured however when Deforest later revealed that Sam was taken to calling him up asking for fighters at short notice who were willing to lay down.*
2. *Although the late Gil Clancey would always assert that, 'Goldman didn't create Rocky, Rocky created Rocky.'*
3. *This was a style, with slight refinements, that would stay with him for the rest of his career, reaching perfection in his bout with Rex Layne in 1951.*

part three   chapter eight

Three Gone Quick

"Nodody'll ever know how good this boy truly is if he keeps knocking them over so damn quick!"

Charley Goldman

It had been some five years since Charley Goldman had last made the three-hour train journey from New York to Providence, then he had come to oversee the penultimate bout in the career of his featherweight Joey Archibald in the Rhode Island Auditorium (*where else could it have possible been?*). Neither man knew then that this was to be the last time that Archibald would feature before his home crowd (*Joey had been born in the city some twenty-nine years earlier*), but the decline of this once talented boxer had been irrevocable since his last great night in 1941 when on the evening of May 12th he had regained the world featherweight championship from Harry Jeffra, the man who had taken the title from him the year before.

Since that fight Archibald had participated in no-less than nineteen contests, he had won only once, and that was back in '41, he was destined to lose this one as well, on points; like most of his losses, forty-two in total, he was hard to stop. His next and last bout however would see him knocked out, in three by the unknown Doll Rafferty. This was only the eighth time he had the immortal KO in his defeat column, yes he was definitely hard to keep down, but then he found it hard to put others down too, of his sixty victories only twenty-nine had failed to go the route.

Gone for now were Charley's halcyon days in Providence when Joey was king. Day's like the evening of April 18th, 1939 when Joey had come to the Auditorium as the reigning New York State world featherweight incumbent (*recognition he had earned in the ring six months earlier when he had defeated Mike Belloise for the vacant crown*), in order to contest for universal recognition against the National Boxing Associations holder, Leo Rodak.

The fragmentation of the title, something which would be taken to extremes during the latter half of the twentieth-century, had occurred due to the abdication of the incomparable Henry Armstrong. Against Rodak parity would once again be restored to the featherweight division. Archibald had gone into the bout as the underdog, yet against the odds he had secured victory; that had been a great night of jubilation for the city, that night everyone danced to Joey's tune, yet in the words of Goldman himself, "When you're dancing good everyone wants to be your partner, but when you start tripping over your feet you dance alone."

Although Archibald never truly danced on his own as his career became terminal, the heady crowds that surrounded him inevitably drifted, yet his rooters in Providence remained firm until the end, however they too were gone now as Charley alighted the train at the Providence station where he was greeted by an exuberant Allie Colombo, Rocco, as was his way now, was asleep at Alvina's.

"It was a great thrill to have Charlie (*sic*) here," recalled Colombo, "Finally it was like we were on are way."

Goldman, had made the trip to Providence strictly on Weill's orders, he personally had not wanted to be quite so involved at this stage, "I only began working Rocky's corner so early because that sumbitch Wergeles had lost favor with Weill, I mean fancy not telling him that his boy was banging out everyone he met!."

Indeed Chick Wergeles had made an unfortunate oversight in not being the one to inform Weill of Marchegiano's progress, he was instantly removed from Rocco's corner, from now on Charley would be with him all the way. It was not the complete finish of Chick's association with Rocky however, later he would be linked to the fighter as a public relations officer, sometime co-manager, and recipient of a major chunk of Marciano's contract to the tune of ten-percent.

The brilliant little trainer, who at the time was heavily involved with the promising middleweight Laverne Roach, who had been named rookie of the year in 1947 - and whose tragic death would be a public spectacle in 1950 before a capacity crowd at the St. Nicholas Arena, New York - probably believed his initial feelings that this was a waste of his time at this stage were correct for the amount of time he actually spent in his charges corner on that balmy day.

Jimmy Meeks, for a long time incorrectly titled Weeks, who had turned professional in 1946 had begun his career in a promising manner, notching up a string of eight victories, four inside the distance, in his first nine starts, the only blemish being a draw in his second outing. Yet by the time he met Marchegiano on the evening of Monday, August 30th an inevitable decline had set in , in fact he wasn't supposed to be facing Rocco at all that night for the new Brockton sensation was set to face one Al Bryant, a big, cumbersome heavy from New Jersey but for the second time in Marchegiano's fledgling career his named opponent decided not to make an appearance, fortunately Meeks was on standby and stepped in for a quick pay day.

Rocco steamrollered over the hapless Meeks in little more than two-minutes of the opening round, knocking him over twice into the bargain, on the second occasion referee Sharkey Buonanno had to forcibly intervene, leading him to comment later, "I had to grab his (*Rocco's*) arm…, I could hardly hold it. Never have I felt such power!"

After the bout an unenthusiastic Goldman replied to a small gathering of reporters from Brockton when asked for his opinion on their aspiring professional, "I can't give no opinion, the fight was too short." Then, as if in the hope of sounding at least a little keen he added, "He sure can punch. He's a little crude as yet to be sure, but what I like almost as much as his punching mite is his poise…I believe he'll go far."

Silverman himself would comment later on Marciano's short right hand that leveled Meeks, "As awkward and clumsy as the kid looked, he could deliver an accurate punch. The kid was hitting guys right on the button."

Providence Journal reporter, Michael J. Thomas, was far more ebullient however when he claimed in his piece the day after the brief skirmish that, "If punching power will do it, Rocky Marchegiano may one day become the world heavyweight champion."

It was a bold statement, one that may have been aroused by his reporting that the crowd that night had roared for Marchegiano, "…as the multitudes used to hail Jack Dempsey."

This was to an extent true, Rocky was beginning to pick up an eager following in Providence now, it was one that would continue to grow and explode into almost mythic proportions later when the then Marciano exploded onto the national stage. Author Wilfred Diamond would sum up this growing appeal when he wrote (*in; This Guy Marciano, 1955*) that, "The one thing that makes Rocky's fights fascinating and makes him the idol of the fans--there is never one moment when he is in the ring that you can take your eyes of him--The payoff might come at any moment. If you look down at your programme or light a cigarette…the curtains might be rung down while you're at it."

Nicky Sylvester, who was at the majority of his friends earliest bouts remembers how he and the rest of Rocco's growing entourage would shout "Timberrrrr" as Marchegiano first set up and then rung down the curtains over one opponent after another.

"The bomb is always there," continued Diamond. "And the fuse is burning--and in one split second it explodes and the fight is over. It's waiting for that split second that makes the Rock's fights sensational--you're always on the edge of your chair."

For Meeks though there would be neither raucous crowd to encourage him on nor eulogies to his power retrospectively composed. Instead he toyed with the sport for another two unsuccessful years before vanishing from history in 1950 with a knock out loss to Sylvester Salter.

Rocco's next bout was scheduled for a fortnight later, thus he returned briefly to New York where Goldman was attempting to iron out the faults that were slowly being corrected, however at this time Charley was preoccupied with more pressing matters for besides the promising Roach he also had a hand at this time in training the outstanding Cuban welterweight, 'Kid' Gavilan who had recently gone the distance not once, but twice against the incomparable Ray Robinson. Gavilan had dropped the decision on both occasions to the then welterweight champion, the second over the full fifteen rounds with Robinson's title at stake [1].

For the Brockton heavyweight now it was work, work, work. When he wasn't training with Goldman at the CYO in New York he was at the Y.M.C.A in Brockton hitting a heavy bag with his bare fists [2], or training at the estate of Ross Murray. "I didn't get no tutoring or anything. I didn't even have anyone to spar with (3)," recalled Marciano of his time at the estate.

All other past times now were relegated to mere hobbies, something to do when on rare occasions he had a chance to relax. Baseball, for so long his driving ambition would from now on be merely a game he toyed at with his brother 'Sonny', a promising player himself, everything else was gone, including his place on a Brockton bowling team, he maintained the discipline of throwing the 10-pound ball would wreck his forearms for punching.

Little is known of official opponent number six, even his name has become something of a mystery, some records tab him as either Jerry or Gerald Jackson, some even reported him to be Humphrey Jackson, birth name Humphrey Pennyworth, a name he allegedly changed when the moniker became immortalized by the oafish, oversized friend of comic book hero Joe Palooka, from the little that we do know Jackson had a modicum of talent, at least in his amateur days for he had claimed no less than five consecutive New York Golden Gloves titles before turning pro. Jackson was a big man too, against Marchegiano on that Monday, September 13th he weighed in at a scale groaning 254lb (*outweighing his adversary by some 70-pounds*), it was a bulk that must have caused a tremor of seismic proportions when his inert form was unceremoniously dumped on the canvas after just over a minute of fighting.

The Jackson enigma continued on. No one is really sure how many fights he had, some believe he turned professional in 1946 and of the handful of fights on record the only names that stand out are Marciano's, Wade Chancey, he of Rocky's try-out before the unscrupulous eyes of Weill and Goldman fame, and, in December of 1948, a five-round decision loss to Coley Wallace. This bout with Coley is made the more interesting by the fact however that the match-up was billed on an amateur card, Wallace not turning professional until two years later.

Marchegiano's next appearance on the following Monday, September 20th, would be a watershed for him on his rise to the top of this the hardest game for this would be the final time he would be billed under his birth name of Marchegiano. In the corner facing him was a fighter who hailed from Boston by the name of William 'Bill' Hardeman, a recurrent loser who had taken part in only seven bouts since turning professional at the beginning of 1948. Of these contests he had emerged victorious only once, a decision over the undersized Harry Bilzarian. However he had been stopped just once and this perceived ability to take a punch, along with his size, six-foot-one and a trim 206lb's, seemed to warrant him, at least in the eyes of Sam Silverman, a chance against Rocky. Others were nevertheless more skeptical. Manny Almeida, who although, on paper at least, was still partners with the smooth talking promoter, voiced the opinion that, "…Hardeman was chosen simply to feed another piece of meat to the monster that was Marciano."

Obligingly Rocky appeased his appetite and devoured Hardeman in the first stanza, and he did it with some panache. 'Despite his hasty exit,' reported *The Brockton Enterprise-Times*, 'Hardman (*sic*) was one of the toughest men Rocky has met. Whereas normally Marchegiano applies the deep freeze with one punch, usually his bomb packed right cross (*nicknamed "Old Reliable"-authors add*), Rocky had to work harder than his Kayo Monday night

'The veteran ringman, Hard(*e*)man, came out of his corner planning to box and wanted to fight in close. But Rocky refused to oblige. He danced around the heavier Boston boxer, moved in fast to strike, then pulled away. On one of his bomb runs Marchegiano planted four or five straight left jabs on Hard(*e*)man's head and the end was near. Rocco followed up with four more left and right jabs, Hard(e)man dropped his hands and then took a solid right to the chin which dropped him into a corner where he took the final count.'

It seems that being digested by Marchegiano was too much for the Boston boy, he fought only once more when three months later he was again served up as an appetizer for an eager audience, this time in his home town. Again he failed to last a round of the scheduled eight against the promising Willie James who would himself get to within a sniff of true contender status in the ensuing years.

After this show Rocco was destined to adopt the name that would invade the public consciousness, a persona that would eventually lead to being used as a synonym of all that is good, all that is tough, and all that can be achieved through sheer damn guts and self-belief. From now on Rocco Marchegiano would metamorphosis himself into Rocky Marciano.

Notes:

1. *Later 'The Cuban Hawk' would defect from Goldman's camp and eventually, in 1951, win the coveted welterweight championship, his leaving however never left a bitter taste in Charley's mouth, it was all part of the game.*

2. *"Art Bergman, a fireman I knew who was a terrific puncher, gave me the biggest, heaviest bag I ever saw. It weighed 180 pounds. The normal bag weighed forty or fifty pounds. I'd had trouble with my hands before. Art told me to punch the bag with my bare fists, and that's the way I hardened them up."*

3. *This is not strictly true, although he had no professionals to test himself against he would however spar with his own fifteen year old brother 'Sonny', or his friend and sometime corner man, 'Snap' Tartaglia.*

part three **chapter nine**

Marciano

"My real name is Marchegiano, it's my fathers' name and my brother's name. They're not going to change it because of me. And I'm not going to change it. I wouldn't want them to feel bad [1]."

Rocky Marciano

It was not unusual for those who aspired towards fame to change their names during the twentieth-century; it was in fact a custom that was quickly adopted by all those who were promised to be laid before the public eye. Actors and athletes alike were quick to rid themselves of a name that failed to elicit certain responses from a public keen to associate a certain personality to their chosen star. Image was everything. Hence the rather dour sounding Norma Jean became the sirenesque Marilyn Monroe. Archie Leech became the debonair Cary Grant. Whilst the almost effete Marion Morrison was turned into the rugged, masculine, John Wayne.

In boxing the reasons for a change of name were not so readily to be related to image alone, after all these guys did not need to exude the illusion of masculinity or allure that beset the movie stars, what they did in the ring was proof enough of their character. Yet still there was often the problem of selling themselves to the public, the old saying of, 'if the name doesn't fit' was particularly true. For instance if Walker Smith had not felt the urge to compete in an AAU tournament when he was under age then he would not have borrowed a friends amateur membership card in order to illegally enter the ring. Forever after he would carry that borrowed name; Ray Robinson *(later the pre-fix 'Sugar' would be added by his future manager who described his style as, 'sweet as sugar')*

Joe Louis sounded better than Joseph Louis Barrow, and as for the young Melody Jackson, he changed to a name more befitting the only man to hold three world titles simultaneously, the remarkable 'Homicide Hank', Henry Armstrong.

Some fighters found themselves stymied by their birth names in other ways. During the early to mid-twentieth century the predominant ethnic classes in boxing were the descendants of Irish and Italian immigrants, these were the names that fit, Dempsey, Sullivan, Braddock, Canzoneri, Galento, LaMotta.

Fighters born Dovber Rasofsky, Noah Brusso, or Gershon Mendelhoff were not going to make it to the big time despite their talent, they did not have marquee appeal, and thus they were changed to Barney Ross, Tommy Burns, and Ted "Kid" Lewis respectively. Under these titles each would attain the championships of their respective weights.

There were some fighters whose names were just too complicated for the ring announcer, press, and fan, to get their mouths around, thus featherweight Willie Papelo became Willie Pep, Stanislaw Kiecal became Stanley Ketchell, and Rocco Marchegiano became Rocky Marciano.

For months now the pronunciation of Marchegiano had been causing chaos for those with the task of introducing him at Providence, it would come out variously as Mack-ge-ano, Mark-a-Jahno, or Marci-ge-ano. Even in the press his name was being misspelt as Markegiano, Marchegino, etc, etc, it was time to address this problem, and the one to do it was Al Weill himself.

After the victory over Hardeman Rocky had been summoned to see Weill at his Broadway office, the reason for the summons had to do with the fact that Al had been asked by his associate Goldie Ahearn to supply a fighter to help fill the card at a show in Washington which had been postponed due to a split lip suffered by one of the headlining protagonists. This had caused a ripple through the field of boxers lined up to fight, leading some to withdraw entirely thereby leaving a gap that needed to be filled.

The ever ticking brain of Weill had kicked into gear and he saw this as an opportunity to show off his Brockton fighter who was knocking over opponents like bowling pins. This was to be the first bout involving Rocky that Al had been directly involved with. It was a leap of faith on his part for up until now he had not seen Marchegiano in action since that day against Chancey some three months earlier, all his knowledge was passed down by Goldman, yet Weill had built his reputation on taking the occasional risk, even if those risks were calculated, and he was taking one now.

Once the New York manager was in complete control he recognized immediately the importance of giving his charge a pronounceable name, Rocky was fine but that last name had to be modified. Several names were muted, amongst them Mack re-emerged but was quickly knocked back, as was Weill's suggestion of March. If he had to change his name then Rocco wanted to keep the Italian flavor. He was proud of his heritage and was rueful of having to assume a name that would not elude to his origin, however, for Marchegiano at least, his manager made a fortuitous call to Manny Almeida.

"Weill called me and said he wanted to change Rocky's name, I couldn't believe it. I told him, 'Are you crazy? This guy's a sensation down here under the name Marciano. What's the matter with that?' The announcer down here (*Harold Warman*) had been dropping the heg out of his name for a couple of fights, so that's how his name came about (2)."

On the outside it was a suggestion that suited everybody, yet later the now Marciano would be fuming for he was worried what his father would say when he discovered the change of name. Why the hell did he have to change it anyway he would cry to Allie Colombo. Eventually he would calm down, especially when his father understood. Rocco even grew to like the name, yet he never changed it officially, even near the end of his life he still signed cheques and contracts under the name of Marchegiano.

On Thursday September 30th, Rocky Marciano found himself in Washington, this was the first time that the quadrangle of Weill, Goldman, Colombo and Marciano would be together, this was the team that with-in four years would have conquered the boxing world.

The headline act that night at the Uline Arena, an indoor venue which was reminiscent of an old oversized airplane hangar which had been chosen due to the threat of a storm brewing on the horizon, was a bout between Sonny Boy West and Maxie Shapiro (*it was Shapiro who caused the previous cancellation*). Marciano was to be in the semi feature against one Don Riffe (*or possibly Raniff*) who hailed from Valley Stream, New York. Yet for reasons never explained it would be a match that never happened.

Whilst Marciano was in the dressing room preparing for the fight he met his adversary for that evening, and it was not who had been billed. Riffe had pulled out at the last minute, his place taken instead by, 'a sad faced Puerto Rican' Gil Cardone. As the pair dressed themselves for battle and awaited the call they broke into conversation. Remembered Rocky, "The poor guy had nothing. His father was sick and he had four brothers and sisters. He had a job and he was fighting on the side. He only fought when he needed the money. I felt sorry for him."

His feelings however did not seem to temper his performance when the bell rang as before the eyes of Weill Marciano displayed the ferocious power of his fists when after a mere thirty-six seconds he exploded a left uppercut to Cardone's chin and leveled him. But there was no quick exit this time for Rocky. When he looked over at Cardone's unmoving form a sudden fear swept over him. As Colombo explained, "It was the first time I got frightened and felt that the man may have been badly hurt."

Gil lay unconscious for almost ten minutes whilst he was attended to by his handlers and ringside physician. "When Cardione (*sic*) finally began to move his head and legs, I felt a shiver rush through me," continued Colombo. "We were both standing beside him. Rocky refused to leave the ring until they brought him back to full consciousness."

For Rocky this was a frightening presage of what was to come, for Weill it was a vindication of his risk. Fortunately for Cardone he felt no lasting effects from the unconditional knock-out, in fact he would keep fighting sporadically for several years, one of the cornerstones of professional boxing ready to take a fight at the drop of a hat, never chasing the big time, content merely for the chance to add to his own probably meager income.

Marciano had received his highest purse to date, some two-hundred-dollars. Sure it wasn't Madison Square Garden money where he could earn upwards of six-thousand but it was going in the right direction.

At this exact moment however the direction he was heading in led him straight back to Providence.

Notes:

1. *Today however the immediate male family members ply their trades under the name Marciano, all except for his son Rocky Kevin who proudly carries the family name of Marchegiano still.*

2. *In fact the name Rocky Marciano had first been seen in print on the morning of January 17th, 1947 in the amtuer bout with Jim Connolly (see part two chapter four and who will come again into the story of Rocky's rise). The name first appeared in print in reference to his professional career in The Providence Journal the day after his first official professional fight against Balazerian before changing back to some mangled form of Marchegiano.*

part three   **chapter ten**

The Contract

"When I signed with Weill it was the biggest thrill of my life. But, boy, if I knew how much of my life I was giving up I would have thought twice!"

Rocky Marciano

Robert 'Bob' Jefferson, who hailed from Brooklyn was a competent boxer, at least in the very earliest stages of his career. Of his first four outings he had lost only to Phil Berman, a promising light-heavyweight who remained unbeaten through the first fifteen bouts, and then only narrowly on points over the full six rounds. This was regarded as highly commendable on Jefferson's part for most of Berman's victims had succumbed in less than two rounds [1]. Prior to his match with Marciano though Jefferson had been knocked out by George Kaplan, again this would prove to be no disgrace as Kaplan had himself hit a winning streak which would follow him right through 1949. It had taken George four rounds to dispose of Jefferson, plus he had lasted the distance against a known hitter in Berman. For the first time since the esteemed Eddie Ross it appeared, on paper at least, that Rocky was being tested.

Technically this Monday night fight (*October 4th*) should have been billed at light-heavy, Jefferson scaled a mere 172-pounds to Marciano's 178, the lightest he ever weighed when stepping between the ropes and it showed for Rocky seemed tight. Maybe he had over trained, burnt himself out in the gym as Jefferson achieved what so far only Epperson and Quinn had done, last out the first round.

The fact that he lasted was down to his evasive skills, the smaller, sleeker, and swifter fighter was able to step out of range on several occasions, even leading Rocky to miss by wide margins with his thunderous punches. Nevertheless in the second round Rocky exploded into life and found his target, knocking the otherwise resilient Brooklynite down twice, both times for counts of nine. On getting to his feet from the last knock down Jefferson was groggy and reeling, referee Ben Maculan had no option but to put an end to the slaughter with a mere thirty-seconds remaining in the stanza.

For Jefferson this night marked the end of the road, at least in terms of promise. He promptly lost his next two tries, again by stoppage, before winning one, on points. This was his last hurrah however as he would fight thrice more in 1948, losing them all. Initially he took a two year hiatus before returning to action in April of 1950. Twice he fought that month, and twice he was quickly disposed of, this was too much, now he called it quits for good.

Rocco on the other hand had notched up unofficial win number ten, nine of those since approaching Weill, all had ended inside the distance, and now Al Weill had little option but to take Marciano seriously, and this is exactly what he did.

On October 8th 1948, a mere four days after his convincing victory over Jefferson, Marciano found himself once more in the cluttered Broadway office of Al Weill. This time however this Machiavellian mentor had his eyes firmly set on complete control over his new pet, the Providence sensation, Rocky Marciano.

To this end he shoved before the fighter an at first glance innocuous looking piece of paper which was inscribed with a swiftly composed and even swifter glanced at proposition of contract. Weill added his name almost nonchalantly to the bottom. Unthinkingly Marciano eagerly followed Weill's lead adding his own name to the sheet with an exuberant flourish of the pen. This act, which to Rocco no doubt signaled a new beginning, would bind the two men together for the next decade.

Notes:

1. *Remarkably in November of 1948 the unbeaten New Jersey sensation, Berman, announced his retirement. "I gave boxing an honest try and now I'll be looking for something else to do," he told reporters, however the lure of the ring remained strong and he soon returned, sporadically, over the following three years. He finally called it quits for good in 1951 when he was knocked out for the second time in three fights. "This guy was a serious threat to Marciano," remarked Manny Almeida. "He was doing in the big city what Rocky was doing here -in Providence-. But in the end he lost heart and Rocky's just kept getting bigger."*

part three   **chapter eleven**

The House of Sin

"That place was like something out of a movie, everywhere you looked there was something going on. People thought I was crazy for living there, but I liked it just fine!"

Rocky Marciano

Now that Marciano had finally found himself under the official guidance of Manager Al Weill events began to change drastically for the former laborer. Already Weill had attempted to take his family name from the fighter, now he would attempt to remove the family influence altogether. As Almeida recalled of his sometime associate, "He (*Weill*) hated anybody from distracting his boys. Family, girlfriends, anyone without his consent. He would vet everyone in that boy's life and if he felt they were wrong for his fighter he would do his damndest to cut them out completely!"

To this end Al informed his new acquisition that before he fought again he would have to serve an apprenticeship under the watchful eye of Charley Goldman, and not from the distance of Brockton, no, not this time, Weill wanted him close. He told Marciano that from now on he would be spending more time in New York, away from distraction, away from his family. However Al Weill may have been shrewd in business, but as a reader of characters he was way off, at least when it came to Rocky Marciano [1].

Family (*'La Famaglia'*) where many generations from the same family co-existed under the same roof, where the father worked and sacrificed himself for the good of the children and expecting the same from them in return only when they were able, was everything to Marciano, as it was for all Italian children from time immemorial. Indeed the family unit was so strong that as the offspring grew and moved out they would not stray far, their connections were binding. Being part of this unit meant that you were protected, cared for, loved. And the biggest part of any family was the Mother. Yes Rocco was intensely loyal to his Mother and to his heritage, at least at the beginning, yet slowly, inexorably, he would be amongst the first to pull away, to become a modern Italian where roots were still strong but the ties that bind were loosened.

But this slow moving away would not happen yet, sure he had broken with tradition by choosing for his bride-to-be someone outside the cultural clique in Barbara, she of Irish descent, yet still he loathed being parted from his comfort zone. He was reticent of being removed for too long from his own indomitable family.

Immediately though the Brockton boy, keen to advance himself, had no option but to acquiesce to his managers demand. Thus he returned to his hometown briefly to break the news of his departure; Weill wanted him to stay in New York for at least a month, a month that would be spent fine-tuning the already monumental changes that had been made by Goldman. Pasqualena by all accounts pleaded with her son not to go, she had lost so much time with him during his years in service of his country, yet Rocky knew he had little choice this was his last chance to make something of his life. Besides it would only be for a short while, he would be back. Little did Marciano know at the time that this would be the start of his wanderings, the start of a life which would keep him separated from his family for months at a time.

The beginning for him on his road to success would lead inevitably to a decline in his private life that would never truly be reversed. Still at least he would have Allie with him, Allie who acted as a sort of umbilical back to his hometown and back to his roots. Wherever Rocco went he could look at Allie and remember where he had come from as he looked forward to where he was headed now.

Often it was a great comfort to him to recall the warmth of his past, yet at others it remained a burden recalling the hardships both he and his family had gone through, and swore he would never go through again. "He would bleed without protest and ache without complaint if he could be called champion," wrote journalist Jimmy Cannon, "Obscurity was all he feared."

The pairing of Marciano and Colombo headed out for their prolonged sojourn in New York in the same manner that they had first arrived some four months previously, in the cab of the uncomfortable, dilapidated, constantly rattling truck driven by Bill O'Malley [2]. Their destination this time was not the dazzling, vibrant belly of Broadway but rather the austerely comfortable rooming house of Ma Braune and into the waiting arms of Charley Goldman.

Work began almost immediately at the CYO with the astute Goldman piecing together this chunk of proverbial rock. However he moved with caution now, Marciano was coming along just right, he was winning, that was crucial to Charley. The trainer was brutally aware of the shortcomings that this wild fighter still possessed but was reticent to tinker with his basic style. "I'm not gonna fool with him too much," Goldman was quoted by the late Everett M.

Skeehan. "When a fighters winning big, a trainer's got to be careful he doesn't do nothing to foul him up."

He was nervous about Marciano's infighting though, as he reportedly continued in Skeehan's, Biography of a First Son. "He has to learn to fight onna inside. His arms ain't long enough. A good boxer'll murder him at long range...When we go for the big guys, he'll have to get inside and take advantage of those short arms."

To this end Charley proverbially killed two birds with one stone for at the same time that he was working with Rocky he also had at the CYO one Cesar Brion, an Argentinean heavyweight who himself was unbeaten in the professional ring. Yet at three years older than Marciano his experience was vastly superior to Rocky's, as was his technique.

Brion was in training for bout with the mediocre Jimmy Walls and needed a sparring partner, one who was resilient enough to last against him. Brion was regarded as a rough tough spar mate by all those who had stood against him at the gym and few were willing to trade blows with him for long. In Rocky Goldman had the perfect foil for not only would it give Brion someone to tee off on but it would also give Marciano the opportunity to put what Goldman was teaching him into practice.

For a week the pair battled it out in the ring, their sparring sessions were regarded as wars by all those who witnessed them. Brion it was agreed got the better of Rocky in most of the exchanges, however the Brockton bull managed to barrage the bigger Brion into the ropes on several occasions. Each time this happened and Marciano began to pound away too vociferously on the Argentinean Goldman would call time. Brion was a tall talented boxer, the fact that Rocky was able to get inside and bully him about proved to Goldman that this kid listened. "You never had to tell Rocky anything twice. The thing I liked best besides his right hand was that he was always trying to improve."

One morning Goldman arrived at the CYO with a young twenty-seven year old who had imbued himself in boxing and was eager to make a name for himself as a trainer, his name was Angelo Dundee [3].

The future elder statesman recalled his initial meeting with Marciano. "I was the new kid around the Block in NY and Charlie (*sic*) would bring me to family type restaurants on 9th Avenue…he told me about this kid from Brockton he was training at the CYO, shortish, stooping shoulders, two left feet but oh how he can punch. (*Charley*) took me to the CYO with him and Rocky walked in with a small canvass bag, (*he*) worked with Keene Simmons that day.

"Charlie (*sic*) was having him (*Marciano*) do an exercise where he bent his knees completely down, almost touching the floor with his butt, and then came up punching. And this boxer called Rocky would do it and end up with a left hook or a right hand every time."

He continued his feelings on the man who would become a close friend, "That great desire to win was so evident in the guy. I could see it right from the beginning. And I could see the progress. Rocky came along remarkably well, because he had a great teacher. In each trainer's life there always comes a greatness with one certain fighter, for Charlie (*sic*) Goldman it was Rocky Marciano."

Dundee at the time lamented that Marciano based himself at the CYO rather than at Angelo's second home, namely the legendary Stillman's gymnasium on 326 West and 57th Street, New York.

Just as Dundee was to become an institution so Stillman's had been one for decades, for as New York was the heart of boxing so Stillman's was its soul. The gymnasium itself had been opened in 1910 under the name of Marshall Stillman in order to help rehabilitate ex-convicts. Soon it would come under the ownership of one Lou Ingber, a former fighter, sometime private detective, and now a trainer who instead of changing the name of the facility decided to transform his own and forever after would be known as Lou Stillman. By the forties he would be described by one former fighter John Garfield, as, "Sour, 60'sh…and was clearly fed up and burnt out (*he*) was all crust."

By the time Marciano had begun his inexorable rise this building had become a mecca for the sport that was second only to baseball in popularity. Every champion, want-to-be-champion, or just plain hangar on had passed through the thick iron entrance doors. From here they would ascend the steep dingy stairs to the second floor where the main gym was housed with its two raised rings, cubicle rooms flanking the walls for managers to make their deals, and on up to the third tier where the heavy bags and speed balls were housed. Here the boxers could vent their vanity by watching themselves in the full length mirrors that lined the walls before retiring behind a door which barely clung to its ancient hinges in which lay the dilapidated locker rooms where a boxer's privacy was marked by mere plywood screens, at least for the name fighters. Here they could lay on the massage tables for their obligatory post workout rubdown, a simple luxury but one that was envied by those less fortunate who had to share a space filled with green metal lockers where they could house their belongings and a long splintered wooden bench was their changing room. The shower room too was simply that, a room, with one rusted shower head to cleanse them, and the only light, a small grime encrusted window.

Here Lou was most definitely in charge for when he wasn't at the gate charging enthralled boxing voyeurs the obligatory 25-cents to witness their heroes performing within a mere arms reach of them thus adding to the stank atmosphere made from a mixture of stale sweat, blood, and leather, he could also be found meandering in and out of the twin rings shouting insults at everyone. It seemed he hated them all, big names and nobodies. Backed up by .38 caliber pistol which was slung loosely about his waist he would routinely escort out the undesirable, dumping them out into the street where a sign read, 'No Loitering'.

It was here that Goldman felt most at home, here that he forged his fighters (*and here that Dundee, "...worked corners with him and watched and learned"*). Yet never had he so far brought the man who would one day be regarded as his greatest triumph that is until Marciano yearned to train on a Monday, the only day that the CYO was closed.

Charley had kept Marciano away from Stillman's through sheer embarrassment. He believed that the fight crowd would disparage his charge, ridicule him for his awkwardness, scoff at his apparent lack of tutelage, but now he realized he had no choice. The thought that the place at least would be quite on this day nevertheless helped to soften the blow.

Indeed it was quiet that Monday in October when Marciano first entered the legendary gymnasium. Apart from the trio of Rocky, Allie and Charley there was only a handful of trainers and fighters populating the space around them. One of the men there was a big heavyweight named Gene Gosney who was in preparation for a make or break bout with the ascending star that was Roland LaStarza. Gosney and Marciano were made to fight each other that day, as Colombo recalled, "He (*Gene*) was a slugger just like Rocky, and from the minute Goldman began the fight they went after each other.

"There were no knockdowns with the big gloves, but the few people that were in Stillman's got a real kick out of the way these fighters went at it. When the bell sounded to end the second round they were still punching, and Charley Goldman and myself had to jump into the ring and break them up."

It was a good honest workout for both men and Marciano would later remember his encounter with Gene as, "One of my toughest sparring sessions ever." It was a session that would not be repeated though for Charley would continue to steer his boy away from Stillman's until he had broken into the big time and could no longer be hidden away. By then Marciano was no longer the butt of jokes, at least not amongst those who were at the grassroots of boxing and had seen him close up in the ring.

The impromptu clash seemed to have made an impression on Gosney too for he went into the bout with LaStarza on the night of December 10th, 1948, primed and ready. He promptly stamped his authority over the favored LaStarza by smashing the previously unbeaten Bronx boxer to the floor twice in the opening round for long counts of nine. Unfortunately for Gene however it appeared he was a bleeder for by the end of the sixth his eyebrows had been clinically sliced by the clever LaStarza, the referee had no option but to stop the fight. After this Gene slipped quietly away, but LaStarza would spin around the boxing firmament, a star getting brighter and brighter until eventually he would crash headlong into Marciano himself.

Goldman must have felt quietly content that he had managed to evade the unforgiving glare of the boxing gods that day at Stillman's. The Brockton boy had performed OK and, thankfully, very few had seen him, yet the grapevine in the pugilistic world was long, in fact it extended as far as Los Angeles where Al Weill was spending his annual two-week vacation. When he returned he would confront the diminutive trainer with thunderous spite.

There is a train of thought amongst the fight community that the real reason Marciano was kept away from this iconic gymnasium was due not to Goldman's wish to avoid the disparaging comments of his fellow artisans but rather that Weill was worried that he would lose control of his new potential prospect.

It was an open secret that boxing at that time was in the vice like grip of an underworld influence that would not be lifted until the Kefauver hearing almost two decades later, and the favorite poaching ground for these predators was Stillman's itself. Here the likes of the notorious Mr. Gray, the underworld czar of boxing and his various minions would haunt and hustle any clients they thought would be willing to accede to their demands. Most would eventually succumb, for if they did not all knew that any career in the sport to which they had devoted their lives would be washed away overnight leaving them hanging hopelessly on the lower tier of the professional ladder, relegated to club fights for meager crowds and even more meager purses. Or worse, they may end up, like Ray Arcel the famous fight trainer and bastion of order, with a lead pipe wrapped around their head. It was in fact Arcel himself, a man who detested the mob controlled atmosphere of his beloved game back in the so called 'golden years' who in a 1972 interview summed up Weill's fear.

"Weill, who we all knew was on the take, had been taken for a ride himself by those influences who ran boxing into the ground back in the thirties and forties, so he was protective of Marciano in the early days. Not through reasons of charity though, he just wanted to wait until he could use the boy as a bargaining tool, fetch a higher price and have complete control of the situation. Weill was a businessman first, a manager second. So he kept him (*Rocky*) close in the early years until he had built him into something special and those influences had no choice but to keep Weill in the loop."

But if Weill was mad at Goldman for acting without first consulting him he was even more irate at his charge for having the temerity of moving out of Ma Brown's without his explicit consent (*yes, even though Weill was not the ogre he was believed to be he still could often be overly exertive as he tried to assert his influence and control over fighters*).

"She was a nice woman," recalled Marciano of Mrs. Rosa Braune, known affectionately as Ma Brown, "And her house was clean, but we didn't like it because there was no life there, and it was too far uptown. We didn't have much money so our only relaxation was walking around."

Usually that meant walking around to the CYO some seventy-five blocks away. Someone once came up with the foolish suggestion that Rocky should take the bus, but that was ludicrous to the man who would walk rather than pay a fare. Instead it was Roy Cavanaugh, one of the truck drivers who would sometimes ferry Colombo to New York whilst Marciano rode with O'Malley, who came up with the perfect compromise. He informed Allie that during his stays in New York he would often find a room at a Y.M.C.A over on the corner of West Thirty-Fourth Street and Ninth-Avenue, near Manhattan. The rooms were a dollar-seventy a night, with two sharing that was a mere 85-cent apiece. Plus the Y had the added advantages of being central to Weill's office, the CYO, and Broadway (*the impressive Madison Square Garden was also but a stone's throw away*). Also, and this was the decider, the building was equipped with a gym of its own. Without hesitation the pair moved into this impressive looking fifteen story brick edifice bearing the legend, 'Sloane House Y.M.C.A' in vast illuminated letters pinioned to a sign running vertical down one corner.

The William Sloane House, to give it its full grand title, had been opened in 1930 and named after William Sloane who had, before his death in 1922, been the chair of the Army and Navy International Committee plus an upstanding member of the National War Work Council of Y.M.C.A. The building was intended initially, and in order to honor Sloane's memory, as an inexpensive boarding house for military personal visiting the metropolitan city. However as the second world war ended in 1945 numbers of servicemen dropped leaving many of the staggering 1500 rooms vacant, thus it was opened to the public in general. For a while the building kept itself clean, visitors would use it for its intended purpose of providing affordable accommodation whilst they stayed and explored or merely passed through, however soon an inevitable decline began to set in as more and more it began to metamorphosis into a microcosm of New York itself. The small cramped rooms would be the hangout of pimps and hookers, drugs and violence seeped through the long faceless corridors. Perverts would slice slits into the curtains of the communal showers to peer at those inside. Garbage was tossed uncaringly out into the pit, a large concrete slab of nowhere land around which the building seemed to be molded (4). There were rumors that there was more than just trash out there in the growing pile, bodies too were spoken off in hushed tones as being buried within the mess.

For sure murders had already taken place inside the brick belly. Down in the vast L-shaped laundry room a woman had been murdered, sexually motivated most thought. Other deaths had occurred via suicide, there were some very lonely people there (5).

It was into this swiftly rotting carcass that Marciano and Colombo came in November of 1948, and they, Rocky particularly, liked it just fine. So what if it was a dump, so what if the lives lived within were not quite the saintly ones envisaged by those back home. New York's underbelly was a stagnant one, the neon covering that greeted casual visitors and peered out of post cards and tabloid sheets was a charade, all in the city knew it, deep down, but they loved it just the same. For now, at least, the dark ones kept their world to themselves, if you didn't want in then fine, go your own way with a smile, and Marciano walked through it all with a smile as wide and infectious as his mother's. Others lives were their own business, besides he never spent long in the place, he was always out, either running around Central Park, training at the CYO, eating out in a cafeteria at Columbus Circle, or trawling Broadway with Allie in tow chatting up the showgirls who were parading on the Mike Todd show, 'As The Girls Go', whilst keeping his eye out for the occasional celebrity who may be foolish enough to wander into the street at night.

Despite the fact that Marciano liked his new lodgings there was the problem of becalming Weill who wanted Marciano at the boarding house so that he and Charley could keep an eye on him, make sure he was being looked after and keeping strict to his regime (*something that neither fighter and manager needed to worry about*). Again however Marciano would assert his independence thus solidifying the feeling that he was uncomfortable with Weill treating him like an errant child who needed guidance. Marciano explained the problem of traveling between the CYO and his former room. Plus the place was cheaper. Weill calmed down, gave in, and allowed the boys to stay where they were.

After his tirade, which seemed to accomplish nothing anyway, Weill informed his fighter that he had a fight lined up for him on the night of November 29th back in providence. Marciano by this time was no doubt chomping at the bit, this was his longest period of enforced exile since turning pro some four months earlier. When he heard the name of his opponent it is easy to imagine a wry smile creasing his rugged face, for he had history with the man he was set to face.

Patrick Connolly was a huge powerfully built man from out of Boston, yet his ginger hair, which gave him the nickname of 'Red', belied his Irish-Celtic origins. The two fighters had met before in the ring on at least one occasion.

Whilst Rocky was using the facilities on Ross Murray's estate just outside of Brockton the self-made magnate thought he would surprise his erstwhile guest with some sparring partners, one of these was Connolly himself. The two fought it out over three rounds and Marciano, as was sometimes his way, looked awful. The bigger, heavier Connolly reportedly forced Rocky all over the ring. "He really embarrassed me," said Marciano later, "All my friends were there and he made me look like a fool. I just hoped that one day I'd get a chance to meet him in the ring (6)."

And now he would, yet the fact that Rocky even managed to climb into the ring at all that night was a minor miracle in itself.

Notes:

1. *Now we can understand that Al was not acting out of megalomania but more as he believed that he knew what was best for his fighters, by cutting out as many distractions as possible the better the boy's chance of achieving their potential in their chosen sport, as it was most would have only short career's, their family could wait a little while whilst their boy made some money for the future, Marty Weill again; 'Weill (saw) to it that the fighters received the money due them...he advised them wisely, none of his champs were financially forced into making a comeback once they gave up boxing.'*

2. *Marciano had sorted this ride himself; it was an early instance of his saving money, why pay when you can ride for free? This attitude would cost him more than he could have imagined in the end.*

3. *Angelo Dundee and I corresponded over a period of some nine-months between mid-2010 through to early 2011 and it was in this period that he composed the short forward to this first volume. Sadly Angelo passed away on February 1st, 2012 just as I was completing the final stages of preparing this volume for release. I cannot thank him enough for his time and belief in this project, I just wish I could have fulfilled his wish of sending him a copy of the finished work, I hope that I have done justice to his memory in some small way.*

4. *If you were lucky you would gain a view out onto the street, unlucky and you would be on the other, dark side, overlooking the pit itself.*

5. *The city of New York would eventually give up on the former jewel in the Y.M.C.A crown in the nineteen-eighties, the entire building converted into private apartments during the nineties. The houses of sin never die they merely evolve.*

6. *Was this the man Jim McMullen was referring to when he recalled seeing Rocky in Lynn against a "...big redhead. (part2 chap7)" Some historians believe that it is. What is a fact however is that Marciano and 'Red'*

Connolly did indeed meet in the amateurs when the then Marchegiano knocked out on January 11th 1947 (part2 chapter4).

part three   **chapter twelve**

The Fight That Nearly Never Was

"When he got in the ring against this kid I realized he had more than a punch, he had a brain too, then I began to believe in him."

Charley Goldman

The pair of Marciano and Colombo returned to Brockton after their New York adventure via Providence where Tony Tartaglia had driven them home. The journey from their exile in the big city which would leave a lasting impression on them both, especially Rocky, was nevertheless nowhere near as eventful as their travel back to Providence just a few days later.

The morning of November 29th was a patchwork of ice and snow as temperatures in Massachusetts dropped below zero. Despite the adverse weather however Rocky knew he still had to be in Providence by two-o-clock that afternoon for the ritual weigh-in. Tartaglia had promised to drop by and give the boys a lift, Allie's car, he felt, was not up to making the journey. Conditions were treacherous but Tony was confident, he had just purchased a brand new 1948 Desoto sedan and felt that he would have little problem traversing the almost ice rink conditions, it was a confidence misplaced.

The car that morning was full. Alongside Marciano and Colombo in the back was a mutual friend, Joe Fidele, whilst riding up front with Tony was his younger brother George. At first the ride was easy enough, that is until they stopped at lights near the bridge that brought them into East Providence. As the lights changed and they pulled away the car began to skid wildly. "The next I knew," recalled Colombo, "We smashed into the side of a truck coming the opposite way. The two front doors flew open and Tony and his brother George disappeared."

"I was stretched out on the pavement," remembered Tony Tartaglia, who had been thrown face first onto the asphalt yet amazingly suffered only superficial damage. He watched as, "…the car skid(*ded*) crazily down the street towards the bridge abutment. It looked like it might go over into the river."

Now Colombo came into his own, all three remaining passengers who were in a car without a driver, had been slammed back into their seats by the force of the collision with the oncoming truck. Allie, desperate to avert a catastrophe leaned over the front seats and grabbed the emergency break, pulling as hard as he could. The wheels of the Desoto locked sending the car sliding some more on the ice before bouncing off a guard rail and eventually, after seemingly careening forever, coming to a halt.

The police were soon at the scene. Remarkably it was only George Tartaglia who was taken to hospital that day, he had suffered concussion when he'd been unceremoniously dumped out of the car, everyone else was apparently unhurt. At first Colombo, erring on the side of caution advised Rocky that they should call the fight off, everyone involved were shaken.

Besides they were late for the weigh-in now. Marciano however was adamant that he would not call the fight off. He wanted his chance to show Connolly that the sparring match was an aberration; in the ring, for real, Marciano was a totally different animal. Luckily for the fighter a passing motorist gave the four casualties a lift into Providence, dropping them at Alvina's house and leaving 'Snap's' new pride and joy an abandoned wreck which had to be towed away.

Once at Alvina's Marciano ate his usual hearty steak dinner before, amazingly in light of the near tragedy, falling asleep. Meantime Allie had phoned Manny Almeida and replayed the accident, Almeida advised Colombo to bring Rocky to the auditorium at seven where the Rhode Island boxing commissioner would examine him.

Thus at the appointed time Marciano turned up, was looked over, and pronounced fit to continue. However all was not that simple for after he had awoken from the two-hour nap that afternoon Rocky had trouble moving. It appeared that his back which had been injured all those years before from falling out of the cherry tree had finally given out on him, helped no doubt from the jarring force of the crash that day.

The incident aside though Rocky had recently been experiencing stiffness in his lumbar region, yet he had put this down to merely pushing his body too hard in training, it would work its way out he reasoned, however now he was in pain. It may have been fortunate for him that it was a commissioner who gave him the once over that evening and not a physician or the bout would no doubt have been canceled. To Rocky it may have appeared that he had staved off once again the infamous *'Malocchio'*, or evil eye that he believed had plagued him since childhood.

"Once in a while mom went to see Mrs. Lucy Parziale to fight off *Malocchio*…It's like some kind of curse. The only way to get rid of it is to see someone who can break the spell, like

Mrs. Parziale," Marciano would recite in his ghosted autobiography which appeared in *The Saturday Evening post*, issue dated September 29th, 1956.

"Mom would take something that I used against my body, like a T-shirt, and give it to Mrs. Parziale. Mrs. Parziale would fill a deep dish with water and dip a tea spoon of olive oil into it. Then she'd recite some words and dip her finger in the water. If the oil didn't spread out, mom knew nobody was putting the evil eye on me. But the more this oil spread, the more people were giving me this *Malocchio* (1)."

Whatever the reason for the automobile incident, accident or design, Marciano would seem to be followed by this malevolent evil eye all of his life (*his back would plaque him for the rest of his career*). Yet this night he somehow made it to the bout, despite Allie having to stretch the lower and middle ropes apart so that his friend could gingerly enter the ring.

The fortitude that the now Marciano showed in entering the ring this night was perhaps more down to his exasperation at the ups and downs which had led to him not fighting for pay for eight long weeks. Originally he had been scheduled to face Don Riffie once again (little is known of this perennial no-show *Riffie, or Riffe, from looking at his record he appears to be another of those ever present journeyman who flourished at the time, winning some and losing more, his record is filled with names no-one now remembers*), this time in Boston on the evening of Monday 11th, October, but this had been postponed until the following week due to a cold suffered by the headliner on the card, namely former Marciano victim Bobby Quinn (*despite his ferocious and decisive defeat to the Brockton battler Quinn, or rather his handlers, still held some sway in the local rings*). Rocky thwarted for now had returned to New York to work out his frustrations and in doing so had damaged the knuckle on his right hand once again forcing him to pull out of the meeting where he was set to face not Don Riffe as intended but rather Jimmy Freeman (*If little is known of Riffie even less is known of*

Freeman, his record is sparse, however he does hold the distinction of holding the young Cuban Nino Valdez to a draw over six-rounds in 1948).

Marciano would be forced to rest up for three long weeks, at least in terms of using his fists, but Rocky could not just sit around. "He was always on the go, always moving," recalled Angelo Dundee. "Even when he was injured he had to do something to stay in the game, that's why even after his long layoffs he still had the stamina to compete, despite the rust, and boy did he rust quicker than most."

The problem was not just boredom whilst he was out of the ring, it was that he was also not getting paid, he desperately wanted to earn money, money to pay his family, to pay back his friends, and more importantly to prove that fighting was a means of escaping the realities of a mundane existence, so now that his date with Connolly was made he wasn't going to let anything else stand in his way.

Before the bout however Rocky sensed the need for urgency when he confided to Allie that he, "wanted to get this one over with quick, he really was worried that his back would give out completely."

This, coupled with his opponents feeling that he had got the better of him in their sparring sessions [2] seemed to spur Marciano on when after a mere 57-seconds he caught his opponent flush with a right hand to the jaw and the Irish descendent crashed to the floor where he was counted out (*Rocky must have had the one round priest for this one*).

In fact so swift and decisive was Rocky's victory that Connolly only got to throw two punches, both of which missed, before he was set up and knocked over. James managed to rise at nine but the referee, on seeing the now familiar glassy eyed stare called the proceedings to a halt immediately.

For Connolly it was the sixth setback against eight wins, all six losses coming in his last ten outings as a pro. Like the majority of Marciano's early opponents he would struggle gamely on for a further twelve-month's before calling time on his career, one that initially promised so much. In his final year before the crowds he would partake in seven more bouts, losing three; at the end he knew his fire was gone.

For Marciano this was win number eleven, ten under the auspices of Weill and all coming with-in the distance and none going beyond the third round. When Weill, who had remained in New York, was informed of this victory by Goldman he decided it was time to show off his new prospect; and he had just the show to do it in.

Notes:

1. *This was not the only superstitious practice Marciano, or at least his family, practiced, for as Rocky continued, "Before every fight...Barbara...went to the priests at St. Coleman's church and got one of them to bless my boxing shoes. Then she'd mail them to me. There were three priests - Rev. Leroy V. Cooney, Rev. Richard O'Donovan and Rev. John Morrissey. They used to take turns. One would bless my shoes and I'd knock a guy out in the first round, the next fight another might do it and I'd take two rounds. Then the third would do it, and it might take me three or four rounds. We always said we wanted the one-round priest to do it."*

2. *And there was more than just one meeting between these two for the pair had sparred each other on numerous occasions, it has emerged that they had regularly met not just at Murray's estate but also in New York, plus this James Patrick "Red" Connolly was –as already stated above- the same Connolly that Rocky had knocked out in the amateurs back in January 1947. The local press would have us believe that they were, 'the best of pals' but Connolly derision and Marciano's contempt seem to imply that this was probably a piece of spin used to sell the fight in Providence where both had ties, Rocky through his string of victories and James due to the fact that he once worked in the City as a plumber's apprentice -when boxing was really big the most innocuous of connections would be used to tie a prospect to a place in order to build a following.*

part three   **chapter thirteen**

One Step forward...

"This was the fight where it should've started to happen. But the kid turned amateur on me, and blew it!"

Al Weill

Arturo Godoy was one of Weill's most successful heavyweights before Marciano had come into his stable. The Chilean born Godoy had in fact caused a sensation way back in February of 1940 by taking the fight to the seemingly invincible Joe Louis for the full fifteen-rounds in a valiant challenge for Louis' heavyweight championship before a capacity crowd at Madison Square Garden. What made this the more remarkable was that the champion, in his ninth defense of the title, was coming off seven straight knock-out victories, only Tommy Farr in the champions first defense had lasted the full route, yet on this night not only was Godoy still standing at the final bell, but many felt he deserved the victory. Still, by now Louis had become a beloved figure by fact of his destruction of the perceived Aryan threat, Max

Schmeling, so there was no way they were going to take the belt away from Louis unless he was carried from the ring.

No one was more surprised by Godoy's showing than Weill himself, he had built the fighter up on a veritable who's who of nobodies since Godoy had based himself in America late in 1936. Before his alliance with Weill however he had fought the former world light-heavyweight champion Tommy Loughran no less than three times with honors even, drawing the first encounter, losing the second, yet gaining the third. This was way back in 1935, five years after turning professional in Cuba. In 1936 Godoy had starched in four rounds former world heavyweight challenger, Louis Angel Firpo, the man who had knocked Jack Dempsey out of the ring back in 1923. But this was nothing really to brag about for Firpo was now forty-four and at least a decade past any semblance of his prime.

The only real name on his record previous to the bout with Louis was the burly, human barrel, Tony Galento. Galento was a man who spat in the face of boxing pleasantries, simply fouling and bullying his way through opponents. Remarkably the immensely rotund Galento gained with this "technique" a genuine popularity, especially when, in 1939, he planted Louis on the canvas in his own attempt to wrest the crown from the champion (1). Godoy held two six-round decisions over this barrel chested bear of a character.

Because of his remarkable feat over Louis, Godoy was granted a rematch some four months later. This time Louis had the measure of his man and dispatched him in the eighth. It was the last time Godoy would get a crack at the title despite remaining as a contender, or at least on the fringes, for several years. However, by 1948, both Louis and Godoy were getting older. Sure Louis was still the incumbent champion, but he had just come through two tough wars with Jersey Joe Walcott and now was contemplating retirement. Before he went for good however he wanted to cash in on his title so he reverted to exhibitions, a popular way for a fighter to squeeze those precious extra pennies out of an audience who otherwise would not get the chance to see them in the ring. Thus since his last bout against Walcott two months previously Louis had been planning a barnstorming tour of the U.S (*this would turn out to be his farewell tour as champion*) and it would begin against his old adversary Godoy at the Convention Hall, Philadelphia, on the evening of December 14th.

For Marciano this date had been earmarked by his co-conspirators as the most crucial event in his still somewhat fledgling career (*originally however Marciano was promised an appearance in Madison Square Garden, the mecca of boxing, on the undercard of what turned out to be Ezzard Charles' successful defense of the heavyweight title against Joe Baksi*). Weill, forever the opportunist, realized that this event was the perfect time to show off his new find whilst saying the proverbial farewell to Godoy. In as much he had begun a campaign to bring Marciano to the attention of the national press. "He announced to us," recalled journalist Jimmy Cannon, "that we were about to see the next heavyweight champion fighting in the guise of Marciano. Few of us took notice."

Yet Al was confident, hadn't his new "sensation" been knocking over everyone he had faced so far. Just to be safe however, the fighter Weill chose to face Marciano that evening was a man who could only be described as a part-time boxer at best.

Gilley Ferron had taken part in his first known paid bout back in 1945, since then his career had been sporadic to say the least, this bout against Rocky would be only his eighth outing, of his previous seven he had won only three, so Weill was most definitely erring on the side of caution on his day (*originally the name put forward to face 'The Brockton Brawler' was one Abel Gonsalves a man who despite his somewhat potted record was still capable of putting an end to winning streaks, just ask Ralph Regan who was being groomed for great things prior to meeting Abel in '48 and was swiftly dispatched inside of a round*). Few could really blame him, he did not want to take a chance on Marciano not bulldozing through another foe and thus tarnishing the managers inflated image that he had spent the last few weeks blowing up like a balloon.

As a way of demonstrating the importance of this bout Marciano was not allowed to return home to Brockton prior to the fight as usual, instead he was escorted by Weill and the mysterious Chick Wergeles via car to Philadelphia.

On the journey Al kept on at Rocky how this was his chance, the good, the bad, and the downright ugly of boxing would be in attendance, including Harry Markson, head of the 20th Century Sporting Club, then the major power in the sport. If he (*Marciano*) impressed tonight then the path forward would be smooth and glittering, Rocky however was nervous.

"I was excited at the prospect of fighting in front of all those big people," Marciano would explain in 1958. "And especially at the chance of meeting Joe Louis who was one of my idols. But he (*Al Weill*) was getting me on edge. He never was the most comfortable man to have around, and this fight was the first time he tried to run the show...It was hell."

Right from the moment that the quintet of Marciano, Goldman, Weill, Colombo and Wergeles arrived at the maze like Convention hall and Civic Center on Civic Center Blvd Weill began barking orders.

"He was like a wild man," recalled Colombo. "I couldn't believe a guy that jumpy had already managed three world champions."

The over energetic manager did manage to calm down enough however to introduce his charge to the legendary Joe Louis, describing him to the implacable legend as the next heavyweight champion.

"Boy I wish'd the ground would open up and swallow me when Al said that," recalled Rocky. "Here I was meeting my hero man to man and he (*Weill*) goes and says something dumb like that."

This had not been the first time the men had met though for Marciano had once been introduced to the great man whilst the former was serving at Fort Lewis where Joe was involved in an exhibition at the base. Unsurprisingly Louis showed no sign of recollection, and why should he, during his later years in the sport he was no doubt introduced to thousands of those talented and also-rans who dreamt of following in his massive footprints[2].

Rocky's childhood friend Izzy Gold remembered an earlier meeting between the two, "He (*Louis*) was a guest referee at the Brockton Arena one night and we followed him to the men's room. He went in a stall and I boosted Rocky up then he boosted me up, then Joe Louis looked up and saw us and when he came out he gave us a buck apiece. So that was one of the biggest things in our lives [3]."

Once the requisite ceremony of the weigh-in had ended (*a ceremony which was more an opportunity for the opponents to size each other up for many in their early careers this was the first chance for the opponents to meet*) Marciano retired swiftly to his dressing room. This was only the second time that he had been forced to hang around the arena prior to a bout, yet he still expected to continue his routine of napping before he entered the ring. Weill however did not concede his possible future star such a liberty, this constant haranguing and cuckolding stirred Marciano more than once. "If Rock didn't get his couple of hours before a fight he felt cranky and wound up," reflected Colombo. And now Marciano was getting wound up.

"Right through the warm-up (*Weill's*) yelling in my ear." Marciano reflected, "I was getting tighter and tighter. Everyone was telling me how important this fight was, I kept thinking, 'Why can't you all just get the hell out and leave me alone, I know what I'm doing.' But I didn't say anything I just allowed myself to get tight."

The pressure was not let off by the overeager manager when the bout finally got under way either. For the first time Weill was working the corner and from the opening bell all Marciano could hear was the almost creaky hinge like voice of Weill yelling, "To the body, to the body!"

Now Rocky was confused, he was tired, he tried desperately to make the moment work for him as Weill had wanted for he knew that this was his big break as he had been reminded all day. Too many times in the past he had let his chances slip away, this time he would listen, he would hit to the body. As he did however Ferron neatly picked him apart with counter-punches. Marciano began getting frustrated and wild, especially when after a minute of such treatment he felt the unfamiliar warm tacky flow of blood slither down his face (*this was a sensation that he would get used to and learn to ignore over the years*). He had been cut just beneath the left eye by Ferron's stinging, slicing blows,. But far worse than this he was being made to look stupid:

> In between rounds I got angry at myself, I was blowing this fight and if I kept listening to Weill I would end up losing it. I should have put this guy away already. I said to myself, 'C'mon Rocco take this guy out.' So I went out the second round and fought my own fight.

So Marciano followed his own advice and did just that. Forgetting everything he had been taught he reverted to his youth and simply swung away, charging at his foe with the zeal of a street fighter. Not giving a damn now to what his opponent was throwing back, the only thing he cared about was victory.

He swiftly overpowered his foe and took control sending the twenty-pound heavier Ferron to the canvas. Gilley though was game as well. He rose tentatively only to have his left brow smashed open by a slashing right from a rampant Rocky. This was followed by another huge swinging clubbing right, the punch that would later be dubbed "Suzie-Q".

"**S**uzy (*sic*) was christened, and nurtured, by a bachelor, a woman hater," chronicled British journalist and author Harold Mayes in his 1956 biography of Rocky Marciano. "A wizened little man," Mayes continued, "Charlie (*sic*) Goldman is his name…Never, never has anything been able to descend on an unprotected jaw with such speed, force and fury."

No one is really sure where the name originated. There are those who believe however that the name of Rocky's mythical Sunday punch was given by *Brockton Enterprise and Times* sports editor Victor C. Dubois who came up with the tag line after listening to the popular song 'Doin' the Suzie Q' released originally in 1936 by jazz musician Lil Hardin Armstrong:

>Now, come gather 'round us folks,
>
>Let us tell you 'bout this swing,
>
>Let us tell you 'bout this dance invented just for you
>
>Now, you swing over here,
>
>Now, you swing over there,
>
>For you swing on out and do the Suzie Q.
>
>Now, come and give yourself a treat,
>
>Watch these babies shake their feet,
>
>What they doin'?

They're doin' the Suzie Q.

From whence-ever her origin though Ferron did not care for the punch (*described by boxing historian Bert (Randolph) Sugar as, "A right hand from hell!"*) that would be born here as it crashed heavily against his skull and sent him to the canvas. Once more he rose, shakily, to his feet (4).

Marciano, sensing the end, wildly attacked, half-punching, half-pushing the tottering Ferron to the floor once again. This time the referee had seen enough, he called a halt to the carnage at 2.21 of this the second and, for Ferron, final round. Gilley walked slowly, unsteadily to his corner. It would be the last time he walked this route for some four months as he recovered from the battering.

For Marciano, the victor, he too would remain out of the ring until the following March...

Notes:

1. *Galento would be mercilessly taken apart in four by Louis which led him to comment immortally afterwards, "My coiner assed me to fight clean. I shouldna listened, if I'd fought my own fight I'da moided the bum! (sic)"*

2. *Marciano at this time had no such pretensions. "It wasn't until about my twentieth fight or so that I really began to believe I could make it all the way," he commented after his retirement.*

3. *It seems the boys had a penchant for following fighters into men's rooms, for another incident relates how the boys followed Tony Galento, also visiting Brockton, when Galento saw the boys he allegedly asked who was the toughest, the boys all looked at a young Rocco, again the garrulous fighter greased the impudent kids palm with a shiny coin.*

4. *Ferron had the dubious distinction of being one of the rare individuals who ever would be able to stand after "Rocky's equalizer" had landed; certainly one who didn't was Jersey Joe Walcott on the night that "Suzie Q" became immortalized.*

part three   chapter fourteen

...and Two Steps Back

"The legs of his baggy trunks were too wide and too long, and some suggested he looked like a burlesque comedian impersonating a fighter. Here in Philadelphia...the crowd ridiculed him as he fought earnestly, but clumsily, in the ring."

Bill Libby

Marciano had won the bout, and won decisively, yet still Weill was beside himself. Rocky had made him look bad, or so he thought. For days now the usually astute Weill had been going around New York and Philadelphia proclaiming the coming of a new king, after Marciano's performance however, the sloppiest since his formative bouts, the fight crowd who should have been in deference to the ascendant's claim to the throne, instead derided him (*see above*).

"We all thought Weill was starting a gag with this Marciano kid, and we wished he'd share the punch line with us," said Jimmy Cannon commenting on the thoughts that were no doubt shared by the majority of journalists in the immediate aftermath of the, on the surface, abysmal display.

"He may not look pretty," returned Goldman at the almost complete blanket disparaging. "But he looks better than those other guys flat on their backs!" To Weill, privately, Charley was quoted as retorting, "Let them laugh, the last laugh will be on us."

Still the otherwise normally careful manager, who brought his fighters along following a certain distinct arc, had been viewed by some as rushing headlong into euphoria over this still underdeveloped fighter, unusual for the otherwise staid Weill who would bring his boys along slowly at first before pushing them into the faces of the press. The almost universal criticism of Marciano may however have been more of an attack on Weill himself, Rocky was merely the unfortunate outlet for the writers vitriol.

It was an open secret amongst the boxing cognoscenti that there was no love lost between Weill and the media of his day, mainly brought about by Al's own domineering attitude once he had control of someone the journalists wanted to write about. Added to this was the fact that he had his favorites amongst the press, his acolytes, those certain few to whom he would pass a few bucks beneath the table in exchange for sweetening their rhetoric when they came to write up a fighter. Then, as now, it was the media who made a man, especially a fighter, and just as quickly destroyed them [1].

In an era where television was still a fledgling medium, and then only preserved for a few, readers were influenced by the words printed in black and white on the broadsheets of the day. Never was this more evident than when Joe Louis defended his heavyweight championship against Max Schmeling in 1938, then the press took an almost godlike role painting the previously highly regarded Schmeling as a dark Aryan devil whilst in contrast Louis became glorified as the savior of the world whilst the pair fought under the shadow of Adolph Hitler and the very real threat of Nazism. The two principles in this drama would never fully recover from this vivid portrayal.

Sure Marciano was not being quite so poetically muted, however, what the press were compiling in words now would stick with him through the majority of his career. Even now in the present day we are, some of us, guilty of judging him by the pen of those who have gone before.

However, in reflection this bout was not the catastrophe it has been painted to be, at least in as much as characterizing Marciano the man and the fighter. Yes he was sloppy, at one time he threw a punch so wild that he scraped his knee on the canvas. But in one respect this was a defining bout in his career, for there he was in the first round getting beat, plain and simple. He was hurt, he was cut and bleeding, the corner had confused him, his mind temporarily was not on the fight, he was, in essence, staring defeat in the face. And yet he pulled it around through sheer will, battling back against blood, against bruises, against injury, and he was injured, that is what kept him out of the ring for some three months and added to the despair in the immediate aftermath of the bout.

In the first round, in desperation, Rocky had thrown a roundhouse right which had thudded off the taller Ferron's skull; he had winced but carried on. Adrenaline pumping, the pain in his gloved fist became a mere inconvenience, yet when the gloves and bandages came off that fragile hand of his began to immediately swell. Colombo wanted him to go to the hospital straight away but Rocky was more interested in watching Louis fight Godoy (*Louis won the six-round exhibition five rounds to one*), and held off the inevitable inconvenience of visiting a doctor until he returned to Brockton the following day by which time the hand had swollen to almost twice its normal size.

At first Rocky was reticent, those hands of his were always swelling after a bout sometimes they would take days to regain full movement. Colombo was adamant though that this time something was wrong, he was more than aware of his friends previous injuries and he worried, if Rocky had fragile hands then that would be that, future ended before it had really got a chance to begin unless they got the problem sorted now. After badgering from all in his corner Rocky was taken to a New York hospital where his hand was accessed, the prognosis was bleak. He had chipped a bone in his right thumb that would need an immediate operation to remove the splinter, after which his hand would be set in plaster. News that once again he was sporting a cast on that hand was met with concern by the Brockton press. 'That injured hand that Brockton's Rocco Marciano suffered in winning a knockout victory down in Philadelphia Tuesday night may be more than just a mishap that athletes suffer during the course of competition in various fields of sport,' reported *The Brockton Enterprise-Times*.

'For this,' the paper continued, 'is now the third time within a year that Rocco has injured that same duke and to those in the fight game this an indication that the Brockton belter's hand may be what is known in the fight trade as "brittle."

'Boxing experts have predicted a great future for Rocco of Brockton. He's the kind of fellow that could give boxing a terrific shot in the arm…But his boxing future depends on his hands.'

At first it was hoped that the cast would be worn for only a matter of a few weeks, with rest Rocky should be back punching again in a month, but it didn't happen. In fact it would take over two long months of more diathermy treatments, more physio, before Marciano would be fit to box again.

At first Weill was devastated by the news, this seemed another hammer blow to his intentions for this Brockton boy, not least was his fighters showing which had been viewed by the boxing fraternity as a charade, but now it appeared that he was so damn clumsy he had even broken his hand in the process.

After weighing up how best to negate these setbacks Weill informed Rocky to keep up his training in Brockton, no glove and bag work obviously but keep the fitness levels up and to call him when the hand was ready.

It looked like it was going to be a long hard winter.

Notes:

1. *'I'll tell you a story about Al Weill,'* said journalist Jimmy Breslin to ESPN presenter Dick Schaap. *'Someone was passing bad checks -under Al's name-, so they brought (Weill) into the grand jury...and said "would you just sign your name so the grand jury can indict the guy for forging your name." Al Weill takes an envelope out of his pocket and he signs his name...They hand it to the district attorney who hands it to the jury. They all look, they see the signature and the last guy turns the envelope over. The envelope said "World Telegram the boxing writer $75", he had the list of all the boxing writers in New York City who were getting paid under the table.'*

part three   chapter fifteen

Reflections

"Marciano is a fighter who needs to fight. He gets stale and rusty if kept under wraps for too long!"

Charley Goldman

As 1948 began the then Marchegiano could not have imagined how far he would come in just twelve short months. In the winter snows of that New Year he was just an amateur, and a fledgling one at that, fighting was merely a way of venting his frustrations at his perceived lot in life, a last gasp attempt to make his way in a world that he saw as an unfair wilderness of lost chances and missed opportunity. He did not truly believe that one day he would be champion, not then at least, but his desire was fueled instead by making a living in something more than laborious back breaking tasks that he had witnessed eating away at his father. To him fighting was a way simply to bring pride to the name of Marchegiano, a means of reaffirming his status as that rough, tough, powerful kid who was still the mythical "King of the Hill".

Ruggedness and the search for manliness were the predominant factors in Marciano's makeup, he was constantly harping on about its properties in interviews. "Boxing is a great sport, it brings out the manly qualities in you and teaches you about the characteristics needed to make it, sacrifice, commitment, a rugged nature."

Yet as the year moved through its inevitable course Rocco Marchegiano began to exhibit a tenacity of will in his endeavors that stood out. A year that had begun merely as a means of venting himself in the hardest of games had begun to transform into something more permanent. He was proving his character not just to himself but also to others, and perhaps it came as much of a shock to him as to those viewing his ascent in boxing that he was displaying something remarkable, something unique. Marchegiano did indeed have something special.

He had first shown these attributes prior to his appearances in Lowell when Jim McMullen had seen him in action and was so impressed by his against-the-odds victory that he immediately invited him to fight in the Lowell championships. This was the first instance of Rocco being in the right place at the right time. The unknown green-as-grass fighter went on to win the whole show, then moved on to take the New England title too, then on to New York where all but the judges felt he had defeated the overwhelming favorite Coley Wallace. Indeed he was showing he had that special something which elevated him above the norm.

The omens it appeared were favoring Rocky now, perhaps he had at last found his way out after so many disappointments. Even when he damaged his hand and was forced to pull out of the Olympic trials this became a blessing for it allowed him to hook up with Goldman and Weill. Within seven months of the year he was fighting professional. Fight after fight he had won, and he had been the last man standing each and every time.

It was perhaps this knowledge, or at least belief, that for once he was achieving something with his life that even minor setbacks could not put a halt to his momentum, thus he did not linger on yet another injury to his fragile hands, sure they were an inconvenience, sure they had caused him to look bad in his last bout against Ferron, but hell, he was still a novice in the professional ring. Weill had built him up to be something more than he currently was and the pressure of that proved to be burdensome, but that ideal which Weill sowed in the minds of the boxing purists, and more importantly in the mind of the now Marciano, would be something for him to live up to.

It was an image he was keen to cultivate, this powerful machine that was knocking out everyone it faced. Marciano had a future now and he was determined not to let it go, this new year of 1949 [1] was earmarked as the year that the boxing world would become sure that Rocky Marciano was a viable force in the sporting cosmos, and, to his credit, he almost made it happen.

First he had to heal his hand. Under the guidance and care of Dr. Del Colliano the injury came along well *("They really were the most troublesome pair of hands I have ever dealt with," the good Doctor would confide)*, a series of diathermy treatments [2] aided in the process. Plus Rocky's unusual but really quite brilliant use of his mother's washing machine to supplement the weekly visits to the Brockton hospital helped.

"He would open up the lid, pour in some Epsom salts, and just plunge his arm into the swirling water right up to his elbow," recalled Colombo. Rocky also had an extra weapon in his armory to assist with his recovery, most afternoons he would visit Al Norling, physiotherapist at the Brockton YMCA, who massaged the hand and ensured its flexibility. This was all free to Marciano, his favorite currency. As Norling commented dryly at the time, "Why should I take his money. The poor guy hasn't got any!"

"Now Rocky is his own doctor," contended Dr. Del Coliano, adding, "(*He is*) exercising his wrists and fingers a couple of times a day as I showed him." Indeed Eugene Sylvester would recall watching Marciano later in his career gripping each wrist with his opposing hand and making tight fists in a rhythmic repetition, "I said to him, 'What the hell are you doing?' and he replied that he was strengthening his wrists!"

The fighter did not just limit himself to plyometric exercises either for he continued to train just as hard as before. He laid off visiting Charley for only a matter of a week or two as he relaxed, to a degree (*as we now know Marciano never relaxed completely*), over the holiday period that winter, before returning to Goldman (3).

"We put Rocky back into the gym again to see if he had forgotten anything and to smooth out some of the flaws that had shown up in his early bouts," recalled Charley in Bob Cutter's biography The Rocky Marciano Story (*published in 1954, this was the first official biography of Marciano*). Goldman continued, "I gave him hours of shadow boxing and was always cooking up things to give him better form. And when I say shadow boxing, I don't just mean moving around to warm up. To be of any use, shadow boxing must have a purpose and be done with a great deal of concentration. Every move, every swing taken - they're there to drive home a point.

"Rocky listened carefully, better than a lot of other guys I've tried to teach. He never undid outside the gym what I tried to do inside it. In fact, Rocky has always tried to add to the program I lay out for him. The fellow's a phenomenal trainer - for example, he's a glutton for roadwork, which other fighters generally look on as the worst part of training. Yes, Rocky really benefited from that short layoff."

On Marciano's return to Brockton he kept running. "We left the house at eight every morning even when it was snowing so hard that we couldn't see the road, and in the afternoon we shoveled out the yard and boxed," said Colombo. Here Marciano took the lessons he had learned from Goldman home with him, he was no longer content to sit and wait for his hand to heal instead he applied himself as never before to practicing the routines that Charley had so dutifully taught him.

"Rock trained hard before," recalled Colombo, "But now he had a purpose and he really went for it."

But if Rocky was a man now striving for his future he was still first and foremost a son, a son to a mother who did not want her child to be in pain. Pasquelena, who had never wanted her eldest to be a fighter in the first place, stepped up her pleas for him to quit now citing once again his hands. She reminded her son that it was only a few weeks previously that he had experienced problems prior to the break. Whilst sparring at the CYO in New York the knuckles of his left hand had begun to swell leading Dr. Vincent Nardiello, New York State Athletic Commissions official physician to pronounce that Rocky was prone to water on the knuckles. This was a condition that could only be eased by draining the hand each and every time this occurred, and it would occur often, in fact it was a condition which would plaque Rocky for the rest of his professional career. Now his beloved mother had the broken bone to add to her arsenal. Marciano was however unrepentant, there was no way he was going to walk away now, his mother had no option but to acquiesce. Deep down she knew that her son would forever regret the decision if he had.

Sooner than expected the hand healed and Marciano was pronounced fit to resume donning the gloves once again. Thus, in early March 1949, Rocco returned to the CYO in order to begin tentative sparring. Weill was keen to get his tiger back into the ring and begin rebuilding the fighter's record after the lackluster debut before an unenthusiastic crowd in Philadelphia. With this in mind the manager had lined up a bout on the penultimate Monday of the month thereby giving Goldman enough time to iron out the creases from the enforced sabbatical, but from the first session of sparring Goldman was more than a little concerned.

"The first time he stepped into the ring I knew we had a fighter who needed to fight as often as possible," recalled the astute trainer.

"The kid was way off with his timing, worse than usual. Despite all the shadow boxing it's no substitute for the real thing, and sparring is just a game compared to the pressure of fighting inna ring before a crowd.

"A kid of his advanced age as well accumulates rust faster than a younger fighter and it takes longer to wear off [4]."

Truly Marciano was a fighter who needed to fight. There is little doubt that in these initial sessions he was protecting his hand, but the passing of time would show that the longer Rocky laid off between fights the rustier he became. "He collected rust quicker that a can in the rain," commented one acerbic journalist.

"Sparring ain't real fighting," Goldman would reiterate later in his charges career. "It don't matter if you spar a thousand rounds, when you are in the ring for real them rounds do not mean a damn. It's in the ring that you got to put it all together. Forget for a moment what you got to do in sparring and it's a powder-puff in the face. Forget in the ring and you're on your pants."

Marciano would come awful close to proving this potentially career shattering truth in his very next bout.

Notes:

1. Which had begun with seeing him actually rated by the New England Association of Boxing Commissioners as a viable contender for the New England heavyweight championship, then held by Bernie Reynolds.

2. A method of physical therapy that involved generating heat in body tissues via high-frequency electromagnetic currents.

3. Hank Cisco the former middleweight who came under the management and tutelage of both Weill and Goldman prior to Marciano's emergence recalled an unusual treatment that Charley Goldman had for swollen and painful hands, one that I have little doubt he used on Marciano; Hank recalls the treatment and the incident leading up to it. 'I had a fight in N.J...Charlie (sic), Marty (Weill, Al's step son) another fighter and myself drove to the fight.....in the dressing room before the fight Marty (Weill) insisted he wrap my hands...Charlie (sic) in respect to his father (Al Weill) let him wrap my hands...I dislocated my thumb because he wrapped them to tight...bones did not have any place to go, luckily when I unwrapped my hand the thumb went back in place but the pain remained...on the way home Charlie told the driver to stop at a food store, he went in and came out with a big loaf of bread a box of salt and a bottle of vinegar. When we got back to Brown's house we went to Charlies' (sic) room he got out a big bowl took all the inside of the bread put in the bowel poured a lot of salt on the white bread then poured the vinegar on top and then started to mix it up till he made a paste out of it, then he got the paste and covered my right hand beyond my wrist then covered it with a towel and Pinned it so it would not move when I was sleeping. I went to bed (and) the next morning the pain was not as bad. I did It for one week and it did the job, the Goldman magic worked'

4. Goldman still thought Rocco was twenty-four while Marciano had in fact turned twenty-five the previous September.

part three					chapter sixteen

Requiem for a Heavyweight

"Win as he did, Marciano hardly looked like another Jack Dempsey on this occasion. He showed no boxing skill whatsoever, left himself open to attack, and his punching dynamic as it was, was crude and aimless."

Michael J. Thomas

Like many of his early opponents the name Johnny Pretzie has become a mere biographical footnote in the rise of Rocky Marciano. At first glance the only distinction this fighter seems to hold is the fact that he lasted into the fifth round against the man who was being hailed now as the 'Massachusetts Man-eater', 'Brockton Strong boy', 'Sir Punch' or 'The Blockbuster from Brockton' (*this last title had not yet been morphed into the more famous 'Brockton Blockbuster', that would come later*). Yet, akin to all the names on the roll of victories, Pretzie was far more than a mere footnote.

This Boston based heavyweight, who due to his incredibly hairy physique would be described as a "werewolf", held a unique distinction in the annals of boxing for he was the only man to enter the competitive ring against both a relatively young Rocky Marciano and an equally relatively old Jake LaMotta.

His bout with the mythical 'Raging Bull' in 1954 would prove to be amongst one of the latter's most controversial fights in a career of controversy (*see below*). The "fight" dragged Pretzie to his lowest point in a sport he had committed himself to since childhood, whilst conversely Johnny's appearance against Marciano on the night of March 21st 1949 would be close to the pinnacle of his career, at least in the professional boxing ring.

Pretzie, to quote the *St. Petersburg Times* of April 26th 1943, was, "Of Armenian parentage and was born at Cambridge, Mass. He was (*a*) four-letter boy at Watertown high school, attended Providence college and Northwestern university a short time and received an offer to be an athletic coach at Iowa State university, but was unable to accept. A great halfback at Watertown, he was offered a football scholarship at several colleges. He played first base in the Boston park league and became a subject for diamond scouts."

Despite his seemingly all-round athletic ability, Johnny (*born John Pretzian*) decided to turn his attention to boxing basing himself in Boston [1] where it seemed that he proved something of an amateur sensation.

St. Petersburg Times again:

> After mixing in several minor gloves events…Pretzie first came to general notice back in January, 1940, when by a one-round knockout over Walter Strow of Wilmington at Boston arena, he won the chance to

compete in the annual state championship. He dropped the tilt on points, however. As a member of the Boston crew in an intercity tourney in May, 1940, at the arena, Pretzie competed as a heavyweight but again failed to emerge.

Then, determined to climb up in the fistic world and irked at losing his two important first fights--losing does not appeal to him--Pretzie began his streak of 25 wins. In the twenty-sixth in the golden glove championships at the arena he hurt his hand with a vicious left hook that eliminated Esterino Cimeno of Providence in the semi-finals, but at the same time eliminated himself. He was forced to default to Howard Thompson, class victor, because of the smashed bone, which caused for insertion of a bone plate.

Pretzie was discouraged and out of competition for some time due to that injury. He damaged his hand again when he swung back through the ropes too quickly, but he won a decision by sheer courage over Pete Louthis, former Buffalo national amateur champ who had trimmed an all-American.

In the New-England all-American championship in November, 1942, at the Boston arena, Pretzie score a sensational KO over Paul Conley, South Boston former grand nationals champ and holder of several titles.

Pretzie timed one punch wrong in that heavyweight windup and nearly broke his thumb--it swelled to three times its average size. And all that with the eastern all-American finals coming up.

However, putting Conley out of the running in two rounds gave Pretzie the chance to compete in the all-eastern finals at the garden where he trimmed Wally Verbanic of Cleveland in the semis and stopped 250-pound Chuck Jennings of Buffalo in two rounds to win the all-eastern title. Pretzie was fighting at 187 pounds then. He tips the scales at 195 now.

Pretzie then became the amateur king of swat and realized an ambition. His terrific left won him the all-American crown. When he met the big fellows in the windups at Boston gardens last December…Pretzie kayoed Charley Riggs of Pittsburgh in one round and knocked out Eddie Kaminski of Chicago to capture the belt.

During his tumultuous amateur career Johnny had achieved some thirty-three knockouts victories in thirty-five successful bouts (*twenty-six in a row helped by his lethal left hand*). During this concussive string Pretzie seemed in no rush to turn his attention towards the paid ranks, instead he made his living by working as a welder at a local Boston shipyard. That is until the Spring of 1943 when he at last decided it was time to serve his country.

He enlisted in the U.S Army air corps reserve at the rather advanced age of 22, serving out his time in St. Petersburg with the 603 training group (*hence the interest in the local press*). By the Fall of 1945 he was back on the streets once more (*his military career is unavailable to this researcher*) and planning now to emulate in the professional ring that which he had achieved in the amateurs, namely an unprecedented string of knockouts.

At the outset he looked as if he would just do it.

William Bell, Charley Lomski, and Clifford Mann all capitulated and fell in short order and it seemed that Johnny was advancing fast through the paid ranks. The fight against Mann was a headline 10-rounder before Pretzie's home crowd of Boston (2), for such a novice fighter to be headlining was almost unheard of (3).

Pretzie however seemed to be a crowd pleasing fighter who shared a similar style with 'The Rock (*he would be compared facially and in build to Marciano*).' At least this was the perception as witnessed by an article which appeared in the New Hampshire *Plymouth Herald* on the morning of November 17th, 1945:

> Despite his third straight knockout in as many professional starts, followers of Johnny Pretzie were convinced today that the hard-punching Boston heavyweight needs plenty of polish before meeting any of the higher ranking sluggers.
>
> Pretzie…was outclassed by Cliff Mann before he connected with a series of left hooks that dropped the New York(*er*)…three times in the third round.

It seems the fans saw the writing on the wall for in Johnny's very next fight he was stopped in the tenth and final round by Jay D. Turner.

In an almost immediate rematch Pretzie gained revenge over Turner, knocking him cold in the sixth and, for a while at least it appeared that he had got his career back on track. But he hadn't.

He entered the ring ten times after his revenge victory over Jay D. back in 1946 and immediately prior to his meeting Marciano in 1949. Of those ten engagements he lost five, including to former Marciano conquest James Patrick Connolly.

He did however manage to gain a victory over another shared opponent in the form of Bill Hardeman whom Rocky had starched in the first. Johnny took the full six-rounds to gain a win on points.

Definitely by the night of March 21st Pretzie's star had started to wane.

However, due to his sensational amateur career there were those who still had faith in Pretzie. After all he had won his last two outings in a row, this night against Marciano would be seen as the third try on his perceived comeback into prominence, indeed many felt that Weill was making a mistake in pitting his fighter against a man with so much experience, someone who still carried undoubted power in his own two fists, especially as Marciano was still plagued with the nagging insecurity over his own brittle hand.

"I was wary of this fight," commented Sam Silverman. "I really thought Johnny had a chance to stop the ride and I told Weill so. I seriously thought this was a major test for the kid. I honestly thought he would lose."

For the first four-rounds it seemed Silverman was absolutely right.

This was to be Rocky Marciano's first main event at the Rhode Island Auditorium in Providence (*and the first in which he would be paid on percentage of the gate rather than a straight sum, a sin of his growing popularity*). After nine previous appearances the crowd finally got their chance to see their adopted favorite top the bill, and what a wild night they had. The fight was scheduled for ten, no-one believed for a moment that it would go that far.

In the first two rounds Pretzie (*who had, it is alleged, taken the bout at three days' notice for a paltry $500*) proved his superiority as he battered the over eager Marciano. Punch after punch connected to Rocky's unprotected jaw, the crowd roared. They expected a knockout in this fight but then they always did when Marciano was in the ring. This time however it looked as if it would be Marciano who would fall.

Recalled Pete Fuller who was in Pretzie's corner for this bout (*see footnote 1*), "Johnny really handed it to Rocky in those first two rounds. I really thought that my kid was going to knock the guy out." Yet the Brockton fighter took all that Pretzie had to offer and began to trade with the older man in the third, at the end of which an exhausted Pretzie sat dejectedly in his corner.

It appeared that buoyed by his two successive victories the Cambridge native felt assured of another one this night, and, after being appraised of his opponents ability to end bouts quickly had decided to take the fight to him. The problem was that in so doing he had expended himself to the limit. Now it appeared almost as if pretzie was willing to do the unthinkable, he was willing to quit.

Jackie Martin, his soon-to-be ex-manager pleaded with him not to, if he did not go out for the fourth he would forfeit his pay, he would leave with nothing! Grudgingly Pretzie continued on. In the fourth Rocky took over completely, the rust which had accumulated over the previous three months finally fell away, much to the relief of his corner, which included Al

Weill. Goldman admitted later that he, "had been nervous when I saw Rocky taking all those punches, but the fact that he took them and came back showed the kids heart."

As Marciano began to bang away at the fast fading Bostonian Al Weill again showed his almost sadistic side as he giggled like a schoolgirl at Pretzie who had started to fall apart. Finally, after over two-minutes of continuous punishment he finally fell, more through exhaustion than a punch. Pretzie managed to make it to his feet, which proved his gameness after he had almost ended the battle himself whilst sat on his stool at the end of the third, but, in hindsight, perhaps he should have stayed there.

The fifth round was the final straw. Pretzie was hammered to the canvas three times before referee Dolly Searle had seen enough and called a halt to the massacre at the one-minute and forty-six second mark.

Marciano had won, yet he had been forced to go farther in a ring than he ever had before, plus all agreed that he didn't look pretty doing it.

But then Marciano never did.

At least Johnny had walked away with his pride. To all those who knew him it was almost inconceivable that he had been so close to quitting for he was regarded as a tough, rough house fighter who relished the chance to do battle. This last fact was eventually proven by the amount of times he got up to face the hammering fists of Marciano.

There would be other nights for him in the future, his fans believed, where he could rebuild his career despite his age (*he was born in 1920*). Initially though Pretzie seemed to suffer from the fate dealt most opponents who had the misfortune of facing the man that reminded author Wilfred Diamond of "…a bulldozer wading into a hillside." Of his next five fights he lost them all, four inside the distance, yet by late 1951 he had begun to experience a brief renaissance.

He did not win all these bouts, but he did gain the reputation as something of a spoiler. First he defeated Lee Oma, a highly regarded heavyweight who had, in his previous bout, challenged for the world heavyweight championship. Next, to prove that he still had dynamite in his gloves, he knocked out the durable and underrated Pat Comiskey who had been campaigning at the highest level for nearly a decade. But by far his greatest triumph had been over Jeff Dyer, an up and coming young fighter who had previously beaten Pretzie. Dyer had lost only twice in his short career and was touted to go all the way by those who had seen him in the ring.

Despite his triumphs however Pretzie was eyed as nothing more than a convenient stepping stone, someone with name enough to mean something when he faced Dyer. Yet this stepping stone cracked young Jeff into unconsciousness by the end of the seventh round [4]. For Pretzie this was his last hurrah, over the next three years he would only stave of defeat twice more, both in 1954, which led to his most inglorious moment against Jake Lamotta.

The Pretzie, LaMotta match was made for the 11th of March 1954 at the Legion Arena, West Palm Beach, Florida. From the moment the bout was scheduled there were eyebrows raised from within the fight fraternity. Pretzie was some twenty-five-pounds heavier than LaMotta who had once worn the world middleweight championship after defeating a one armed Marcel Cerdan back in 1949. He had managed to keep a tentative hold of the title for two tempestuous years before losing it to the incomparable Sugar Ray Robinson in a bloody brawl known forever after as "The St. Valentine's Day Massacre" (*February 14th, 1951*).

LaMotta and Robinson were no strangers to each other (5), in fact this was their sixth, and final, meeting. Incredibly LaMotta had actually beaten his foe in their second encounter. The image of a lithe Robinson being hammered through the ropes by a young prime, aggressive LaMotta is an indelible one (6).

Controversy surrounded LaMotta all his life. He claimed that in order to get his much deserved shot at the championship he so craved he was forced to throw a fight against the inferior Billy Fox. Later he would be consistently hauled before the New York State Athletic Commission on charges of not trying against opponents which left a stain on what could have been a glorious career (7). Again, in the bout with Pretzie, there would be such charges by the Florida Boxing Commission, this time however they were directed at his opponent.

In the bout itself Johnny hit the floor no less than six times before the referee stepped in during the fourth round; invariably though something stank, Pretzie's purse was held up, the fans and Florida Commission felt that Pretzie kept falling down. Not one of Lamotta's punches most agreed had seemed to land flush (8). The cry of "Fix" reverberated around the arena, and there seemed to be an argument for this when it emerged Pretzie was actually earning some small change as a strong arm man for the mob. The claims eventually came to nothing, but for both fighters this was the end. Lamotta fought only twice more before retiring for good. As for Pretzie, this was his last bout; he never entered the ring with gloves on again.

He was not through with boxing however, for he continued on as a trainer for several years whilst earning a living by doing that which was the calling of most boxers who failed to keep their earnings from the ring, namely enforcer, security guard, or bouncer. Pretzie tried his hand at them all as he wandered through life until 1989, when, at the age of 68, he fell into an argument with an off duty Housing Police Officer in a Boston bar. The pair went outside where Pretzie wanted to settle the dispute with his fists. The off duty officer, perhaps aware of the old man's reputation, decided to pull his gun. Whether by accident or design there was a bang, a flash, and Johnny Pretzie fell dead.

It was a tragic end to the life of a remarkable man who had skirted so close to the edge of greatness. Alas for him Johnny found that he missed that one vital ingredient which elevated his former opponent Marciano into the stratosphere and left Pretzie, quite literally, looking up[9].

Notes:

1. *A move he made primarily to further his ambitions, for, as he recalled to Pete Fuller, the same man who had turned down the chance to oversee Marciano's career the previous year, and who was in the corner the night Pretzie met the rising Brockton fighter, "Johnny always admitted that he loved his home town of Cambridge, but knew he could not have made it there. Boston was where boxing thrived. He came here to grow, but it was close to the town where he was born, and he went back often."*

2. *Where he had settled after his demob in order to work with the highly ranked manager and trainer Jackie Martin, a man with whom he would have a quite public falling out soon after his bout with Marciano.*

3. *However not as remarkable as 1956 Olympic champion Pete Rademacher who in his professional debut challenged Floyd Patterson for his heavyweight title in 1957. The Olympian even had the temerity to put the champion on the canvas in the second before himself being yo-yoed off the mat some six times before being halted in the sixth.*

4. *Both Dyer and his career never recovered from the shock as he floundered around the professional ring until 1957.*

5. *Which led LaMotta to comment, "I fought Sugar so many times, I'm surprised I'm not diabetic."*

6. *This was the only time sugar Ray lost until he met Randolph Turpin in 1951 by which time he had run up a record of 128 wins, 1 loss, and 2 draws!*

7. *We remember LaMotta now through the outstanding movie of his life "Raging Bull" starring Robert De Niro, this depiction of his life -based on his own memoirs- has left him, for better or worse, revered.*

8. *Which were never regarded as that powerful to begin with, even in his prime.*

9. *There was so much more to the Johnny Pretzie's story after his retirement, for more see 'Johnny Pretzie's Requiem..' an article by John Powers that appeared in The Boston Globe, August 18th, 1989...(for this article –and others- I have to thank those at the reference desk of The Boston Library).*

part three   chapter seventeen

Artie and the Jimmy Boys

"Why waltz with a guy for ten rounds if you can knock him out in one."

Rocky Marciano

Marciano's remarkable string of stoppages was drawing himself attention not just from the fans and the press but from the local Rhode Island Boxing Commission, they were, to quote from *The Brockton Enterprise*, 'somewhat concerned over the Brockton boy due to his rapid climb and sudden prominence'. There was a feeling that Rocky was finding his fights a little too easy, that he was perhaps being groomed for a shot at the championship sooner rather than later, indeed his name had already been linked with the biggest prize in sport; 'It is agreed among the fistic experts', wrote Michael J. Thomas in *The Providence Journal*, "that the noations top five young heavyweights are: Roland LaStarza and George Kaplan of New York, Harold Johnson of Philadelphia, Rocky Marciano of Brockton and Phil Berman of

Philadelphia. It is believed that any one of the five will lift the world heavyweight championship within two or three years.

"Never in the history of boxing has there been such a golden opportunity for a young heavyweight with a punch. The leading title contenders of the moment are all 'old men.' The public awaits the arrival of a young challenger worthy of the name. Fame and riches await such a lad."

Rocky's recent stoppage of Pretzie had risen eyebrows, hadn't he been out of the ring for three months with a broken hand? So why was he able to finish his man off! Hell, his hands seemed to be oh so brittle full stop and yet people were crumbling when he threw them in fury, was something up, was he being built into an attraction, was he being made more than he was? The Rhode Island Commissioners were coming out and saying that full faced, there was no overt accusation that both Al Weill, in cohort with local promoters Almeida and Silverman, were building this boy up, choosing him by dint of his remarkably brief but explosively spectacular amateur career in the local rings.

In an attempt to ensure that Marciano was facing opponents who were viewed as viable opposition 'The Little Rhody' commission took it upon themselves to draw up a list of names whom they deemed acceptable to face the rising star, these and only these would be approved. Two of their deputies Charley Reynolds and Tony Petronella reported that they didn't wish to appear unfair to Marciano but, "they will take every precaution against Rocky getting soft touches for his bouts in Rhode Island."

Petronella elaborated, "we realize that Marciano isn't ready to take on name fighters. He's still in the process of development, but at the same time we aren't going to be duped into giving him easy matches. We're not asking him to meet the best or near best, but we will insist on fighters whom we deem capable of testing him. We have a job to do and it will be done."

If Rocky got past any of the names on this list in the same devastating manner then the commission would have to concede he was the real deal (*see footnote 6 below*). Weill, Almeida and Silverman ruminated over the names and swiftly chose one, it was an opponent that they had penciled in twice already back in '48 but each time the deal had fallen through, but now it was concrete, Rocky Marciano would most definitely be facing off against one Artie Donato.

To his fans in Red Bank, New Jersey, he was known as 'The Rumson Tiger', but it was a sobriquet meant with tongue firmly planted in cheek for Artie Donato was no tiger.
In his very first professional outing back in June of 1946 Artie had been stopped in two rounds by one Johnny Phelan who was giving away some fourteen pounds[1]. This inauspicious beginning did not get any better for by the time Donato met Marciano on the evening of March 28th, a mere week since Rocco had seemingly struggled against Pretzie, the New Jerseyite had been involved in just fifteen bouts, winning only nine. Of his six losses no less than five had been inside the distance against such unknowns as Jimmy Walker, Phil Alston and sometime Marciano punch bag, Wade Chancey.
Artie did have his moments however. He managed to do the double over both the roly-poly Jack (*La*)Cacasio and slightly trimmer Tony Jess. Both these victories came via the full route, in fact only two fighters had fallen victim to this seemingly claw-less 'Tiger'. These unfortunates were Oscar Mimms and Matt Mincey, neither name, with respect, conjuring up an image of terrible fighting men, nevertheless the Brockton press tried their best to make him sound more than he was by mentioning that he had been top contender 'Jersey' Joe Walcott's chief sparring partner in 1948 when Walcott had tried for the second time to wrestle the crown from the great Joe Louis. The fact that he made the Rhode Island list at all

is remarkable but then of his previous victories five had come in succession before this noght so perhaps there was the hope that he was finding some kind of form…

Against Marciano though Donato at least tried to put up a fight, he sped out of his corner throwing, and landing, a series of left and rights. Rocky was so stunned that he could only reply with a single right to the jaw which was fortunate for - as if to prove both that his hand had healed and that 'The Little Rhody' commissioners concerns were unfounded- this was the only punch he needed.
Artie went down so hard that he bounced an inch off the canvass before settling back down in a seated position to be counted out[2]. The entire bout, including the count, lasted a mere thirty-three seconds!

Artie only fought twice more after this, both stoppage losses, before he too, as with so many of the conquered names early in Rocky's career vanished into obscurity [3].
Donato's last bout against one Tommy Gomez on St. Valentine's Day 1950 was perhaps; no, in retrospect definitely, a foregone conclusion for Gomez (*who ended his career with seventy-four victories, sixty-four of those within the distance*) was a fighter who in many ways was the yard stick by which Marciano himself could be measured or if not then at least the perfect example of that something which set this seemingly awkward and clumsy slugger Rocky apart from the field. As journalist Whitey Martin recorded of Gomez in the spring of 1952:

> The Gomez story is another saga of what might have been, a poignant tale of a fighter who lacked just one ingredient in his bid for fame…We first met Tommy around 1941 through Pete Norman, sports editor of the

Tampa Tribune, who naturally was rather high on the young heavyweight (*Gomez hailed from Tampa*). Gomez had been piling up an impressive list of quick kayos (*and*) they weren't all dropping from fright They were being tagged.

We found him a stocky, muscular young fellow, quiet and confident and with large, strong hands… 'I can knock out anyone I can hit,' he said, and you know he wasn't bragging; just stating a fact.

The above could have been used, and was used regularly, to describe Marciano. The only difference was that Rocky had the ingredient which poor Tommy lacked. For Gomez, filled with so much potential and power could give it, but, to quote Martin again, "He couldn't take it too well." This is where the Brockton fighter had his advantage over the other guys who seemed to be making waves in the heavyweight division of the late forties and early fifties, a time when the boxing public craved new blood after the lengthy reign of Joe Louis.

Names such as the Canadian Earl Walls, nicknamed 'The Hooded Terror' who despite a poor start to his career had found his rhythm by the early fifties and was racking up victory after victory. Bob Satterfield, a six-foot Chicagoan famed for his lethal right hand. Clarence Henry from Los Angeles, hailed by many in early 1949 as, "The most exciting prospect to come along since Joe Louis." George Kaplan who between 1948 and 1950 had tallied up nineteen successive victories, Rex Layne, the Utah farm boy, Roland LaStarza. The names (*which included at one time Marciano's nemesis Coley Wallace*) could go on and on, so hungry were the boxing fans for a new hope that any fighter who had scored a series of wins, whether against names or nobodies was pounced upon.

Yet each one stumbled when push came to shove, they either tripped each other up or discovered that when it came to stepping up to the plate against a seasoned campaigner they lacked that essential something which raised Marciano above the crowd (*Marciano himself stopped two of them in their tracks*). They just didn't have it, they couldn't take it. Yet it is an irony that despite Rocky's success', despite him steamrolling all before him, the national press didn't really latch on to him until he had defeated Carmine Vingo in 1949, and then would drop him again like a hot potato within the year. Still, for now, Rocky proverbially kept his head down and waded swiftly on.

James (*Jimmy*) Walls was served up next after the Donato debacle, Walls was perhaps the epitome of that unfortunate individual who was used to pad a promising fighters' record. Before Walls met Marciano on the night of April 11th, again in Providence, he had entered the ring some twenty-five times and exited on only five occasions victorious. However he had managed to scrape together two wins in a row which probably came as more of a surprise to this Englewood, New Jersey native than it did the fight crowd, by dint of this he had been approved by the 'Little Rhody' commission (*he was not the first choice however, or even the second, the original palns had been to face tough Gene Gosney but he was unavailable, then Philadelphian Tony Gangemi had been approached but his license had been suspended*)[4].

Jimmy tried his best on the night against Marciano though. Certainly he was honest in his endeavor, even managing to win the slow opening round according to the judges. In the second stanza however, despite, or possibly because of, Walls daring to go toe-to-toe with Marciano, it began to fall apart for the reckless Jimmy. He was staggered time and again, yet somehow he managed to survive for the full three-minutes. In the third he wouldn't be so lucky (*or maybe fortune favored him, depending on your point of view*) as Rocky buried a devastating left deep into the hapless boxers gut forcing the wind violently from his body. Walls was completely incapacitated and the fight stopped at the 2.44 mark by referee Dolly Searle.

Remarkably Jimmy campaigned on for another seven years, even managing to outdo himself in the three months between October 1953 and January 1954 by winning no less than six bouts in a row. Nevertheless this was a false dawn for of his next and final sixteen appearances he won only once more. Yet his record, particularly during the fifties, is a veritable who's who of heavyweight boxing from that era. Notable amongst the names he faced, aside from Marciano, were Roland LaStarza, Cleveland Williams, Nino Valdez and future champion Floyd Patterson. Of course Walls lost against them all but what stories he must have had in his final years.

For Marciano he would next face a Brooklyn, New York, heavy by the name of Norman Evanson. Norman it appeared had a bit more to offer than Marciano's previous opponent, at least on paper. Of his previous twenty-four outings, Norman, now renamed Jimmy Evans, had notched up no less than eighteen wins, thirteen of these via stoppage. But alas Evans was coming off two defeats in a row. Marciano, for his part, was determined to make it three.
By all accounts the fight on the evening of April 2nd was a cracker whilst it lasted, Rocky actually won the first round, unusual for him unless he knocked his opponent out (*which he had achieved no less than nine times already*). Evans gained parity by winning the second with a deft bobbing and weaving style that seemed to briefly confuse Rocky who found his opponent rolling with his punches and countering with hard, crisp shots in return. In the third

however Marciano had his foe figured, and, according to *Providence Journal* reporter Michael J. Thomas(5), "Marciano, sporting a new left hook, showed a much more polished attack. He didn't waste as many punches as in past."

Indeed Rocky seemed in this third, and what proved to be final round, to be actually targeting his shots rather than just throwing from all angles. The result was immediate. Evans was clinically taken apart by short, sharp punches, until referee Ben MaCulan had no option but to pull the surgical Rocky off a glassy eyed Evans who by this stage was hanging limply against the ropes offering no defense. Amazingly a minority in the crowd actually booed the conclusion to the fight; some of these blood crazed cronies believed MaCulan had been too hasty in calling a halt to the affair. A small group even stormed down to ringside to complain vehemently to members of the Rhode Island Boxing Commission who were in attendance. But all thankfully to no avail. Heck, the commissioners weren't going to overturn the referee's decision especially as that arbiter of justice inside the ring had only been acting on their very specific orders. To quote Thomas again:

> Further fighting would have been useless and could have resulted in injury to Evans. Maculan (*sic*) furthermore was following instructions from the commissioners who weeks ago warned the referees to take immediate action as soon as Marciano had an opponent in danger (6).

This was a remarkable line from these boxing beaurocrat's, it appears that so concerned were they by the power displayed by the incredible Marciano that they feared a tragedy may come from his small, but thunderous fists(6). Just a few short months later when Marciano went to

New York and thus beyond the boundaries of New England's jurisdiction, these men's fears seemed to have been fully justified.

Yet those in the crowd were unaware of this new stipulation and continued to rage, it is little wonder then that in later years Marciano would grow to despise those elements of the boxing crowd. In fact he would become almost vitriolic in his disgust of these, as he called them in his retirement, "blood mad hungry guys who have no right to attend boxing. All they want is to see people hurt, they have no concept of the sacrifices these boys have made to put on a show for them like the majority of decent boxing folk have."

These thoughts were for later however for immediately after his victory Marciano was jubilant at win number sixteen (*fifteen since officially turning pro*), all won within the distance. So far Marciano had never gone beyond the fifth round. He had the advantage of Al Weill at last firmly ensconced as his manager and busy paving a path towards, at the very least, bigger paydays before larger crowds. Locally at least people were beginning to pay attention, even his conquered opponent Jimmy Evans (*who completely disappeared from view following his mauling by Marciano*) was filled with praise claiming Rocky was a better prospect than the highly touted LaStarza whom Evans had battled valiantly back in 1947 before losing over a hotly contested six-rounds.

Back in the here and now however, everything seemed to be going smoothly for Marciano, but as seemed to be the way there was to be a major shift in his professional life, one that would influence the remainder of his career, and it would happen right away.

Notes:

1. Phelan was such a nondescript that this bout was his only verified encounter.

2. A picture taken at the exact moment that Artie came crashing down shows the hapless fighter gazing at his conqueror with an expression that seemed to say imploringly, "Why did you do that? I was having so much fun."

3. I find it sad that these fighters who crumbled to the canvass on Marciano's rise are so unknown, they are men who had lives to live, families to feed, who were left hurt and bleeding, strewn wreckage, road kill on Rocco's highway to the throne. Most now are but shadows, wraiths walking the halls of Fleischer's mythical fistic Valhalla, for some we know not even the date they came into this world nor the date they left, we have only names to prove that they were ever here at all, I hope through this work they may find recognition in some small way.

4. As Manny Almeida explained at the time "Those fighters on the list just weren't available for one reason or another. One was ailing, another wouldn't fight in Providence and some others Marciano's handlers refused to accept. I lined up others, but the commission refused to approve them. For a time it appeared I wouldn't make it. In fact I was on the verge of giving up when I was informed of this guy Walls. He had beaten henry Bernstein, Norwegian heavyweight, the previous week. It looked as if he would fit the picture and fortunately the commission saw it that way."

5. Thomas was a close friend of Rocco's and would spend time with the fighter before each bout, becoming one of Marciano's staunchest campaigners through the early years.

6. This ruling was brought into force after the Rhode Island boxing commission had to conced that Rocky really could hit after he began disposing of those on their list (see above) and goes a long way to explaining why many of the Brockton phenoms victories, especially in Providence, were technically classed as stoppages rather than clean knockouts, the referee's just were not willing to take a chance.

part three   chapter eighteen

Uncle Mike

> *"Every important boxer in the U.S...must fight either for Mike Jacobs, or with his approval...He has beady eyes, a dead-pan face, a gruff voice, a set of badly fitting false teeth. In a business where profanity is a high and useful art he is superbly profane...He is also feared."*
>
> *Anon. Life (June 20th 1938)*

By the late Forties Michael Strauss Jacobs had been the king of boxing for almost two decades. He sat supreme and unchallenged at the head of the fabled Twentieth-Century Sporting Club, then the most powerful force to be unleashed on the pugilistic world. Jacobs (*born March 10th 1880*), a former street hustler in his native New York, had begun his rise to prominence when barely into his teens when in the late 1890's the astute newspaper and candy seller had managed to wrangle a deal which allowed him to secure tickets for the numerous boats and ferries that traveled from the metropolitan mainland to Coney Island. Later he would move onto scalping tickets for the famous theatre's of Broadway (1). He was always on the lookout for a good deal, always on the hustle.

For almost twenty-years the chain smoking Jacobs contented himself with moving smoothly through the fledgling entertainment field before eventually branching out into promoting cycle races and circuses, but always the murky shadow of boxing fell over him.

As early as 1904 he had become associated with the famed promoter Tex Rickard who would assist Jack Dempsey to three separate million-dollar gates. At first Mike would help with ticket sales, handle the money, small things, nothing fancy, no grand dreams. After all back then boxing was sewn up by Madison Square Garden which at the time was in her second incarnation and stood at 26th and Madison Avenue (2).

Fortunes for Jacobs moved up a gear however with the death of Rickard in 1929. Having taken the lessons learned by the remarkable promoter, and through inheriting a small stable of Tex's fighters, Mike began to promote his own cards. Initially his cards were held at New York's Hippodrome over on 6th Avenue, it was not long however as the shows began to turn a profit the fabled Garden, now situated on 8th Avenue in her third and most famous guise, came calling.

As was the way, when competition could not be beaten it instead became engulfed, the beast devouring its prey. Only this time the prey would begin to eat away at the beast from the inside for Jacobs was tenacious, not for him second best, or even amalgamation, he wanted total control, and within seven years he would get it.

The transformation began in 1933 when Jacobs, along with sportswriter Ed Frayne, the ultra-talented Damon Runyon(3), and Bill Farnsworth of the powerful Hearst newspaper chain, colluded to birth the Twentieth-Century Sporting Club; its main purpose to break the monopoly held by the Garden. Working from within now Jacobs began to add to his boxing stable, and in 1935 he would make his most propitious move when he took control of the up and coming sensation that was Joe Louis.

This son of Eastern European immigrants (*via Ireland*) knew a good thing when he saw it, if he didn't he would have ended up a two bit street corner merchant swapping rags for dimes. In Louis he realized the potential to sew up boxing. Jacobs, now being dubbed 'Uncle Mike' built this talented fighter into a phenom (*it helped that Louis really was that good*).Together they filled out shows in the Garden. Louis' popularity became so vast that 'Uncle Mike' opened a ticket office at 225 West 49th Street to accommodate the burgeoning demand from fans to see the new sensation.

This office was slap bang in the center of the stretch of pavement on West 49th between Broadway, where Jack Dempsey owned a popular restaurant, and Eighth Avenue where stood the fabled Garden. This one time innocuous looking piece of real estate was now the hub of boxing for between those two New York landmarks the good, bad, and downright ugly of the sport of boxing congregated. Some were making deals, some waiting to be seen, others merely drowning themselves in the various bars that lined this stretch which would from now on become known as, 'Jacobs Beach'.

In 1937 Mike Jacobs ascendancy over the Garden was complete when his fighter (*Louis*) claimed the heavyweight championship of the world, for the man who owned the champ owned boxing, in short order the Twentieth-Century Sporting Club took over complete control at Madison Square, and Jacobs took over sole ownership of the Twentieth-Century by buying out Runyan and forcing Frayne and Farnsworth out onto the proverbial street (*it seems 'Uncle Mike' had no qualms about stepping over whoever got in his way*).

Over the next decade no fight would be sanctioned nor fighter get a look in at the Garden without the express consent of Jacobs; Joe Louis would continue to rule as champion as thousands flocked to 'Uncles Mike's' events and all seemed to dance to his tune. Yes, all seemed good in the house that Jacobs built. However as the 1940's rumbled inexorably on through war and uncertainty, time itself began to catch up with both promoter and fighter alike. First in 1946 Jacob's suffered a stroke (*from which he would never fully recover*), then in 1949 Louis, already showing the definite signs of decay announced his retirement. With Mike's empire beginning to crumble about him his beloved 'Jacobs Beach', that bastion of the boxing world, was in crisis; it would not be long before it was invaded…

Notes:

1. *That this was a pure piece of business may be attested to by the fact that he had a tendency to fall asleep when he and his wife Josie occasionally attended the shows themselves.*

2. *The original building had been converted from an old passenger depot for the New York and Harlem railroad in 1874 by none other than the great showman and hokum peddler P.T Barnum before being razed then raised again in 1890.*

3. *Runyan (an adulterated boxing fan) was a writer whose prose would almost single handedly shape our concept of nineteen-twenties New York.*

part three   chapter nineteen

Mr. Gray

"Carbo was slick, he would fool you into liking him, then tear out your throat!"

Jimmy Breslin

For over a decade there had been a shark circling around the outer edges of 'Jacob's Beach' sniffing blood and licking its maw. At first it waited patiently, feasting off the crumbs that fell from the main table and into its path. These scraps did not appease this silver-grey clothed beast from the depths for long, no sir, for this creature was growing ravenous, and this creature was a cold blooded killer!

Paulo Corbo had been born on New York's lower east-side in 1904. The son of Italian immigrants he had very little going for him as a child, thrown at birth into poverty he learnt quickly that the only way to make a life was to fight and steal for it. It was no surprise (*much to his beloved mothers' shame*) that by the time he was eleven he had already experienced the inside of New York's State Reformatory. In his youth the diminutive Corbo was little different from the thousands of others in the big cities slum districts who scrabbled to make some money merely to survive on a day to day basis.

However as the years passed, Corbo (*who had by this time changed his last name to Carbo*) began to show a truly terrifying edge on those unnamed hoodlums with whom he grouped together when in 1928 he was arrested for the murder of Albert Webber, a taxi driver who refused to acquiesce to Carbo's demands for tribute money. Yes, in a short time the little street hood had stamped his name as a wannabe gangster. The incredibly short spell he served in the notorious Sing-Sing prison (*thirty-miles from New York on the banks of the Hudson River*) for the reduced charge of manslaughter on Webber, would serve as a badge of honor and grant him access to the inner sanctum of New York crime.

Carbo, by now attempting to hide behind a myriad of assumed names including Paul L. Carbo, P.J Carbo, Frank Fortunati, Frank Marlow (*even 'Jimmy the Wop', which he detested*), and his personal favorite (*the one which stuck*), Frankie Carbo, found himself working as a hired killer for the notorious bunch of mercenaries who were collectively known by the rather macabre label, 'Murder Inc'. This motley band was headed by such luminaries of the underworld as Benjamin 'Bugsy' Segal and Louis 'Lepke' Buchalter. Their job, to wipe out all competition, if the price was right, and it usually was.

During 1927 through to 1940 they turned New York into a virtual war zone as bodies piled up and blood ran through some of the most glamorous streets of the city.

Frankie himself was alleged to have been involved in at least five murders, including that of the former ring leader 'Bugsy' Segal who had fallen from favor. Yet despite being arrested time and again he somehow defied prosecution and remained free. The fact that he did so is not that remarkable when we remember that this was the era of prohibition where everyone was in the pocket of the man with the most money, or the most guns. Everyone from the lowliest officer on the beat to the chief of police and even the Mayor of New York himself, was on the take, so it is no surprise that the man now known as 'Mr. Gray'[1] should be allowed to roam free.

By the end of 1933 New York's underworld was hit by the news that prohibition was being repealed, it ended thirteen years of a dry America, and, it was hoped, the monstrous vehicle that had made men such as Al Capone rich and, incredibly, feted. By cutting the throat of the mobs main asset to making money, the government assumed, these insects who had fed off the nation's vices would scurry away. They were wrong. These men may have been unscrupulous, but they were also smart, they knew where the big money lay and at this time it lay in gambling. Whether it be small time deals in saloons and bars or big money sports, major players in the mob quickly moved in to play that game, only they stacked the deck in their favor for they would not be merely dealing the cards, they would own them. Thus with a rapidity which was startling they moved into the three big ones immediately, baseball, horse racing, and boxing.

These sports, the top three in America, had always had an element of hoodlum activity at their base since their earliest days. Where there was money to be made there were those willing to bend the odds in their favor, only now the influx of the underworld became almost pandemic as they infested each and every quarter of the big three money making sports.

The way they did it was simple in its way and a throwback to the protection rackets which were honed on the streets of the major cities in America. Essentially they bribed, brought off, or muscled their way into each empire. Took over contracts, moved in legitimate names, or at least names that were clean of any criminal activity, then simply sat back whilst others controlled the strings. But they weren't dumb for they did not attempt to influence every game, every race, or every match, that would have been suicide. Instead they took their cut out of the clean mugs (*those whose only crime was to consort with the mobsters*) who faced the press and public pleading innocence, then they waited for a moment to move. Usually this meant building up a team, or horse, or fighter, into a position of prominence, working on the public trust that a certain result was expected, then bang, they would strike, piling money into the outcome in the form of legitimate bets, always making sure the result went their way. They would secure that result through intimidation or promise of greater glory down the road to those involved.

Frankie Carbo made his first tentative grubby steps into boxing at the exact moment that the mob faced the transition from lords of prohibition to czars of sport, when in 1933 he was given 'a piece' of future middleweight champion Babe Risko by New York crime lord Vito Genevese. It was the beginning of a remarkable reign as Carbo began to seek his own empire starting with Madison Square Garden [2].

But this scheming, manipulative killer was not content with one mere fighter he wanted to run the whole show. Yet whilst Jacobs was in the proverbial catbird seat he knew he couldn't quite get the deal done, for although 'Uncle Mike' was not averse to bending to pressure from the doyens of crime he did have enough clout to stop them taking over completely, and the mob knew it. However they also knew that Jacobs could not hang on forever, thus mercilessly they chipped away until the strain to keep his empire together took its inevitable toll on Mike. By 1949 Carbo, that shark waiting in the water was ready to attack, and when he did it would be hard and final.

Carbo knew, following the protocol which had proven so successful, that in order to gain complete control he needed a stooge, a malleable, clean cut, fresh faced puppet to front the show. Luckily for him there was just such a man waiting in the wings, someone whom the mob had been grooming for just such a role, and who, for his own part, was more than willing to comply. Thus enter stage left James D. Norris, and with him came a new era in boxing...

Notes:

1. *He picked up this, his most famous monicker due some said for his penchant for wearing suits of that color, others that it was testament to his hair which had taken on a salt-and-pepper hue from an early age.*

2. *Here he became such a familiar figure that in 1936 when he was arrested for the murder of Max Hessell and Max Greenberg two competing bootleggers who had been 'dealt with' in mid-1933 the police, knowing that he would be in the Garden picked him up off the street as he emerged after a watching a bout.*

part three   chapter twenty

The Golden Boy & Octopus Inc.

"Jim Norris was a nice guy, but he just had a thing about gangsters!"

Bill Cayton

James D. Norris was a man who was born with the proverbial 'silver spoon in his mouth', or to be more accurate, a solid gold one. From the moment he entered the world (*November 6th 1906*) he'd had it easy owing to the families trait of grinding out a fortune by sheer graft and bloody-mindedness, a gift that he would not inherit.

His father James E. Norris had been the benefactor of his predecessor's ownership of a fleet of sailing boats out in Ontario, Canada. The senior Norris had transmuted this beginning into the growth and distribution of grain when he decided to strike out on his own and move to Chicago when still in his early twenties; it had helped that he had been raised on the family farm, giving him a head start in the knowledge of crops. But his biggest interest would come not from such cereal production [1] but from a youthful interest in hockey.

Whilst his son was still a child Norris began to dabble in the growing sport of Ice-Hockey (*another immigrant, like himself, from Canada*). He had himself played conventional hockey years before and yearned to be involved in some capacity as he grew into adulthood. Thus he promptly went out and invested in several teams that were thriving in the Illinois area. Later he would also purchase the stadiums in which they played, becoming, by the nineteen-forties the most influential figure in the fledgling sport.

His son however seemed to show no inherent ambition to follow in his fathers' formidable footsteps, for although named as a member, and even president, of several companies Norris junior rarely ventured into any offices for he seemed content merely to squander his enormous wealth in the numerous horse tracks and brothels of America. It was in these dens that young James D. (*or Jim to his friends*) became acquainted with the underworld figures who would seduce his senses of adventure and danger, remaining with him for the rest of his life.

For years now Carbo had been courting Norris (*the pair had first met each other at the dog-tracks*), in fact they all had, his father's name gave him great credibility, the perfect front for the mobbed up guys. Often Jim was coerced into signing his name to a letter of credential, or even offering up bail money, to friends of friends for friends. Rarely did he really know who he was doing it for in the first place but he was nevertheless happy to comply because it allowed him to remain in the seedy underworld that he got his kicks out of being a part of.

As life rolled on for Norris it was all one long party, he showed no real interest in earning a living, hell, he didn't have to, even as he turned into his forties, he was as laid back as ever over a career. That is until one fateful morning in 1949 whilst out playing golf in Florida with the immortal Joe Louis. An opportunity was presented to him on the usual golden platter.

Louis, the incumbent champion since 1937 had finally decided to quit boxing in March of that year, despite not having defended his title since the previous June he knew time was up on his remarkable reign. His final two defenses against 'Jersey' Joe Walcott had convinced him of that (*most, including Louis himself, felt that he had lost the first tussle with Walcott*), but the great champion was not going to be allowed to enjoy the fruits of his labor as many felt he deserved for during his service in the Armed Forces whilst the second world war played out its course Louis had given exhibitions for the troops for which he was paid (2). Being the great patriot that he was Joe immediately donated the purses to the war effort, as a thank you the American government, who had not been paid their tax cuts from these events, demanded reimbursement. Louis, to whom money poured out of his pockets like water, was now almost broke.

A solution was dreamt up, or so it seemed, by Harry Mendel, a former press agent. The idea appeared simple enough on the surface. Under the grand title of Joe Louis Enterprises sign up the four leading contenders to Louis' vacated throne, face them off in an elimination tournament, promote the shows and rake in the profits, what could be simpler. Now that Mike Jacobs was ailing and had himself decided to call it a day after his meal ticket, Louis, had called it quits, there was no real legitimate competition to tying up the top four, however the initial sponsor (*an unnamed Florida Hotel owner*) had pulled out of the deal so now Mendel suggested Norris.

Jim Norris was no stranger to boxing, although it was never his sport of choice (3), so he was at first reticent to take the reins of such an adventure. He had no business acumen at all, so he suggested that he should at first speak with someone who had. To this end he approached Arthur M. Wirtz who was the business partner of Norris' father.

Wirtz was pure business and he knew a good deal when he saw one thus he attacked Louis and his partners hard in an attempt to hammer out the best deal. Louis in turn was in no real position to bargain, he was desperately in need of money to pay off his debts thus within days the formidable International Boxing Club was born out of the ashes of Joe Louis Enterprises which sold out for the measly sum of $150,000 in cold hard cash. Louis himself however would be kept on as official spokesman for the newly formed organization in return for ten-per-cent of all net profits, yet the fix was in, for in the first few years the IBC strangely made barely enough to pay their expenses.

The newly formed organization moved fast. First they secured the Polo grounds in New York from the swiftly folding empire that Jacobs built, then they acquired the rights to hold bouts in stadiums outside New York, and to cap it all they quickly signed up the two leading contenders for the heavyweight crown in 'Jersey' Joe Walcott and Ezzard Charles. But Wirtz knew that they needed to be more than a one trick pony, they needed a stable of fighters to secure their ascension to the top of the fistic pile, this is where Carbo saw his opportunity and pounced.

Frankie and his 'associates' now had parts of a whole plethora of boxing talent and they would gladly give them over to the IBC for a percentage of the gate and the rights to the fighters appearing on the foundling medium of television. Of course, at first Wirtz was reticent, but Norris agreed, what harm could it do anyway they were all going to make a pile of money, at least those at the top, the little that trickled down to those below was meaningless (*this included Louis, whose cut was so paltry that he was forced to return to the ring in 1950*).

Only a matter of months after forming the IBC promoted its first heavyweight championship fight between Walcott and Charles at Comisky Park, Chicago in June of '49. With Charles victorious, Jim Norris, and more importantly Frankie Carbo, had the heavyweight champion of the world. Their takeover was complete especially as weeks before they had captured that other jewel in the boxing crown, Madison Square Garden.

This bastion of the boxing world quickly folded, or to be truthful, was absorbed. Firstly Norris, through the influence of his formidable father who actually owned shares in Madison Square, leased the building for boxing shows off the fading 20th Century Sporting Club which still operated despite Mike Jacobs' retirement. Then with stunning swiftness he ostensibly took over the whole shebang. Some of Jacobs' old hands were kept on by the new organization; however the joint matchmakers at Madison Square, Nat Rogers and Tex Sullivan were quickly ousted. This meant that Wirtz and Norris needed a new man to make the shows at 'The Garden'. It would be none other than Carbo himself who suggested just such a man, someone who knew boxing inside and out, someone who wasn't averse to doing what needed to be done to put on a good show, and even better, had played the role of matchmaker at 'The Garden' before.

That man was none other than Al Weill.

Notes:

1. *Nor from the cattle ranches he owned which were worth, it was estimated, near $200 million.*

2. Louis *was a great propaganda tool for the Allies after his decisive victory over the German Max Schmeling in 1938.*

3. *But it has been rumored that he dabbled in promoting low key boxing shows back in his native Chicago as early as 1936 fronting them it is alleged, for Carbo himself.*

part three   **chapter twenty-one**

Family Ties

"Who the hell else would I hand him (Marciano) over too if not my own flesh and blood!"

Al Weill

Al Weill consistently sought power in one form or another, and he was never averse to sidling up to the people who could give it to him. He had done it back in the thirties when Jacobs was king which had allowed Weill to hold the reigns at 'The Garden' back in the golden age, an age defined by the emergence of Louis as the biggest drawing card in the sport since Jack Dempsey. But Al didn't last long, for although he craved prominence and would seduce those he thought could give it, he still hated to be dictated too.
"If anyone spoke to me, the way I speak to my fighters," he once said, "I'd crack them right in the nose! (1)" This was one of the rare times that he admitted his acerbic tongue could be as brutal as his fighters' fists. "But," he continued as a way of explanation, or at least self-

assurance that he was justified in his mannerisms, "I only tell them the way it is, and they listen, and I make them rich. If they don't they leave town and will never make it!"

So back in the thirties he severed ties with Mike Jacobs and the 20th Century Sporting Club because he had his own ace up his sleeve in the form of Lightweight Lou Ambers. Ambers took his portly manager (*and trainer Charley Goldman*) to the championship of the world on no less than two occasions in the late thirties, but despite this managerial coup Weill felt slightly deflated for Ambers was good, but he wasn't catching the world on fire. Now he had a second shot at the biggest job in boxing, matchmaker at Madison Square, the prestige this would bring him was pure dynamite.

At first news of Al's new position was greeted by the press, rather remarkably, with a sense of optimism (*one can only wonder how many palms he greased to be accorded such muted enthusiasm*).

"He has handled scores of fighters and served as matchmaker and promoter in many places. He knows all the answers. According to his colleagues he has made and put away more money than almost any other half dozen guys in the business," gushed International News Service journalist Milton Carver at talk of Weill's re-ascension to the top. "Strange as it may seem to anyone not connected with the peculiar, sometimes baffling, prizefight business," he continued, "He is proud of his long career in various capacities around the ring. 'For 35 years I've been involved in it without a break,' he (*Weill*) said. Like a man recounting a long career as a business tycoon...He now will begin to lead that double life peculiar to the boxing matchmaker. With half the managers and fighters Weill will be applauded as a great man, and he will be reviled and attacked by the others...But anybody who thinks the man known as 'The Vest' will worry his head for a moment about these minor problems is slightly touched. He will be the most unworried man in the business."

However Weill did at least have a small concern and it came in the form of what he was to do with Rocky Marciano.

It was a rule, unwritten, yet as solid as concrete, that no matchmaker could manage his own fighters. This was seen as a conflict of interests, and it was this very ruling that had led Weill to favor Ambers over a decade earlier. Back then however he knew without a doubt that Ambers had talent and would take him to a title. In Marciano he was still not completely certain in the boys' true potential. Should he cut him loose and pray he never made it or should he find a way to hold on, just in case. Thus Weill had the biggest decision he had ever had to make before him, the resolution of which would either make or break him down the road.

Marciano himself would later recall the outcome of Al Weill's decision. "When I was training in New York, in the CYO gym on 17th Street for a Providence fight…I got a phone call. It was Weill, and he said, 'Come on right up to the office. Stop everything you're doing there and get up here. It's very important.' When I walked into Al's office, there were three other fighters there, the only ones he had outside of me at the time. Weill sent then out as soon as I got there. 'I'm the new IBC matchmaker,' he said. 'I just released those guys. I'm not managing them anymore.' He opened a drawer and pulled out a paper and passed it to me. 'Sign it,' he said. I didn't even read it. I don't know to this day what it said. I signed it and Al put it away. Then he says, 'That's a private agreement between you and me. But if anyone asks you who your manager is, tell them Marty.' "

So Al had played his cards, laid them out and prayed that Lady Luck would not trump him, he would hand Rocky over to 'Marty'. This seemed like a good, safe, solid bet for the 'Marty' in question was none other than Marty Weill, Al's very own stepson. It was nepotism of the highest order from Al, and it was also immensely shrewd, for Marty, a man with limited experience in the fight game, would not only keep Marciano just within the reaches of his stepfather, he would also be willing to give him back when the time was right. Al knew that, Marty knew that, even Marciano knew it, and, so it appeared, did everybody else in boxing.

"After Al and me signed this agreement," continued Rocky, "Marty was around for all my fights, but he was never my manager. We weren't fooling anybody. Everybody knew my real manager was Al, and he didn't try to hide it."

Yet even though Marty was to all intents and purpose purely a puppet manager he and Marciano still went through the formalities of signing a contract to bind them together (2). Yet it seems that the agreement between the fighter and new man in charge was the most beneficial of Marciano's career (3). Marty himself would keep very quiet about his dealings with the legendary Brockton heavyweight, yet he did reveal a small detail of their contract together when in 1993 he responded to the allegations that Marciano was being fleeced out of earnings by his late stepfather. "During that time (*in which Marty was the manager of record*) Rocky had some two dozen bouts and was guaranteed two thirds of any money he earned as a fighter!"

Indeed it seemed that things were stacked in Marciano's favor now, for as bigger pay days loomed he could look forward to higher percentages in his pocket, and with Al concentrating on business elsewhere he would be allowed to concentrate on fighting. Of course things would not be that easy, but right now Rocky, as was his way, put these political maneuverings behind him and concentrated on his next scheduled appearance back in Providence.

Marciano was on a roll now, fifteen wins in a row since officially turning professional. Every time he entered the ring he was, Rocco felt, assured of a knockout (*as did his growing entourage of fans who adored him for this*). So far no one had extended him beyond the fifth, nine had not even lasted beyond the first. When Marciano's next opponent was named there was nothing in his opponents' immediate record that suggested that the outcome would be any different this time out.

Sure the guy had never been stopped, but then he hadn't turned that trick on many either. In fact of the eighteen victories in his first twenty-bouts only five had failed to go the route, and now, the last seven in a row had that dreaded capital L appended to them in his win/lost column. But like the forty-nine names who sprawled across the record of Rocky Marciano there was far more to this opponent than mere statistics on a piece of crumbling, faded paper. In fact he would do something that many were beginning to think was impossible, he would keep Marciano in the ring for a full thirty-nine minutes.

Notes:

1. *It is an irony that Weill often was himself the recipient of just such treatment.*

2. *At least that is until big daddy Al was ready to tear it to shreds.*

3. *This contract would eventually last for three-and-a-half-years.*

part three   **chapter twenty-two**

The End of the Beginning

"I had never seen him (Rocky) fight, but looking at his record...they were mostly one or two rounds. I was hoping that after five or six rounds he would get tired and fall down."

Don Mogard

Don Mogard was once considered by many as one of the best Canadian heavyweights of all time. High praise indeed when you consider that his compatriots included former world heavy champ Tommy Burns and the truly outstanding Sam Langford. As time has passed however Mogard's reputation has become overshadowed somewhat by such luminaries as the hard-as-nails, yet inevitably tragic, Arturo Gatti, plus, by default, the sometime frustratingly brilliant Lennox Lewis [1]. Today Mogard is almost forgotten, even in his native country.

Born Donald Edward Mogard on August 12th 1925 in what was then the small almost overlooked village of Hampstead, New Brunswick, as a child he showed no outward interest in becoming a fighter stating that there was, "No history of boxing in the family." Yet he did admit that, "We always had a set of boxing gloves at home (*ostensibly for he and his two elder brothers, Robert and Carl to sort out their differences*).

"I left school at 15, worked on a farm for three months, but didn't like it much as the cows had dirty habits. So I went to work in a timber camp until I got a chance to work in a stone quarry," Mogard recounted to journalist Ron Olver in 1990. "At 17 I joined the Air Force, training as an air frame mechanic."

In a brief autobiographical letter penned in 1989 Mogard writes in his own inimitable style:

> I never saw a boxing ring until I joined the Canadian air Force (*sic*) in 1943 and was sent to Montreal Quebec for training
>
> I finally ended up at Mountain View airport a bombing and gunnery training center in Ontario and there was a little P.T.I corporal there whose main interest was boxing Vic Bagnato was his name he had been a good amateur but he had a couple of brothers who were pro's (*sic*)

During Don's service for his country he remained stationed in Canada thus he never saw action in the war that was raging throughout Europe (2).

For many of those who survived, if not all, the second world war changed lives dramatically, for Mogard it was no different (*yet perhaps not quite so dramatically*) for through the guidance of corporal Bagnato the young New Brunswickian found himself inevitably gravitating towards the amateur ring. Remembered close friend and compatriot Solly Cantor, "He lost the verdict in his first ever bout as an amateur, then racked up eleven wins in a row.

Three of them concluded by knockouts. He also scored major wins against Ernie Prosser (*one of Canada's outstanding heavyweights*) and Oren Safir, the Dominion heavyweight champion. He also kayoed Grundy Aylmer for an RCAF title. As the new champion, he kayoed Gunner Sauve, the Pettawawa Army champion - and Mike Jeles (*American Diamond Belt champion*)."

> I finally got out of the air force in 1946 and after a holiday at home I went back to Toronto (Vic Banato's home town) to see if I could make it as a boxer.
> Had a couple of fights in Toronto (3). Then went down to Patterson N.J with (*manager*) Bill Daley he had quite a few Canadian fighters down there (*sic*).

Despite his initial tentative start, drawing and then dropping a decision to Sauve, Mogard seemed to be realizing the potential he had shown as an amateur by racking up fourteen straight wins over the next twelve months (*including a revenge win against Suave that left them all square in their own personal tourney*). All seemed to be going well until he ran into the perennial spoiler of many hopefuls in the late forties, Roland LaStarza.

LaStarza was the poster boy of the heavyweights'; a handsome college educated New Yorker who was being groomed for the top. Since turning professional in July of 1947 the former standout amateur had notched up twenty-six victories in a row (*Roland's career is covered in more detail in later volumes*). He was a consummate boxer, testament to this is the fact that thus far he had only stopped his opponents from going the full route eleven times.

For Mogard this was a big step up in class, but for many it was a step that those who witnessed the bout thought he had navigated magnificently, yet the records show that he came out on the receiving end of a dubious decision. Don, as was his way, took the plaudits that followed in his own usual stride. Never one to brag or boast about his accomplishments, never one to complain even if he knew he had been wronged he later recalled that Marciano himself approached him after their own bout regarding the tussle with LaStarza, "Rocky saw the *(fight)* and said he thought I won it but I think he was just being polite."

The pair went at it again in November, in between which Don defeated Jimmy Walls for a second time. On this occasion there was little dispute, LaStarza won, and won convincingly (4). For Mogard however this bout would mark the beginning of an irreversible slide. Whatever spirit the Canadian had for boxing seemed to be waning for before his veritable war (*and in retrospect possibly finest hour as a professional*) with Marciano in May of 1949 he had performed before eager audiences no less than six times, and lost them all.

If events were going wrong inside the ring outside at least they were turning in this jovial Canadians favor (5):

> The first person I met when I got to Patterson was Lee Savold the gym was up 3 flights of stairs and 16 stone fat old Lee was puffing a little when he got to the top. He wasn't fighting anymore and just spent his time in the gym training some of the boys. He got pneumonia a few months later and when he recovered from that he had lost all his excess weight and decided to make a comeback[6].

After a couple of fights in the States he came over…to England to fight (Bruce) Woodcock (1948) Solly Cantor (*a respected lightweight and friend of Mogard's: see above*) came over with him then he lost the fight on a foul and came back to the States and arraigned for a return fight in 49 and Daley decided to bring me along with him also Frankie Cortese a pretty good welterweight.

That's when Daley got me a fight with Marciano -probably to pay for the boat fare as I never got much out of it.

When Marciano and Mogard met in the Rhode Island Auditorium on the evening of May 23rd it was the former's fourteenth appearance before what was swiftly becoming his home arena, for Mogard it would be his first and last showing in the Auditorium. The voluminous theatre like interior was swarming with fans of the Brockton fighter clamoring to witness his ascent up the heavyweight ladder. There was a palpable sense of excitement, an excitement generated by the man who was being labeled by *Providence Journal* writer Michael J. Thomas as 'Sir Punch'. Almost everyone in attendance prophesied a victory for Rocky, most expected it to be swift.

Yet despite Mogard's record of nine losses in twenty-seven outings he had never been stopped, in fact he had not even been off his feet, the man was durable and teak tough, Marciano would have to be at the top of his game to stop him. Thus Rocky was keen to enhance his reputation by stopping the unstoppable, and in his eagerness to do so he very nearly blew the fight.

Marty Weill was now in Marciano's corner for the first time in his official capacity as manager (*although The Brockton Enterprise would erroneously report that Marciano was once again under the guidance of Chick Wergeles*) and he would recall his new charges opening assault, "Marciano's punching reputation pulled in another sellout for Manny Almeida. They had come to see their new hero make another easy hit…Marciano, shortly after the first minute, nailed Mogard with two sweet right hand shots to the face a little high, but good punches."

Mogard did not go down, instead he countered with a right to Marciano's jaw, a real good punch. A guarded look flashed across Marciano's face. This had never happened before. When he hit a man with a right the man was supposed to go down. Mogard didn't do that. He came back, and hit hard too. When Rocky returned to the corner, he asked Charlie (*sic*), "What do I do now?"

The crowd applauded but restrained any thoughts that something was amiss. Sure their man Marciano had made better starts, he looked sloppy in there, but then he always did; so what if Mogard did not do the decent thing and fall down when Rocky "lowered the boom," to borrow a phrase popular at the time. Perhaps they would get their moneys' worth tonight, perhaps this one may go a couple of rounds.

They settled down to the second round, better not go to get that beer, it may be over by the time they got back, too many had been caught out like that before, but they wouldn't have been this time. In fact there was a heck of a long way to go. For Mogard it was a necessary haul through a savage storm. He had done it before, though perhaps the weather had not been quite as rough, for Rocco however it was to be a veritable marathon.

"As he (*Marciano*) was about to throw his left he dropped his right hand ever so little," continued Weill remembering the second round. "Mogard shot over a terrific right to Marciano's face. The punch shook Rocky more than he had ever been in his young boxing life." It was one of Mogard's strongest stanza's with every judge awarding him the round. "The fight developed into one of the most sensational ever seen in Providence. When the Rock and Don went toe-to-toe, smashing each other with everything they had."

It seemed to be a case of an over aggressive Marciano losing his composure as the bout progressed. Round by round he frustratingly harried his opponent, left hook, left hook, his new weapon. Rocky was still throwing his right but it was almost as if he had lost faith in it after its complete disgrace in the opening round, and when he did use it, as Michael J. Thomas reported, "He either missed completely or tossed loops that landed harmlessly (*a precursor of his famous 'Suzie Q' ?*)."

Mogard, tagged by the media as a 'clutch and hit fighter', rewrote the form book as he moved around the ring, dodging, ducking, back peddling, opening up Rocky as he came rushing forward and exposing his opponents vulnerable defense then launching effective counters. In the eighth Don even had the temerity to launch an assault of his own landing freely with combinations, if only he had his adversary's power many must have thought that night, then they would see just what Marciano was really made of. In fact, at certain points Don seemed remarkably to be stronger than the man who was being hailed as the reincarnation of that other Massachusetts sensation, 'The Boston Strong Boy', John L. Sullivan.

Mogard's superiority in strength was evident when Marciano cornered his foe, somehow Don managed to bull his way out, negating Rocky's chance to launch an all-out attack. Mogard was also able to jostle his perplexed adversary in close, yes, without a doubt by the final bell Rocky Marciano knew that he had been in a fight.

The Auditorium was bedlam at the end of the encounter, the invincible Brockton slugger was still there, ten-rounds, no-one thought they would ever see him still in the ring after almost three-quarters of an hour, but there he was, and more important, separated only by the referee as they awaited the result, was his opponent. I can picture him now, the power puncher, stood with head bowed, wondering why he was still there. He always lived by the principle that no matter how ugly he looked in the ring he should make sure that, "Every time I fought I did everything I could to take the decision away from the judges." Yet here he was, waiting…

In all honesty there was only a small group of ardent Mogard fans in attendance who believed that their man had won the fight. Despite the fact that Rocco was off form his constant attack had clearly won him the night, in actuality the courageous Don only managed to pick up two-rounds, the second and eighth.

Looking back this was an important turning point in the career of the future world heavyweight champion, for it was here that he proved he could win a fight by other means than just knocking out whoever he faced. They were not all going to roll over, and when they didn't Rocky needed to be ready to go all the way. Sure some weaknesses were exposed, but these could be worked on, ironed out, improved. What was important was that he had won and won unanimously.

Yet Rocky fell into a depression, he always would after failing to take someone out with the power of his fists. Allegedly immediately after the match he approached Mogard, they shared a dressing room which wasn't unusual for fighter's who were still making a name for themselves. "Why didn't you go down", he reportedly asked, "Because I'm from New Brunswick", came the alleged reply. Although the veracity of this conversation is doubtful, a tale spun to sell Don in his home country. That the pair did talk about other things nevertheless is attested to by Mogard himself, and it had nothing to do with the what, when, why or how of Don's ability to withstand Rocky's punches (7).

In retrospect it is not all that remarkable that Don stayed on his feet, although later he would simply joke to his daughter and anyone else who cared to enquire as to how he managed it that he, "Just stood behind Marciano to get through (8)."

During his career Mogard was never knocked off his feet by anyone, sure the caliber of some of his opponents were suspect, but at the end of the day a heavyweight punch is still something to be wary of. Don battled through well over two-hundred rounds throughout both his amateur and professional career never once tasting the canvass, a remarkable achievement when you consider that even the great Joe Louis was bounced off the mat seven times in his first amateur fight, and even as champion is second only to the yo-yo named Floyd Patterson for the amount of times he had to rise from the floor (9).

Within days following Mogard's valiant stand he found himself on board a boat heading for England as part of the retinue that accompanied Lee Savold who was hell-bent on revenging his earlier defeat to the British and Commonwealth heavyweight champion Bruce Woodcock.

> I had no illusions about becoming a boxer anymore so I thought of it as a working holiday.
> I did quite a few exhibition bouts with Savold in the summer of 49 then Woodcock had a car accident so the Savold vs. Woodcock fight was postponed for another year. Savold and Daley went back to the states. I stayed to have a couple of fights in Sweden and one with Don

Cockell. Savold & Daley came back in 1950 and fought Woodcock again (10). I fought Frank Bell that night (11). After the Savold vs. Woodcock fight we did a tour of Butlins Holiday Camps six of them which we all enjoyed. In the middle of the tour Charlie Henery and I went to Berlin with Freddie Mills (*former world light-heavyweight champion*) and (*his manager*) Ted Broadrib for a boxing match I can't remember who I fought (*Karl Payler, draw*) Charlie and Ray Wilding went back to America with Daley I stayed here as I had just got married12 and we wanted to stay in England for awhile longer. We are still here and I think we shall stop here now. I spent some time in Brighton with Tommy Farr when he made his comeback (*Farr was a welsh heavyweight who went the distance with Joe Louis in the latter's first defense of his title back in 1937, Farr had initially retired some ten years earlier in 1940*) also used to box with Jock Gardener and (*Don*) Cockell as they used the same gym.

…My last fight was with Albert finch and after losing that (*by decision on the 26th February 1951*) I decided to go to work for a living."

"He always told me he stopped boxing because he stopped winning and it was starting to hurt," mentioned Tracey Mogard in our correspondence. Thus the man who had gone the distance with the two most promising heavyweights of his day, Marciano once, and LaStarza twice, slunk away from the boxing scene entirely leaving behind a record of nineteen-wins, sixteen-losses, and three-draws. It was not a record that would assure him a place in the annals of history (*it would however guarantee for him a place in the Canadian Boxing Hall of Fame*) but it was an earnest, honest career.

Don quickly settled into a new career path far removed from his former exploits. With a family to feed that now included two daughters, Jill and Tracey. He first found employment working for an export packing firm. He remained there for a decade before joining the Post Office in 1962 where he would toil away at Waterloo station loading and unloading mail onto trains and trucks, not hiding, but neither living off his past, for twenty-seven years. "He didn't take any promotions that were offered to him because he never wanted to be in charge of lots of unruly lazy men," reflected Tracey.

This unassuming, modest gentle man who had, "lots of friends and no enemies", found a new direction after his retirement, that new direction was golf. "It's a lot of fun, fresh air and no black eyes. That is how I spend my weekends now if the weather is good enough," Don wrote in 1989. Sadly just five years later in 1994, at the age of sixty-nine, Don Mogard, the first man to last the distance with the irresistible force of Rocky Marciano, was gone.

> If I had a chance to do it all again I would collect every
> Saturdays football results and win the pools every week;
> and keep out of the ring (*Don Mogard 1925-1994*).

Notes:

1. Lewis represented Canada as an amateur after moving there in 1977 before returning to his native England to begin a career as a professional in 1989.

2. He came close however, stating in a letter to a friend that whilst he was on a two week embarkation leave pending posting to England the war came to an end.

3. Four, a first round KO of Keith Prosser, followed by a trilogy with fellow Canadian Wilfred Sauve which resulted in a draw and win apiece for the protagonists - Mogard actually lost the first fight by TKO in the opening round when the referee was forced to stop the bout due to a vicious cut, however the verdict was changed to a draw when it was felt that the injury was caused by a clash of heads.

4. This may be more due to the fact however that Mogard was a last minute replacement when the New York Boxing Commission had refused to sanction LaStarza's official opponent Leo Stoll on the grounds that the bout would not be competitive.

5. A testament to Mogard's sense of humor comes from his daughter Tracey Mogard who has furnished me with some remarkable material that made this chapter possible, "Dad had the most wonderful sense of humor, it was only last year (2009) that I realized he was kidding when he said he broke his nose playing tennis!!"

6. Savold would later be retired for good by Marciano, his career is covered later in connection with this bout.

7. For details of their conversation see the chapter dealing with the first Marciano - LaStarza bout in volume two.

8. This version of events became so well known amongst those who either knew him, or at least knew of him, that when Jackie Duggan of the Canadian Boxing Hall of Fame contacted him in September of 1992 inviting him to attend a forthcoming event as guest speaker, Mr. Duggan wrote specifically that, "At the head of the table you may be asked to say a few words, but please don't put yourself down. The people don't want you to joke by saying you stood behind Rocky Marciano. Believe me, you took his best punches and gave him a scare...The other story I read about you was that Rocky hit you with his best punches in the fifth round, an all out assault by hitting you three punches in a row with his right hand, however, you stood your guard and never let on anything hurt you or blinked an eye. You will get a standing ovation for this kind of talk."

9. I wondered if it ever rankled Don that he was remembered more for a gallant defeat rather than any of his magnificent victories, my question was answered by his youngest daughter, "Don was never rankled over anything."

10. In fact Don took part in some six bouts before Savold returned winning one, drawing one and losing the other three.

11. The Savold - Woodcock fight on June 6th 1950 was incredibly labeled as a for the world heavyweight championship by the British Boxing Board of Control, Savold, the victor by technical knockout in the 4th was never recognized outside of Britain.

12. At Caxton Hall, London, June 17th 1950. "Mum's maiden name was Barbara Leah Adolphe Potash nick (she was) born in London in 1928 so that made her 22 when she met Dad," wrote Tracey Mogard before detailing how her parents had met. "Basically...Dad and some and some other sparring partners were lodging at the home of the Sewell family in Seven Sisters Road, their son Danny was a boxer (you may remember his brother George was the actor). My mum and her sister Joan (being cute and blonde) were roped into showing the visitors around London...their honeymoon was actually the exhibitions of Butlins."

part three   chapter twenty-three

Doubly Sure

"When I first started out I was hugely confidant - there were some who mistook my self-belief for arrogance - I really believed that I could knock out any one I faced!"

Rocky Marciano

For Rocky Marciano failure to defeat an opponent in sensational style was hard to take, "I really thought that I had let everyone down, here I was trying to make a career for myself, and now I thought I had blown it. The fans came to see me knock people out, I hated to disappoint them."

"Man, the Rock was really cut up, after the fight he just sat in the dressing room shaking his head, muttering to himself," recalled Allie Colombo. "The way he acted anyone would have thought he'd lost the fight."

For days Marciano was in a slump, his training, usually the one thing that sparked his desire, suffered. Colombo again, "He began to fall apart, just going through the motions in the gym, I really think that Rocky was toying with the idea of quitting then and there. It wasn't until

Charlie (*Goldman, sic*), who Rocky loved, took him to one side and told him that what he did against Mogard was better than a knockout because it proved that he didn't have to knock everyone out, he really was a hell of a fighter, that he could beat anyone over the long route as well as the short, that Rocky's mood began to improve."

"You know," commented Sam Silverman many years ago in a eulogy to Marciano, "I really think that despite all the outward toughness, all the strength and power, Rocky was a real soft touch, a real fragile person. I mean he had this confidence in himself that he could do anything, and when he didn't he seemed to fall into a depression, as if he couldn't understand why he had failed."

In fact so shattered seemed the Brockton fighter's ego, and so concerned were those who steered the course of his career that it seemed the only remedy was to get him back into the right frame of mind, and fast. The only way this was going to happen was to make sure the next opponent was a better candidate to fall under Marciano's hammering blow's than the last, at least on paper.

"I don't want to put him in with someone too smart or with the style to beat him," issued Al Weill to his stepson. "I don't want him to get beat, but we got to take some chances."

That the elder Weill passed on these instructions showed that he was still very much holding the reins, despite the fact that in public Marty would attempt to feign complete control of Marciano he was fooling no-one. "Everybody knew my real manager was Al, and he didn't try to hide it," commented Rocky. Despite the fact that Al Weill was unashamedly flaunting the rules that prohibited a matchmaker from openly controlling the destiny of one or more particular fighters, the various boxing commissions and media turned a blind eye, at least at first.

With the above in mind team Marciano attempted to line up someone quickly, but despite their best efforts, and the intervention of the Rhode Island commission, it would take ten-weeks before Rocky entered the ring again against an opponent who on the face of it was perhaps perfect for their designs, for although few regarded him as a real viable threat, they also knew that he would not completely capitulate either.

Harry Hershel Haft had begun his professional career only eleven months previously when on the sixth of August he knocked out Jimmy Letty in two-rounds. Thus began a very promising start that saw him notch up some twelve victories in a row before losing, on points, to one Pat O'Connor in January of '49. Between this bout and his encounter with Marciano on the evening of July 18th Haft took part in some eight battles, he lost all but two (*including a knockout loss to someone who was definitely now on Marciano's radar, Roland LaStarza*). There are suggestions, most from Haft himself, that the reason for his downturn in fortunes was due to the allegations that his career was determined by those shadowy members of the underworld who controlled the sport during boxing's revered 'golden era.' This may have explained some of the defeats, but certainly not all. At the end of the day the simple fact is more likely that Haft just wasn't good enough. Observed esteemed trainer Ray Arcel [1], "The mob boys knew a good thing when they saw it, sure they ruined a lot of potentially good fighters, but at the end of the day they never shot themselves in the foot by totally destroying someone they thought was a prospect, especially when they had complete control of the situation [2]." Besides, a man of Harry's background was not one to be coerced by anybody.

If ever there was proof of the old adage of 'wrong time, wrong place' it was Haft. Born on July 28th 1925 in the Polish town of Belchatow, Harry was a Jew at a time in history when that religious culture was the most detested in history. At the age of fourteen the insidious war machine that was the Nazi's invaded his home country and began their ethnic cleansing program in order to Germanize all forcibly taken new dominions. For them it was easier to merely eradicate all that was seen as against the benefit of the master race rather than reeducate the populace.

To this end Jews of all ages were systematically rounded up and sent to concentration camps, there to be kept for an indefinite period or merely executed for nothing more than being something other than German. Haft himself was quickly picked up and found himself being moved from camp to camp. It was during his internment that he began to fight, allegedly taking part in notorious death matches that saw one combatant beat insensible another for the perverse pleasures of the sadistic guards. The loser was taken away and allegedly killed, that Haft survived is testament to his ferocity and vicious temper, traits that followed him throughout his life.

In the sometime shocking biography written by Haft's son [3] we are presented with a brutally disturbed character who apparently felt no guilt about killing an elderly couple who had offered him shelter when he had managed miraculously to escape from one period of enforced imprisonment. It is then no surprise that he turned his attention to boxing, a legalized form of violence.

At the conclusion of the war Haft was taught how to box by American servicemen who had liberated a detention centre where the animalistic Pole was then interred (*how he survived the war at all if half the stories are to be believed is, quite frankly, remarkable*).

According to the accounts Haft came to America in early 1948 through the aid of an unnamed American uncle who promptly shunned him upon arrival. Thus, having little avenue of support he turned to boxing [4]. However by the time he met Marciano Haft's career was winding down, this was his last chance to prove himself as a fighter and rebuild his career, a loss here and, he felt, there would be little point in carrying on.

Apparently so determined was Haft to win this one that he got himself hypnotized into believing that Marciano's punches wouldn't hurt. It was a futile effort, one that was exasperated by allegedly being approached in the dressing room prior to the bout by three unidentified hoodlums who ordered Harry to fall down in the first or face the consequences (6). This is a possibility, but whether they were genuine mobsters or merely fanatical fans eager for Marciano to return to his demolishing best is un-provable, yet the former concentration camp detainee took no notice for he did not go down in the first, it would take a little longer than that.

At the first bell Marciano, performing before one of the smallest crowds to have gathered in order to watch him fight, rushed at his opponent. "As usual Marciano was all fury and no finesse. He was in there to deliver the clincher and nothing more," reported John Hanlon in *The Providence Journal* the following morning. "Haft, a "rusher" with little style landed the first good punch in the third round - a hard right to Marciano's stomach. Marciano in turn tested his range with a long right to the jaw, and that was that for the first frame."

In the second both fighters tore into each other, but inevitably it was Rocky who began to take charges, by the end of the round the bewildered 'Animal of Jaworzno (7)' was groggy and laying back against the ropes. It was only a matter of time now, the crowd could sense the impending end of another fighter who was foolish enough to believe he had a chance against Rocky, hypnotized or not.

Hanlon catches perfectly the end of the bout, "Two hard punches to Haft's head - a left and a right - were Marciano's openers in the third. At the halfway mark, Haft rallied briefly, but it was too late. After several damaging blows to Haft's head Rocky delivered the crushers. The first was a left, coming up in the midsection. Then as Haft doubled up from the force of the wallop Marciano shot a short right - down and across - that put Haft out of action."

Harry Haft left the ring to a rousing ovation from the sparse crowd that had gathered, they realized that he had given of his best. This was to be the last time that a crowd applauded him for his fighting heart that had brought him through the war and to this place tonight, for as he walked to his dressing room and out of sight no-one there, perhaps even the defeated boxer himself, realized that they would never see him in the ring again.

In his years outside of boxing it seems that the traumatic experiences during his youth followed him until his death in 2007. Little is known for certain of this period, even his son's biography fails to recount in detail what became of his father. The little we do know is that he went into the fruit business in some capacity and that he was a brutish, bullying man, scarred no doubt by the extreme depravity of his captivity. Does this excuse his behavior? Of course it doesn't, but it goes some way to explaining it.

As his opponent faded out of view however, Marciano was just coming into it, at least on a national level.

Within a week of Rocco's conclusive victory over Haft Marciano's name was linked once again in all seriousness with the heavyweight championship of the world, a title then held by the remarkable Ezzard Charles. The connection came about through a small, almost innocuous piece in the national press that listed three 'Eastern Boys' as possible future contenders for the most revered crown in sports. The first was, almost by default, Roland LaStarza, who was aiming for his thirty-first straight victory on the following Friday (*29th July*). The others were current New England heavyweight champion Bernie Reynolds, and of course, Marciano[8].

When the national media first got news that Rocky was being seriously touted as a possible contender for the championship(9) they scoffed and asked in unison, "Who's he ever fought?" Well Charley Goldman had an answer to that, "He has fought everyone we put in front of him." 'Nuff said!

For the next "one to be put in front of him" Rocky had to wait until Tuesday, August 16th, and that someone was a virtual Providence local; ironic then that the bout took place in New Bedford, some almost forty-two Kilometers away.

Pete Louthis hailed originally from Cumberland, Rhode Island, where he had been born in 1922 yet his links to Providence were strong. As a collegiate he had attended Providence College where he stood out as a star tackler on the football field until his call up into the service of his country in August of 1943 by which time he had already taken part in some ten paid bouts (10). Yet it seems that Louthis couldn't quite make up his mind as to whether he was a professional or an amateur for despite being hailed as a future prospect as early as '43, in 1946 he was accredited as winning an All-Amateur Championship.

Upon his discharge in late '45 - early '46 Louthis, managing himself, racked up five successive wins in a row before meeting the vastly more experienced Lee Savold who knocked him cold in the fifth round. In a mirroring of the vast majority of Marciano's early opponents this began the inevitable sporadic career that saw his losses outweighing wins leading up to his clash with the rampaging Rocky.

Perhaps Pete knew his career was winding down as he was no longer a youngster just starting out on a career, by the time he met Rocky he had been fighting since 1942, now he was twenty-eight with thirty-nine accredited bouts under his belt (*of which he had lost thirteen*). Therefore he had, by 1948, returned to Providence College. Not this time as a student though for initially he took on the post of an athletic coach, specializing in coaching the next generation of prospective luminaries how to box. He liked his new position in life so much that he remained at the College for forty-two years.

For Rocky this was supposed to be another routine fight, sure there was always the concern that he might be caught by one of Louthis' punches that had seen off some eleven opponents out of his adversaries twenty-three wins, but of his last four appearances Pete had only managed one win. However there was a problem, one that had Rocky's handlers in a panic.

Since the auto-accident back in November of 1948 Rocky's back had suffered from a series of prolonged stiffness, for the most part he had ignored the pain that had shot through his spine and combated the effects of the loss of mobility with regular visits to an osteopath in New York, however leading up to this bout his back really began to take a turn for the worse. Allie Colombo became so concerned for his friend that he suggested that Marciano should take a lay off from training for a while. Despite repeated heat treatments issued by Brockton's Dr. Michael Del Colliano, nothing was helping to restore full movement to the muscles. Marciano balked at the suggestion of an enforced lay off, after the setback, as he saw it, of being forced to go the distance against Mogard, the last thing he needed was to break the momentum he had rebuilt through his destruction of Haft. No, he would continue, besides Charley Goldman had magic hands, he had sorted out the stiffness before Marciano's last bout when the symptoms had begun to raise their head, he could do it again. The only problem was that Goldman would not be in his corner when he fought Louthis for Charley was in the West Coast with the Argentinean Arturo Godoy. His replacement was Jack Moore, a sometime promoter and trainer who had ingratiated himself with Al Weill back in the thirties.

Moore, who had picked up the sobriquet of 'Doc' took one look at a stiff, suffering Marciano when he turned up for the weigh-in at the New Bedford Page Arena at two on the afternoon of the 16th of August and decided there and then that the fight should be called off immediately.

Rocky insisted he would be OK he just needed to walk the effects off. Besides the stiffness in his back had been exasperated, he felt, by the journey to the venue where he had been cramped up in the back seat of a car driven by Brockton resident, and mutual friend of both he and Colombo, Johnny Jantomaso. "The pain was so bad," recalled Rocky, "that Allie had to walk me around and around the Arena right up to the time of the fight."

The debilitating condition hardly abated however when it came time to enter the ring. Remembered Rocco again, "I could hardly get through the ropes into the ring, Allie Colombo, my closest buddy…had to stretch the lower rope almost down to the canvas and hold the middle rope as high as he could get it…I had a terrible time for the first two rounds."

The above is borne out by the by-line in the following mornings *Providence Journal* that read 'Cumberland Fighter Dominates First Round'. Then, commented journalist Michael J. Thomas:

> In superb condition and showing no fear whatsoever for his foe's known punching prowess, Louthis amazed the crowd by his dynamic opening-round stint.
>
> He stunned Marciano with a solid right, delivered at close quarters that raised a mouse under Rocky's left eye. It was a clean shot that curbed Marciano's offensive operations for the remainder of the canto, which Louthis won conclusively.

Louthis, unaware of Marciano's disability at this stage, saw his chance and tried desperately to seize on it, but try as he may he couldn't land the telling punch that Thomas believed, "would have cut and closed it (*that left eye which was swelling perceptibly*)." Confidence was building in Pete, he always believed that he could beat his opponent (11), a belief developed through observing Rocky many times when he had performed at Providence (*thus negating the allegation made by Sam Silverman that Louthis, "did a choke," because he was, "petrified of Marciano"*).

Following a pattern that would become almost a standard for Marciano in the future however, as the bout progressed into the third-round Rocky began to get into his stride. The accumulation of punches thrown, although seemingly ineffective to the audience safe beyond the confines of the roped square, were taking there inexorable toll on his opponent. Louthis was perceptibly weakening and Rocky was finding his range. Suddenly a lethal left hook exploded off Pete's jaw, and all the hard work that the Providence alumni had put into the first two-stanzas was undone in an instant. 'The Husky Rhode Islander was lifted off his pins,' commented *The Brockton Enterprise-Times*, 'and he hit the canvass on his back with his mouthpiece flying. Louthis rolled over at the count of four, then raised to one knee, but got no further as the referee continued to toll the full count.'

This was indeed the last fight for the thoroughly defeated Louthis. From here on in he seemed to content himself with his new vocation at Providence College where, in 1950, after earning his Master's Degree from Boston University, he became a fully-fledged Athletic Coach. Just two-years later he graduated to the position of Intramural Director where he took charge of the organization and supervision of all athletic programs for the students at his beloved Providence College. There he remained until just a year before his death at the age of sixty-nine in 1991. That his contributions to the college were appreciated is testified to the fact that whilst still incumbent in his position back in 1980 he was elected into the college's Athletic Hall of Fame.

For Rocky this was win number nineteen. He should have been jubilant, his name was in the national press in association with possible contender status, he had not been defeated, all but one victory had come with-in the allotted number of rounds, but still there was that damn back of his. Surely nothing else could go wrong and ruin his chances of making something of his life both for him and his family. He knew he had to get this problem sorted, and sorted fast, so he made a trip to Boston to see a Dr. Thomas B. Quigley who, after a thorough examination concluded that Rocky's original belief that it was nothing more than a trapped nerve was incorrect. Marciano had a slipped disc, possibly caused by that auto accident the previous November (*see chap;'The Fight That nearly Never Was'*), or perhaps that aggravated the earlier incident where a young Rocco had fallen out of the tree whilst pilfering cherries. His only certain cure was an operation, but that would keep Marciano out of the ring for at least a year at best, if not curtail his career for good. For Marciano this was not an option.

After the ups-and-downs of the previous few weeks there was no way he was going to let something else hold him back so he steeled himself for a long, painful self-recuperation. He faithfully visited Dr. Del Colliano at the Brockton hospital to continue his diathermy treatment. To this he added weekly visits to the local YMCA where in-house coach Al Norling would massage the stiff, knotted, muscles of his lower back. As a supplement Rocky would encourage Allie to pull his legs as he hung from a gymnasts bar in order to stretch out his spine. Amazingly this combination seemed to work for with-in a week or two Rocky's back condition was barely noticeable. "But I never knew when the terrible pain would start up again," reflected Marciano. It was like living with a ticking time-bomb, one that could go off at any minute and permanently put an end to his blossoming career.

Notes:

1. *Who had himself several run ins with the mob, including a lead pipe over the head!*
2. *This was especially true of sometime Marchegiano conqueror Colley Wallace who blamed his failure to get a bout with Marciano in the professional ranks to his mobbed up manager Frank 'Blinky' Palermo who himself would retort later, "Hell Wallace was good, but a shot at Marciano, man, he (Wallace) wasn't even in the same league, everyone knew Rocky kicked his...ass in the amateurs, what was the point."*
3. *Harry Haft: Survivor of Auschwitz, challenger of Rocky Marciano. Alan Scott Haft. Syracuse University Press.*
4. *Some say he did so in order to get his name in the paper and prove to the world, and to his lost love, that he was still alive, although the brevity of his career and the fact that those in his native Poland would probably never read the provincial American papers that reported his brief career may count against this theory.*
5. *One can only speculate the fate of Haft had he ever met this opponent in one of those alleged death matches.*
6. *Haft was not the first to claim that he had been asked to take a dive against Marciano, Johnny Pretzie also maintained that he had been asked to "Fall down" if he managed to cut his opponent and the fight looked like it may go in his favour. This seems a strange request for Rocky was not really considered a bleeder until later in his career and bouts were rarely stopped in those days due to blood flow unless it was gushing out in torrents. There is of course no concrete proof beyond the word of some of his opponents that Marciano was aided by elements outside his control in those early days, and then again there is no absolute certainty that he wasn't either.*
7. *As Haft's former captors had labeled him.*
8. *Rocky and Roland were on a collision course when this article came out, Marciano's handlers knew that LaStarza was the hottest heavyweight on the rise and would need to be passed sooner rather than later. Of his last five opponents all had met Roland and lost to him, but Rocky had beaten them all more conclusively thus gaining a psychological advantage over his New York target.*
9. *Marciano was being seriously considered as a possible contender in June of 1950.*

10. *Of which he won nine, losing at the first time of asking to Ted Hendricks due to a severely lacerated eye.*

11. *Most fell into this farfetched optimism before they faced Rocky, "The thing with him," commented future opponent Archie Moore, "was that he looked so beatable."*

part three **chapter twenty-four**

Tommy G.

"Fighting was a means to an end for me, the means was getting paid, the end was getting beat!!"

Tommy Giorgio

Marciano's troublesome back kept him out of the ring for five weeks and there were many in his close retinue who believed that it should have been longer, but as we know Marciano became rusty far quicker than most due in part to his advancing age and his lack of natural ability, at least in terms of boxing prowess. Thus in order to facilitate the Brockton fighters successful return to action his next opponent was unashamedly hand-picked in order to offer the least chance of resistance. Why should it have been otherwise, after all Rocky was fast becoming a rising star, all but one of his bouts had ended early, the crowds were growing larger at almost every appearance, why take a chance at ruining the kid now.

"Everybody rates a sensational young fighter a lot higher than he actually should be," commented Charley Goldman as if to emphasis the point. "To satisfy newspapermen and boxing commissions (*a stab at the Rhode Island commission who sanctioned this bout*), he's often forced in above his head and sometimes even ruined."

Weill (1) had the exact person in mind to ease Rocco through what might perhaps be a very tentative few rounds in the Providence ring, yet still no chances were taken, in preparation for this night Rocky had sparred more rounds than he had previous to any other engagement.

Tommy Giorgio (2) was the charitable man who was chosen it was hoped, to be the one who would ensure Marciano was not too over stretched in what was seen as little more than a glorified sparring match. The only difference being that neither fighter was expected to pull their punches (*Rocky rarely did in practice anyhow*). On paper Giorgio was undoubtedly the perfect man for the job, of his previous eighteen encounters since turning professional some fourteen months earlier against one formidable sounding Jackie Harris, Tommy had run up a nicely balanced record of nine wins and nine losses. So no he was not seen as a real threat. However, of his nine defeats only three had come within the distance, so he was viewed as fairly durable which would be used as a prime reason should the Brockton slugger fail to take this opponent out. Also, in order to eliminate the threat of an upset should the bout go longer than anticipated Giorgio was chosen for his own perceived lack of punching prowess, of his nine victories only one had folded before the final bell.

The fact that he was far from a killer himself in the ring was evidenced on inspection of Tommy's record which was littered by such names as Jim, Ernie and Percy, none of whom stood out as terrible fighting men (3).

Yet as with all those who faced the marauding Marciano, and whose lot it seemed were to be described rather unfairly, yet not without reason, by *The Providence Journal* reporter Michael J. Thomas as, "no more than the rustic fighters Marciano has bowled over," Tommy's story was far more impressive than his record belied.

Tommy had been born around 1926 or '27, I have never been able to find out the exact date for sure at the time of writing (4). Little is known of his youth except that he was born and raised in Schenectady County, New York. His first forays into boxing occurred, as it did for most youths in the late nineteen-thirties and early-forties, when he was drafted into the U.S. Navy during the Second World War. His first bout took place whilst still in basic training, the next three whilst sailing around the Pacific Ocean.

In January of 1947, Giorgio, now released from the service of his country, capped his brief amateur career with victory in the Adirondack Amateur Athletic Union Golden Gloves Championship in Albany, New York and followed this up in April of '48 with third in the National Golden Gloves held in Boston. Three months later he turned professional.

For his initial start in the paid ranks he defeated one Jackie Harris on points over five rounds before ringing up a small string of victories, all but one over the full route, before suffering two setbacks in a row, again it was decisions. Of his next eleven starts he would emerge victorious only four times, however, such was the vagaries of the sport at the time, his losses didn't really count against him when it came to choosing his opponents, or being chosen for them. Many of the journeymen prevalent in the forties were far more polished than we today can imagine, it is easy to look at their records and see the defeats piling up and imagine that these men were used merely to pad records, to make prospects look good. To some extent there is some truth in this, favored fighters would certainly be fed certain types, a slugger, akin to Marciano may be fed a cutie with a perceived granite chin, like Giorgio, in order to see just how powerful a puncher the boy was. Knock out someone with a chin and everyone hails your power, fail to do so and everyone cheers your efforts yet points out that the fighter has a chin of steel, just so long as your boy doesn't end up on the wrong end of the verdict, or look awkward attempting the feat, then you couldn't lose. However, in reality most of those to whom the prefix journeyman has been tagged were more than that. Each began with dreams, perhaps not of becoming champions, but at least of earning an honest living with their fists. Most, if not all were earnest and sincere in their endeavors, at least at the beginning.

When these backbones of the boxing industry were not being used to bloat the record of a promising fighter (5) they were busy fighting each other, and fight they did. A look at the records of those who fought Marciano alone shows a criss-cross of careers. Indeed the records of future opponents like Ted Lowry, Carmine Vingo, Bernie Reynolds, and Roland LaStarza show them spotted with familiar names, and not always against whom were they victorious which goes to show that not all the journeymen of the day were mere names, some were damn good. It was just that through circumstance their lot in life was never fulfilled, their big chance never came. Injury, timing, life, all these things transpired against them. In essence, putting your fighter in against any one of these tigers was a risk, unless of course you had the fight in the bag as it were, a euphemism for some kind of fakery, a knowledge that one of those in the ring was ready to lay down for an extra few bucks, or a shot at someone higher up the ladder.

Giorgio was one of those earnest fighters, he faced no less than three future Marciano opponents in Carmine Vingo, Ted Lowry, and Bernie Reynolds before he stepped into the ring against his most famous nemesis. Sure he lost to both Vingo and Reynolds but he beat Lowry who was one of the most underrated, most distinguished and most inopportune of Rocky's early challengers. Of this victory there was no dispute, Giorgio was not on a winning streak that needed to be preserved, in fact he had just come off two defeats.

Previous to his engagement with Marciano Tommy came mighty close to pulling of the victory of his career when he faced Bernie Reynolds, a man who was being seriously considered future world championship challenger class.

So against Rocky on the evening of September 26th 1949, once more before an almost capacity audience at the Rhode Island Auditorium, most, if not all believed that the Schenectady native would lose, but most too were no doubt in agreement that the boy would at least try his damndest; and try he did. But Michael J. Thomas was less than ebullient the following morning when he reported the bout in *The Providence Journal*:

> Rocky Marciano, young Brockton heavyweight has completed the elementary phase of his fistic education. The time has come to step him up in class...There was ample testimony of this as the powerful Brockton lad, using a preponderance of left hooks, knocked out Tommy Giorgio...in the fourth round of their scheduled 10-rounder at the Auditorium last night...The New Yorker made an earnest enough attempt, was high on durability and courage and even showed flashes of boxing skill...The end came at 2:04 of the fourth session. Sir Punch[6] finished Giorgio with a right and left delivery after he twice had dropped him for nine counts. The first toll, result of a nifty left hook, came in the first round. This was the best punch of the fight and no doubt many of the 2255 customers...were surprised at Giorgio's recovery. They

usually stay put when Sir Punch catches a foe as he did Giorgio on this occasion.

It was here that the author of the above piece decided to pay Giorgio at least some seemingly grudging respect. "But Giorgio not only got up," continued Thomas, "he fought back. It was the same in the fourth round when Marciano dropped him with a right and a left. Tommy just about made it this time however...the fight was interesting as long as it lasted. Giorgio boxed cleverly at times and made Rocky miss by the proverbial mile. Rocky tossed scores of punches in the four rounds pursuing his foe in his usual relentless manner, but he missed almost as often as he landed...Giorgio also leveled some heavy punches in gamely exchanging with Sir Punch. One right raised a mouse under Rocky's left eye in the first round and another drew blood from his nose in the third. But Rocky dominated the battling throughout and there never was any question as to the outcome."

Indeed the end was now inevitable, yet it was not a clean punch that finished Giorgio however, for as Marciano bulled his opponent into the ropes with a thunderous right he followed up immediately and unleashed one of those murderous uppercuts that he so favored as an amateur. Both Rocky's momentum and Giorgio's bouncing off the rope caused the punch to miss it's intended target and Marciano connected to Tommy's exposed chin with his forearm rather than his fist. So exhausted was the game former Adirondack amateur champ that he fell from the sheer persuasive force of the blow and was counted out.

It was a job well done for Rocky. Thankfully his back had held out for now and there had been no perceptible signs of stiffness, plus it appeared the voices who demanded their boy get back into the ring sooner rather later had been right, any rust that had settled on Rocco's compact frame had been shed quickly and almost effortlessly. For him now it was move forward quickly as just two weeks later he would be headlining once more at the Auditorium. Tommy though would lay off for some three-months.

Tommy's next encounter would take place in the famed Madison Square Garden (*ironically on the same bill as Marciano himself who was making his own debut that night*). Again this was a gallant losing effort, the fight being stopped when he was not permitted to leave his corner for the fourth round by a possibly over anxious referee. Now Tommy's career really began to wind down. Over the next nineteen-months he fought professionally only five more times, losing them all, before retiring in the Fall of 1951 with the less than impressive record of nine wins and fifteen defeats. His main event against Marciano remained (*as it had for so many*) a highlight of his boxing career but not the pinnacle, that had occurred in the Spring of 1950 when he faced the former World heavyweight champion Joe Louis.

Louis had finally decided to retire from his coveted position as heavyweight champion after twelve years as the incumbent holder in 1949, almost fully a year after last defending it against Jersey Joe Walcott for the second time. In his absence Ezzard Charles had ascended to the throne. Charles, a hugely talened boxer had the misfortune of following the mighty Louis to the crown and thus his reign was never popular, yet it was, even by modern standards, hugely successful (*leading historian Bert 'Randolph' Sugar to rate him seventh in his list of greatest heavyweight champions, one behind Marciano whom he rated sixth*). The specific details surrounding these events, and Charles' reign will be discussed in more depth later, yet suffice it to say that the public indifference to Ezzard paved the way for Louis' attempt to do the impossible and regain that which many people believed was his by right, namely the heavyweight championship of the world.

Yet Joe was aging, he knew that he could not just jump right back into the ring and fight that would be suicide against a slick boxer like Charles, he needed to get himself back into shape. This he did by staging a series of exhibitions which toured the whole of the Americas.

"I was what they call in boxing a trial horse," recalled Tommy himself in 1985 when he looked back on his meetings with Louis in Brazil during April of 1950. "Joe would fight us to determine the caliber of existing talent without actually going into a regular bout. I went the distance with him in two six-round exhibitions but they weren't of any consequence. They never entered the boxing books as a bona fide contest."

There seems to be some cynicism in Tommy's words as he recounts this meeting, but then perhaps it has more to do with the fact that he was never really over-awed by anyone. And why should he have been, he knew that not everything you thought you knew about a fighter was always the complete truth, most was a means of selling the boxer who was mere merchandise. Heck Tommy knew all the angles when it came to selling fights and fighters'; he knew that what you saw on stage, in the press, was not necessarily the real article.

Giorgio used this to his advantage after he left the boxing ring for when he had unlaced his gloves for the last time in 1951 he immediately turned his attention to professional wrestling. Yet to Tommy, who gained some forty-pounds so as to create a more fearsome physique, wrestling was all a game compared to his former sport. In order to confirm this he even applied to the American Guild of Variety Artists for a license declaring that he, as a wrestler, was merely an actor and deserved to be a part of the Guild (*thus presaging the later formation of the WWE and its overt fakery*).

"You have to be a good actor to be a wrestler," he declared in the same 1985 article in which he also gave away some of the secrets of the wrestling circuit. "Why, sometimes the hardest job you have in the ring is to keep from laughing at the fanatic fan who is getting all steamed up over the drama in the ring."

Tommy's wrestling career, it seemed, was to follow a similar path to his pugilistic one (7), for by the time he was interviewed in 1985 he had retired from wrestling, never having accomplished any great notoriety in his former profession and was by then earning a living as a self-employed general building contractor. At one time he supplemented his income as a sportswriter for the *Glenville Weekly* the local paper from the town he called home in Schenectady, but that had come to an end too over a decade earlier. Yet he did not seem bitter, life had been good to him, perhaps he had given it his best, and at the end of the day that is all any of us can do.

In November of 1996, Thomas Giorgio finally left the stage for good and the man who had as a boxer faced a future and a former world heavyweight champion and who as a wrestler had entertained the masses during the crucial rise in popularity of the "sport" was buried at St. Anthony's Cemetery, Glenville with very little fanfare. His death, like his life, got scant mention outside of his native Schenectady, which was a shame, for he was one of the real characters of the roped arena...

Notes:

1. *Referring here to Al who still ran the show behind the rather transparent scenes, when I refer to Marciano's 'official' manager of the time, Marty I shall use at least his christian name.*
2. *Sometimes presented with the pre-fix Di which his family shed soon after arriving in the America's from Italy.*

3. With all due respect to each of these who to be fair showed real bravado just to step into the ring, yet people respond to names, there is something primal in associating a type to a title, therefore if someone is called Nevil you expect a certain individual, whereas with Rocky whose name seemed to sum him up you expect something entirely different, as reflected historian Bert Sugar in 2005, ""Just say the name, Rocky Marciano, it resonates strength, there's a name...this is not going to be a piano player this is a boxer pure and simple, it's even more than a boxer, Rocky, that's not a dilettante that's a puncher!!"""""

4. January 2011, the fact that he was twenty-two when he faced Marciano in 1949 attests to this date, even his professional record fails to mention the year of his birth.

5. A situation that many of those knew all too well from the side of once being tabbed prospects themselves.

6. Thomas' new nickname for Marciano, he had yet to pick up the more popular 'Blockbuster Blockbuster.'

7. And intertwine at times too for Marciano even refereed matches in which his former adversary took part on more than one occasion, in fact the two were real friends, accompanying each other on fishing trips when their paths crossed.

part three **chapter twenty-five**

The Tiger

"I often wish that I had lost a fight, just to know what it felt like. Not when I held the championship you understand, but one of those early ones where the decision could have gone either way."

Rocky Marciano

Theodore Adolphus Lowry could have been one of the greatest fighters in the history of boxing; he fought most everyone at heavyweight and light-heavy in his time, beat some, lost to others. He was a cutie, a spoiler, an unknown and very dangerous opponent. If ever there was a synonym for 'journeyman' it should have his biography under it for he would fight at a weeks' notice, a days, an hours if he was in the right place. Yeah, this man should have been one of the greatest of all time; if only he had come along a few decades later.

Born on October 27th, 1919, Lowry's early youth was spent in a depression hit New Haven, Connecticut where local transportation was still provided mainly by horse and cart. At the age of ten he lost his father who doted on his youngest son (*there were four other children*) making life even more difficult for the family. Three years after the elder Lowry's parting the family moved to Portland, Maine where when it snowed it was not unusual to see 10 to 12 feet drifts on the promenade that Lowry described as, "beautiful".

Theodore, now more commonly known by the shortened version of 'Ted', grew up to be an athletic youth, trying his hand at most every sport from skiing to marbles. He was competitive in them all, especially basketball. Yet whenever he was quizzed as to what he wanted to be when he grew up his immediate answer would be, "boxer". Strange then that he did not actually don a pair of gloves until he was seventeen, and only then at the goading of his small circle of friends who dared him to enter a touring amateur show that came to Portland (1). Ted entered, took part in three bouts and won them all. For his efforts he was awarded a medal and a robe, it was one of his greatest prizes since he had won a basket of fruit as a child for winning a sixty-meter foot race.

The young Lowry's jump into professional boxing was meteoric, within a short while of his amateur victories he became a sparring partner for an unnamed middleweight who was in town to train for a crack at the middleweight championship of New England. "I gave him a good workout," recalled Lowry (*in his excellent autobiography: God's In My Corner-Publish America, 2006*). "In fact, the workout was so good that my trainer, Roy Brooks, and former heavyweight champion, Jack Sharkey, wanted to take me home to Massachusetts and train me and make a pro out of me."

Before he could go however there was the prospect of asking his mothers' permission. At the time Ted was earning an honest living on the railroad, bringing home eighteen-dollars a week, of which he would, akin to Marciano, give his mother all but 50-cents. Unlike Rocco however he would habitually ask for more at which he would be rebuked, he didn't drink or smoke, so what did he need the money for anyway. "It took some convincing," added Lowry, "but they (*Sharkey & Brooks*) were able to convince my mother I would be able to send money home."

Lowry's first professional encounter occurred on the evening of August 1939 in Portland, a four rounder that was billed as an exhibition against one Winfield Allen. The debutante gained the popular vote and thus notched up his first victory. Over the ensuing three years alone he would build up the remarkable record of sixty-eight bouts, winning forty-two, losing twenty-two, and drawing four. Along the way he picked up the Maine State light heavyweight championship. He also picked up a nickname, one that would stick with him for the rest of his life.

Ted recalled how at one of his earliest fights in New Bedford, Mass, he fought a man who bore upon the back of his robe the legend, "Rhode Island Champion". Lowry admitted to being afraid for the first time in the ring, "I didn't put up much of a fight that night...he won it easily." The young Portland based professional continued to relate how when he returned to his living quarters that he shared with five other hopefuls they showed their mutual disgust at his dire performance by placing his food plate upside down at their communal table. Stuck to the downside of the plate was a note cajoling him for his poor showing. Over the next week none in the household would speak to Ted, he admitted later that he seriously considered returning home, "No one was talking to me anyway so I didn't care."

At the end of the quiet, uncomfortable week Lowry had a fight booked, so he decided to just go in the ring blindly throwing punches until he got knocked out then call it a day. So he followed his game plan and at the bell for the first came out firing everything he had.

"He never really got out of that corner," wrote Lowry. "I dropped him right there in the first round." When the winner returned to his quarters everyone was full of congratulatory fervor, they had given the now conquering hero the silent treatment, they claimed, in order to make him mad. If that was the real reason then it worked, over the ensuing weeks Lowry kept up the tactic, it proved successful, so successful in fact that the local papers picked up on this all attacking fighter and gave him a name that stuck, they called him 'Tiger'.

Yet the now newly clawed 'Tiger' Ted Lowry almost came undone when he met someone who employed the same tactic as he. "I met up with a fighter who met me in my corner, and it was all I could do to get out of it. I was taken by surprise and did not look too good in that fight." As the humbled, seemingly de-clawed fighting animal left the ring, one of the customers yelled out, "You are the tamest tiger I have ever seen!"

In May of 1943 the "tamest tiger" would be caged for the next three years as he was called up to serve his country. His reminiscences of those years in the military make for remarkable reading and are covered in detail in his own work. Very briefly 'Tiger' Ted found himself part of an elite parachute regiment known as 'The Triple Nickels'. His job was to put out fires caused by Japanese incendiary balloons that strayed into American territory. Promoted to Sergeant he found himself taking part in a three-round exhibition with the then world heavyweight champion Joe Louis who believed that Lowry had the potential to become a champion (*it was, said Lowry, the pinnacle of his entire professional career*).

Released from duty the now former, and citationed, soldier returned immediately to the prize ring where between late 1946 (2) and his encounter with Marciano on the evening of Monday October 10th, 1949, the remarkable Lowry took part in no less than forty-one contests against some of the top boxers in the light-heavy and heavy class (3). This time the results were a little less spectacular. He lost some twenty-two of those contests, seven in a row before he met Rocky. Yet he was still dangerous, and as if to prove it he held heavyweight contender Lee Savold to a draw, plus effectively, according to those who witnessed the fight, beat future light-heavyweight champ Archie Moore only to see the verdict go against him (*it is interesting to note that Archie never faced him again*). Yet his performances were becoming erratic to say the least, for not long prior to facing Marciano he had tackled Tommy Giorgio, and lost.

There were many times in the career of 'Tiger' Ted Lowry when lack of preparation may have caused a subpar performance. Not through any real fault of his own, he was always in shape, but often such was the little notice he needed to be ready to fight that he would never get the chance to study an opponent, gage the style and figure it out. There were times too when verdicts may have been swayed in the favor of his opponent, a fighter on the rise who was more valuable than Lowry, especially as the forties moved on towards their conclusion pushing Ted inevitably towards his thirtieth year.

The once young literally hungry fighter never got his breaks, never got his big chance, whatever the reason, whether poor management, or poor treatment. 'Tiger' was swiftly becoming a filler, someone who was convenient, who could be relied upon to turn up at the drop of a hat. The only thing that was never a given was his performance. He could still pull one out of nowhere, he was still slick, he could still show up the inadequacies in any opponent (4). This was all especially true of the night he faced Marciano. Sam Silverman knew this, he knew it only too well, and it was this knowledge which brought Lowry to Providence that night.

Silverman, who still ran the show at The Rhode Island Auditorium explained, "I was becoming disgusted with Al Weill, and wouldn't have minded getting rid of him. Weill wanted too much money. He was getting twenty-five percent of the gate, but the greedy guy wanted thirty. And Weill was looking at getting Rocky soft fights now that he thought he had

found something in Marciano. But I had to protect my club." Ostensibly the astute promoter decided to bring in the 'Tiger' to defeat Marciano and so put Weill in his place by ruining his dream, "I thought Lowry was gonna lick Rocky."
Claims that Marciano's erstwhile manager was still protecting his fighter were countered by Charley Goldman however, "What Weill has done for Rocky is sensational. From the beginning, he realized that he had a green fighter, slow to learn, but who was worth nursing along, carefully. There were a lot of stories that the guys Rocky fought weren't trying and so forth, but none of those stories was right. No fighter who fought Marciano was held back - they were in there to knock him out if they could."
Yet it was Sam himself who was mostly responsible for the caliber of opponents who faced the Brockton fighter in the first year of two of his career, especially in Providence. "Rocky's fights were all legitimate, good hard fights...Marciano could have lost any number of times in his early fights." To all intents and purposes this was not just a bout that Rocky could have lost, but actually should have lost!

Rocky had looked bad in the past, that was his way, he still had not developed into the tight swarming fighter who would terrorize the heavyweight division later in his career. In fact he would never become a text book practitioner of the ancient art of self-defense, yet he had always, and would always find a way to win. Mostly it was through his own efforts. On this night however the way to victory was found, perhaps, through some force beyond himself.

"I hate leaving the result to judges," Marciano was once quoted as saying, "I like to let my fists be the only judge. When others have control of the results there is always the possibility of some skullduggery." Against Lowry the feeling that there was some form of skullduggery afoot was definitely in the air. Reporter Michael J. Thomas, usually such an ardent supporter of Rocco was amongst the majority of voices who felt that Marciano's victorious streak had been ended.

"There were strange developments and questions left unanswered as Rocky Marciano, undefeated young Brockton heavyweight, was awarded a unanimous decision over Tiger Ted Lowry of New Haven in their 10-rounder at the Auditorium last night," wrote Thomas in the following days early edition of *The Providence Journal*.

He continued, "Marciano, in the first place, did not win the fight as this observer saw it. This reporter gave it to Lowry six rounds to four."

Remembered Lowry, "Rocky Marciano was only 26 years old when I came face to face with him...he was an up-and-coming heavyweight...I was 29 years old with a fairly decent record myself...Although Marciano packed a devastating KO punch, I was not intimidated by him or his reputation. I had more experience than he did and-at the time-more knockouts. If anything I think he underestimated me.

"But there was no fear in Rocky Marciano's eyes as we faced off that autumn night...He was cool, calm and collected, and judging by the ovation he received, he was among friends."

Lowry would continue with his recollections of that night. "I had the feeling they were hand-picking his fights, bringing him along. So I was not intimidated by his record. I did not know until I was in the ring with him that he was all that they said he was.

"I will never forget that night. Outside the air was crisp and cool. Inside, the temperature was rising. The bell rang, and Rocky and I moved towards each other. I did not face him; I gave him my side. I moved in on him and he came at me swinging, right then left. Because of the position I was in, he was unable to hit me with his right or his left.

"Rocky stood in a semi-crouch and just kept swinging; he kept coming at me, relentlessly throwing punches. But I wasn't there. I was able to hit him at will." The erudite and literate Lowry regaled us with the first four rounds of the fight, stanzas that he won convincingly.

As Thomas stated in his own article, "Lowry...came close to knocking out Marciano in the second, third and fourth rounds," when, "...Lowry punched as though bent on making a kill...The wonder of it was that Marciano withstood the punishment.
"Lowry stung him with two terrific rights in the first. He rocked him with two vicious uppercuts in the second, either of which would have finished a less durable boxer. And in the fourth Lowry had Marciano in such a bad way that it appeared it would be only a matter of time before he would complete his kill (5)."
Lowry again on his aggressive foe, "I could tell by the expression on his face that he was befuddled and surprised. He had no defense against me. And he was having trouble trying to figure out my style."

However in the fifth things changed, and changed dramatically, suddenly the 'Tiger' seemed to slow down, to go into a shell. "It may have been that Lowry, nine-year ring veteran, tired. It may have been that he weakened from Marciano's unending body attack, but whatever the reason, there was an appreciable decline in his offensive operations in the second half of the fight and it didn't look good to the crowd, nor to this observer." So reported Thomas again. In fact so reticent did Ted seem at times that the referee, Ben MaCulan three times was forced to warn Lowry to open up, once in the fifth and twice in the seventh, even threatening him with disqualification if he failed do so.
In defense the man facing the swarming bull offered up his reasons for his seemingly reticent attitude to trade punches, or at least his inability to do so. "I think the corner men figured out my style somewhat because he came out fighting differently. Instead of rushing me, he moved around me...He slowed down and began to concentrate on what he was doing. He threw a right and then a left hook. I blocked his right hand and threw up my right hand by my

ear to block the hook. That's when I found out he could punch. He hit me on my arm, and I thought he almost broke it."

From now on the former railroad worker would concentrate on preservation by fading away from his adversary's wallops, leaning back, turning slightly to negate their power, yet all the time picking off his opponent whenever he was able. It may have been this that cost him the fight despite his belief that he won at least two of the remaining six rounds, a point agreed to by those present, save Marciano's corner and, more importantly, those judging the fight itself. Marciano was the, "much busier of the two," reiterated the Providence reporter. "He landed three punches to Lowry's one from the fifth round on concentrating wholly on the body. His aggressiveness was probably what caught the eye of the three officials, but his thrusts lacked sting to be effective. Many should have been discounted altogether.

"The bout ended on an exciting note, with Marciano tossing a punch after the bell and Lowry, seemingly aroused, wanting to continue. The referee stepped in and stopped the overtime hostilities. Lowry came close to flattening Rocky just before the finish with a right hook. Marciano rocked, but regained his balance." Thus saw Thomas whose honest appraisal of the events that night showed the reality of a bout which was way too close for comfort for the unbeaten prospect who no doubt stood nervously sweating in the middle of the ring as he awaited the result. When announced it would send the crowd of 3695 into a frenzy of booing and cries of fix (*the local Brocton paper, who saw their boy as a conclusive winner, commented on the boos of the crowd but only in passing and more due, it was claimed, to the fact that perhaps they had bet on Lowry to win at odds of 100 to 35 against*).

The beaten fighter was magnanimous in defeat. He was used by now to decisions being awarded against him. Yet as he made his way through the Auditorium to his dressing room he must have felt like the deserved winner as many in the disappointed crowd rallied to his side with pats on the back and voices filled with approval at his performance, and equal disgust at the result.

"I don't want to take anything away from Rocky," composed Lowry in his own recollections published in 2006. "He was a good fighter, well conditioned and tough...I know that when I was in the ring with Rocky Marciano, I was in the ring with a fighter -not a boxer- and he was a good one. But -perhaps to Rocky's surprise- I was a good boxer and a smart fighter too. "No one can tell me differently: I know I beat Rocky Marciano in our first fight and, if he were alive today and wanted to set the record straight, he would tell you the same."

Notes:

1. *Lowry admitted that one of the real reasons he wanted to become a boxer was to avenge being knocked to the floor by the father of a girl he yearned to court, he never did get the chance to avenge this humiliation.*
2. *He had partaken in only four fights whilst in the forces.*
3. *Lowry himself could easily move between the two categories scaling in as low as 162lbs or as high as 185.*
4. *As Lowry himself recalled, "Nobody who held a title wanted to fight me. I was what you might call a spoiler. So, I spent most of my time fighting in small clubs."*
5. *"In my impression the bell saved him" offered up Lowry.*

part three

chapter twenty-six

Breakthrough

"I don't envy anyone who tries to write my story because it's really pretty boring, especially in my early career - I mean, all I ever did was train and fight."

Rocky Marciano

The above statement, attributed to Marciano circa 1956, in some respects is absolutely right for that was all he seemed to do from late 1948 through '49, train, fight, fight, train. Even in the periods where he was forced to lay off due to some, what to him was viewed as minor inconveniences, like a broken hand or slipped disc, he still concentrated on improving himself, whether that was strengthening his body, or expanding his mind.

"He did a lot of reading," remembered his youngest brother Peter Marciano, "He wasn't the stereotypical kind of fighter that you may have met back in those days. Rocky was a well read guy."

The one thing that he did not want to be seen as was a brute, particularly as his fame began to spread later in his career. Most pugs and ex-pugs of the time (*as they still are to some extent today*) would be caricatured by the infamous "doe's and dem's" cartoon figures of lore. The oafish, thick skulled, addled brained thugs, sometimes good, sometimes bad, but never really in control of their selves, speaking in slow droning, monosyllabic ways, who populated the media and entertainment industry of the day (*one only has to reference the portrayals of Lenny in the various motion picture versions of John Steinbeck's Of Mice and Men to see clearly what is meant*).

Rocco could never be accused of having a gruff, slow speaking voice, if anything it was the antithesis of the archetype for he spoke with a soft, almost lyrical accent, prolonging his A's and silencing his R's as do many native to Massachusetts. In his local tongue the adopted surname that he would become famous by would be pronounced "Maaciaano".

There would be some who would be more prosaic when describing his particular timbre. "He has no coarseness about him," wrote Nat Fleischer, editor of the Ring magazine, shortly after Marciano had ascended to the title. "He comes across as a shy, typical Momma's boy whose almost angelic voice is not vulgarized by either smoking or swearing." It was true that Rocky no longer smoked, and in public he never swore, but when the doors were closed, or he was in the company of close and trusted friends, he knew all the words that three years in the forces would have taught him, and there is little doubt that he used a few of them immediately after his bout against Lowry.

One can only speculate as to his mood in the dressing room immediately after those evenings events. Judging by previous experience it was probably very black. The only real verified account of a reaction by someone in the fighters immediate circle was from Sam Silverman himself, the man who had sent Lowry against Rocky with the intention of spoiling his perfect record, if only to ruin things for Al Weill (1). For despite his plans seemingly going awry he seemed filled only with praise when he commented dryly to the man who was driving the Boston resident home after the bout that Rocky was, "...one tough son of a bitch. He's going to beat a lot of good fighters."

Silverman was right, Rocky would indeed go on to beat, "a lot of good fighters", but right now the only concern of those who steered his career was that he just beat a fighter, any fighter, and did so convincingly.

The problem was that there was a sudden paucity of fighters available, everyone was tied up elsewhere, at least this is what was told to Silverman, Almeida, and company when they approached to find names to face Marciano. For this reason alone Rocco remained out of action for four weeks before again entering the Providence ring to face opponent number twenty-two who was another of those who believed they had the number of this Brockton heavyweight. The fighter in question had formed this opinion on the evening of September twenty-sixth when Rocky, still working out the kinks in his back, forced out a four-round victory over Giorgio.

Joe Domonic, sometimes Domonick, had been in Tommy's corner the night that Marciano labored to a win. Before the bout Joe had expressed his eagerness to face Rocky, believing that he could beat the upstart, after the bout he was more convinced than ever that he could turn the trick. "Nothing will happen to me," commented a overtly confidant Domonic at the time, "I have met plenty of tough boys before and when I played tackle for Oklahoma University I got used to being roughed around. Rocky Marciano will not hurt me. I saw him fight, and I know what I can do with him. I will go after a knockout, and early."

The prospect of Dominic facing off against Marciano was, it appears, a mouthwatering one, "He looks," wrote Thomas in the *Providence Journal*, meaning Domonic, "as though he'd be the one to test Rocky if and when they (*his managers*) separate Sir Punch from the lesser lights."

It seems that at the time Joe Domonic was being touted as a prospect, one to watch in the Massachusetts area, his two close bouts with New England Heavyweight champion Bernie Reynolds, and the perpetual opponent of all, Roland LaStarza, who he put down twice, plus a unanimous decision victory over former world title challenging Tami Mauriello, had lent him prestige. He was a fighter on the way up when Marciano faced him, despite a recent setback against an unheralded Steve King.

Initially the team that guided Domonic [2], claimed that the defeat to King was down to their boy being stymied by a damaged shoulder, added to this he also had a terrific cold which had sapped his stamina. However, so one sided was King's victory over the allegedly hapless Holyoke native that all that had been built up concerning the future for this former Staunton Military Academy and Oklahoma University amateur heavy king was cast in doubt. There were two proposed bouts tentatively scheduled into Domonic's immediate future [3], the first was against one Joe Baksi, the other, with Cesar Brion.

Baksi and Brion were fringe competitors, both experienced and dangerous, yet both seemed to blow their biggest chances and never fulfilled their potentials. The bout with Brion was to be of particular importance, the winner of that one would be pushed on towards the top, for both fighters this was a huge chance, yet Brion, or at least his camp, pulled out, perhaps after Domonic's loss in such a manner those in control thought that there was little to be gained but a hell-of-a-lot to lose in taking the fight. So Joe was left without an opponent. He contented himself instead with an exhibition against Joe Louis on the former champions barnstorming tour of the country in late October, before bagging the bout he sought with Marciano.

Despite initial reticence from Weill in actuality no matter which way you looked at it this fight was a given, for Domonic it was his chance to both erase the memory of that loss (*his tenth in twenty-nine starts*) and restore his prospects in the professional ring, for Marciano it was the opportunity to respond to the allegations that he was fighting set-ups whose only job it was to look good falling down, and that those who refused made Rocky look clumsy and awkward as he fumbled his way to victory. Domonic was going to test Rocky, there was no doubt about it, most in the press thought that Marciano would have to be at the top of his game to stand a chance in this one (*in fact for the first time a return clause was written into the contract should Rocky lose*)!

A little over six-and-a-half minutes after the opening bell the crowd in Providence had seen enough and began jostling their way towards the ring in order to vent their collective emotions, yet it was neither derision nor scorn which they wished to express, rather euphoria, for it was perhaps here, on Monday November 7th, 1949, that the legend of Rocky Marciano was finally born.

Michael J. Thomas was in ebullient mood as he reported the following day the news that Marciano, now "an embryonic Dempsey" sent the crowd, "into a frenzy by the toe-to-toe milling and Marciano's devastating punching." Within moments of the opening bell it was made obvious that Joe was in way over his head as Marciano literally nailed his opponent to the canvass with a rugged left hook, right hook combination, it was the first time that Joe had been taken off his feet since he had turned professional eighteen months before.

"Joe was up at eight and fought back as Marciano sought vainly to complete the kill," scribed Thomas, before continuing. "It was apparent then that Domonic was doomed to a sad finish...Rocky was poised and sharp. He has shed the clumsiness of past performances and was even boxing with high skill. Overnight he had become a polished performer."

Marciano's improvements were summed up in *The Brockton Enterprise-Times*, "Marciano was more accurate than usual in tossing his lethal blows, never missing his target and refraining from the customary wasteful wild swings. He showed improvement in his footwork that gave more effective leverage to his punch throwing."

The end came in the second; first the helpless Domonic was dropped hard for a count as Marciano relentlessly picked his opponent apart with shots to both the head and body. Then came the end, a long right that sent Joe to the canvass.
"The third time he went down," commented former smalltime fight raconteur Angelo Pucci who attended the bout, "everybody thought he was knocked dead. He was not only knocked out in the second round, he was stiffened like a frozen horse!"
"I figured I could knock him out," offered up the defeated Domonic who had taken fully ten seconds after the count to regain any sense of himself. I didn't dream he could hit like that, that's why I mixed it."
Many years later in his ghosted autobiography serialized in *The Saturday Evening Post* during the latter half of 1956, Marciano gave the reason for his calculated victory. Dominic it seems had made Rocky mad, "He ridiculed me. He said I was nothing but an amateur." Despite his fast growing public image it seemed that it was still not at all wise to cross Marciano.

This was incredibly almost the end of Joe Domonic, he disappears from records and archives like a willow-the-wisp, it seems his defeat at the hands of Marciano was so convincing that he called it time on his career not long afterward, I have found only one verified encounter post-Rocky, in February 1950 when he lost to another touted heavy in Art Henri (*an additional one of those who never quite made it past journeyman status*). Now he truly is nothing more than a name on a record, such is the mystery of Joe Domonic.

Rocky Marciano on the other hand was just beginning to blossom. Soon, in the hope of nurturing this fistic flower he would be planted in Al Weill's very own garden, there to be displayed for all to see, and what a sight he would be.

The garden in question was none other than the one on Madison Square, or to be honest the one on the corner of 50th Street and Eight Avenue.

Madison Square Garden has become one of the most instantly recognized venues in the world, yet the incarnation that stands today is not the original, in fact it is not even on the same site. The original garden stood on Madison Avenue and was the brainchild of that celebrated purveyor of bluff and wonder Phineus T. Barnum who converted a former railroad terminal into an extravagant theater of dreams entitled, majestically, "Barnum's Monster Classical and Geological Hippodrome," in 1871. By 1879 the building had changed hands twice more, becoming first "Gilmore's Garden" after popular American band leader Patrick Gilmore who leased the open air venue in order to hold temperance and revival meetings popular at the time (4), before falling into the hands of the affluent Vanderbilt family who turned the arena over to sports of all descriptions, including boxing. It was they who renamed the structure, "Madison Square Garden".

Soon however the Vanderbilt's would be forced to sell the old Garden before it fell down around them. Fortunately the new consortium that took over razed the building to the ground before erecting a brand new, half-a-million dollar enterprise over the old site. This new building, also named "Madison Square Garden" stood for thirty-six years until she too was torn down and the entire city block upon which she stood was swallowed up by the monumental New York Life Insurance Building which still stands today.

Such was the myth of the Garden however that a third incarnation was already under construction as the second one came down this time at 50th and 8th. Built by boxing promoter extraordinaire Tex Rickard's, and nicknamed "The House That Tex Built" this rather dour, in comparison to the building it replaced, looking construction would quickly become a mecca for boxing fans throughout America who thronged in their thousands to the smoke filled, cramped, three-tiered brick shaped auditorium. Legends were made under her inauspicious roof, they were also shattered. Such was her status for making and breaking careers that by the late-forties anyone who wanted to be anyone in the nefarious fight game knew they had to be seen in that prestigious ring if they wanted any chance at all of making it big.

When Al Weill again took control of her fortunes, or at least of the fortunes of those who graced her stage, it was a given that his most prized possession would one day make his appearance, it was just a matter of time, or more precisely, of timing. It seemed that Al was waiting until his potential meal ticket showed himself, now he had. Still it was a gamble for the last time that Marciano had really been touted amongst the fight cognoscenti back in December of '48 in Philadelphia was, on the face of it, a disaster (*see chap. One step forward...*). Perhaps on reflection Weill had rushed his boy, something that he was rarely accused off at the best of times, or maybe he really had seen something special from the beginning for despite all the talk that there was nothing going in favor of this, as Weill himself would have us believe, one-dimensional fighter whose only saving grace was his punch. Al stood by him, in fact he showed remarkable faith in Marciano (5).

Perhaps there is an argument that Marciano was a far rounder fighter at the beginning than many would have us believe, he had after all proved a sensation at amateur, maybe Weill denigrated his charge, belittled his ability, down played his natural gifts, in order to take credit himself for creating a truly remarkable fighter (6). If this was so then he had incredible foresight, or perhaps not. Official stories of the discovering of Rocco did not begin to appear until 1950 by which time sometime former Marciano manager and press agent *par excellence,* Chick Wergeles, was holed up and employed at the Marciano camp under dubious terms.

"Chick really was a twister of tales," once commented the late Sam Silverman. "He came up with the image of Rocky that the press see today. Sure Rocco was a fighter first and foremost, sure he threw the textbook out the window, at the beginning it was his punch that sold him, but that boy was never as green as Al and Charley (*Goldman*) made out. I should know, I was there!"

Still, assumptions aside, Marciano was deemed ready for the Garden, or more than likely Al Weill was ready to unleash Marciano once again, although under the helm of his step-son, Marty Weill.

On the occasion of Rocky's first appearance at the prestigious venue on Friday, December 2nd, 1949, he was not the main attraction, that distinction belonged to the undefeated sensation that was Roland LaStarza who was making his sixth appearance at the coveted arena, this time against Cesar Brion, the same Brion who pulled out of the bout with Domonic the month before. That morning's papers are filled with gushing praise for the Bronx butchers son, and college educated, LaStarza who was facing the railroad inspector's son from Argentina, Brion. The winner of the bout having dangled before his eyes that richest of carrots, a crack at the heavyweight championship of the world. Perhaps their shot could come within the next three months promised Garden matchmaker Al Weill.

Indeed the top of the bill between the athletic LaStarza and Brion -whom one rather cruel scribe from Missouri's *Daily Capital News* described as, "tall and rather fragile looking, with thin arms and small hands"- was an earnest attempt to inject fresh blood into the heavyweight scene. For too long now Joe Louis' domination had left little room for new faces to make a mark for themselves. Now with Louis retired it was time for younger blood to be transfused into the anemic division. It was hoped that the winner of this one would be the standard bearer who would go forward to revitalize the sport, for as the saying went, "So goes the heavyweight's so goes boxing." There were many then, as today, who believed that if the cream of the crop, namely the heavies, were poor then the rest of boxing would suffer. This was never true for when people found the top division boring they turned to the lower weights and the likes of Marcel Cerdan, Jake LaMotta, Rocky Graziano, Willie Pep, and "Sugar" Ray Robinson.

The main event, that show which was promising to deliver a future champion, was a dud. Most writers felt that on this showing incumbent champion Charles had very little to worry about from either man in the ring that night. LaStarza, predominately a counterpuncher, won the decision over ten-rounds, the first two of which were amongst the most thrilling seen in the Garden, the last eight of which however were amongst the most boring ever seen. Nevertheless the fans, who booed the action given by the two principle protagonists, were given a treat in the scheduled eight-round semi-final, a bout between Marciano and one Pat Richards which stole the show.

Richards, who also went by the moniker of "Irish," had been a professional since October of 1946 when he had taken the decision off one Sherman Washington over six rounds. In his very next outing though the then Pre-Med student studying at Ohio State University who boxed merely to pay his tuition fees lost via stoppage in the first round to Joe Browne, he would not lose again in his next twenty-one starts. Yet there was a shadow hanging over the athletic, hardworking and seemingly sincere Richards [7], and that shadow was the mob. Pat's manager was the notorious Frank 'Blinky' Palermo, a well-known figure with underworld connections, in particular the dark czar of boxing himself, Frankie Carbo.

This connection inevitably leads to questions over the veracity of Richards bouts, particularly the fact that by the time he met Rocky "Irish" Pat had a record that consisted of twenty-three wins (*15-KOs*), six losses, and no-less than five draws. These last results bring to mind that all is not right, one draw, yeah, two even, but five, no-one has five draws. That is unless someone is trying to fiddle the numbers, in essence, making doubly sure they do not lose. Unfortunately Richards' connections taint this bout, for me at least.

Nevertheless that Marciano captured the imagination of all in attendance that night as he blew his opponent away inside of two-rounds, is not disputed [8].

Rocky unceremoniously belted Richards into a sitting position midway through the second stanza whereupon the referee Frank Fullam waved proceedings to an end. Marciano clearly came to fight, the question was had Richards?

There was no complaint from anyone in the Auditorium that evening about the bout ending too early, clearly Richards was in way over his head. Nevertheless any initial euphoria over Rocky's Garden debut was soon put into context by nationally syndicated sports columnist Red Smith when he composed his weekly column entitled, 'VIEWS OF SPORTS' the following Wednesday in which he discussed that evening's event:

A departing customer was heard to say that Rocky Marciano, winner of the semi-finals, could have whipped either principal (*refering to Brion and LaStarza*). Maybe so, for the little athlete from Brockton, Mass., punched handsomely to dispose of Irish PatRichards in the second round. On the other hand, either Lastarza or Brion might have looked like Dempsey against Richards...Marciano, a superbly built animal and a flat-footed hitter, dropped Richards with a right followed by a left hook in the first round. Mr. Fullam, rushed in formenting peace, wiped resin from Richards' gloves and inched aside while Marciano waited. Richards gazed around vacantly, wiped his own gloves on his trunks and finally gave a bewildered nod when Fullam spoke to him. Thereafter the referee was poised as though on springs, leaping in to protect Richards if Marciano so much as frowned. A right put Richards down again for an eight-count in the first round, and when a left to the temple caused him to seat himself briefly on the bottom rope in the second, Mr. Fullam declared an armistice over Pat's puzzled protests. Richards appeared undamaged but Mr. Fullam could bear no more.

Smith was not the only one who seemed to be disparaging the victory; some spoke about how Rocky still appeared to be a little amateurish, even to the point of clumsiness. To these though Charley Goldman replied with not an attempt to hide his contempt; "Let them laugh at him. Rocky can hit and he can take a punch. He lives clean and he can fight forever. He fights the tough punchers and don't get hurt and knocks them out, and he fights the clever boxers and knocks them out too, or at least beats them bad enough to get the decision."

Much as Domonic before him Richards too pales into nothingness after his meeting with Marciano. Indeed after Rocky he does not even set foot in the ring again for some four years when he faces the unheralded Hosea Chapman and is stopped in the sixth, after this there is no more. We have a birth date for him of December 15th 1923, but no news of what became of him after his career wound down, of how he lived, and how he died, assuming of course that he is no longer around (9).

There is little doubt though that all involved with Marciano were jubilant at his success, in particular Al Weill. This time he had kept his championing of Rocky to himself, primarily because no one was supposed to know that the fighter was still his, but even to his closest friends he kept quiet. Now however things were different, Marciano had performed in front of his biggest audience, and received his biggest pay day to boot $1,500. He had also seen in the flesh the one he considered to be his biggest obstacle, the one he had to beat if he was going to make something out of his sport, namely Roland LaStarza.

That LaStarza had been in Rocky's sights for some time was attested to by former opponent Don Mogard who recalled immediately after their own tussle the pair speaking in the dressing room, "I was talking to him in the shower after the fight and he wanted to know about Roland LaSatarza the top young heavyweight around at that time. I had fought and lost to him twice.

Rocky saw the first one and said he thought I won it but I think he was just being polite. I told him he should wait until he had a few more fights before taking on LaStarza."

After his poor showing against Brion Marciano would be next in line for LaStarza, but for Marciano he had two more to get past first.

First up was a return to Providence on the night of December 19th against a real ring worn and experienced trial horse by the name of Phil Muscato who was having his eighty-seventh professional fight since turning to the paid ranks in 1942. Of his eighty-six previous outings he had won fifty-six, included in his resume were victories over the likes of future light-heavy champ Joey Maxim, heavyweight contenders Lee Oma and Lee Savold, and finally the inevitable 'Tiger' Ted Lowry. Yet despite his remarkable record Phil had never managed to claim a shot at the championship, even though he did manage to get as high as number 5 in the heavyweight rankings back in the mid-forties. But he hit a slide, as seemed to be his way, he could not hold together any real consistency. He would win a few, then lose, always getting close before falling away. He must have been an immensely frustrating fighter to manage; in fact he must have been frustrated full stop. Seven years of effort, and all for nothing but memories.

Sometimes memories are not enough, fighters crave the tangible, like belts and trophies, and respect, which although cannot be held in the palm of your hand is still something that must be earned. All who enter the ring want it because fighting is the loneliest job in the world. "Once you're in there (*the ring*)," wrote Marciano, "…there's a terrible loneliness. You can have a gang travelling with you wherever you go, and mobs of guys in your camps, and three or four guys in your corner. But when the bell rings, you're out there all alone, and nobody in the whole world can help you but yourself. It's a thing you got to get used to and a thing you got to understand."

Again a Marciano adversary was touted as a tough test, but this time with some justification for Phil held victories over perennial contenders Lee Oma (*twice*), Lee Savold (*also twice*), and former world light-heavy champ Joey maxim, by dint of these Muscato was the heavy favourite going into this one, however what seemed to be overlooked by all but Rocky's astute handlers was the fact that Phil was on a losing streak now, his glory days were perhaps behind him but still he was vastly experienced and this surely should give the Buffalo native an advantage. Despite the fact that Muscato had been selling his wares in American rings since before Marciano had even donned a pair of gloves in earnest did not mean that Phil was ancient, in fact he was only six months older than Rocky himself. But of course the slightly younger man was also the fresher due to the fact that he had been fighting professionally for only eighteen months. Still, few people could have predicted how convincingly Marciano would take this seasoned campaigner apart.

"The boxing world at long last appears to have the smashing, power punching heavyweight fighter it has sought," eulogized Michael J. Thomas in his latest instalment in the Marciano saga. He continued in full praise of Rocco who, "may only be a year or two removed from world conquest...(*and*)...who punches with the savageness of Dempsey and the wild ferocity of Firpo...Rocky gave a terrific display of punching power in defeating as game a heavyweight as ever has fought here. Tossing power laden overhand rights and ripping left hooks, Marciano dropped Muscato nine times, but Phil was still on his feet at the finish of one of the best heavyweight scraps ever held here."

Twice the game veteran was saved by the bell when at the end of the third and fourth rounds he dropped from sheer exhaustion, he crumpled three times in the second and fourth, twice in the third then again in the fifth and final round. At last the referee Sharkey Buonanno saw sense and called a halt to proceedings at the 1:15 mark of the fifth. At the end all in attendance were on their feet cheering with a mixture of excitement, awe, and amazement. Few could believe that Muscato was able to take the beating he seemed to be taking yet keep attempting to carry on.

"Why the guy remained dangerous until the fourth round," remarked Marciano's trainer Charley Goldman who was becoming a fixture in his charges corner now. "I've seldom seen," Charley continued, "a fighter fight back and toss punches as Muscato did after the battering he took."

It seemed in fact that Muscato was indeed still, "a dangerous fighter at all times." *The Brockton Enterprise-Times* again, 'for spells late in the third and fourth rounds as well as the early going of the fifth canto it appeared the Ward 2 bomber (*Marciano*) was on the careless side. He was over-anxious, driving for the "kill" and leaving himself open. But as he will explain, Rocky knew he had Buffalo Phil in a bad way and only himself realized he could take anything his weakening opponent could dish out.'

As for the game but totally defeated challenger he had this to say, "I'd like to meet him (*Marciano*) again, he's a good prospect and hits hard but I still believe I can beat him." When members of the press complimented Phil on his brave stand he replied simply and with little sign of bravado, "Heck, that wasn't nothing, I've been in tougher battles than that." Tougher battles he may have been in before, but awaiting him after his defeat at the pulverizing hands of Marciano were future world heavyweight challenger Nick Barone and perennial contender Harry Matthews (10). Phil lost both these and called it a day after eight years of struggle and sacrifice, for him it was the end of the road, for his conqueror however the future began to really open up.

"I'll tell you when it really crossed my mind," he replied to reporter Bryan Egan when quizzed as to when he believed he could go all the way to the title. "It was the night of December 19th, 1949. That night I had Phil Muscato down five times (*sic*)...Afterwards, I drove back to Brockton with my pals and then, when we were driving along, one of them said 'You know Rock, you haven't got far to go now.' 'Go where?' I asked. 'To the title,' said he. 'About five good wins and you can be on top of the heap'."

"Then we started figuring who I'd have to get by...Roland LaStarza, Rex Layne, Joe Louis, if he made a comeback, Jersey Joe Walcott, and Ezzard Charles.

"When I got to bed that night I couldn't sleep. That was the first I got round to thinking I could be champion of the world."

For Marciano the future really loomed large now, he dared to dream, at last, that perhaps he could make it, he could really do something amazing. Sadly for Muscato though, his dreams were done.

Phil tried his hand at wrestling in the fifties, apart from that he kept himself to himself until his death in 1991, another one whose voice was lost to the ages. Still at least he had years to at least allow his voice the chance to speak of his encounter with Rocco whereas Marciano's next opponent would never speak of his encounter with Rocky principally because he couldn't even remember it!

Notes:

1. And as the promoter and instigator of the show perhaps exhibit A in defense of a clean result, for if Silverman really wanted Rocky to lose that night then the judges would have no doubt acquiesced to his wishes and not courted the unpopular reaction that they received by giving Rocky the nod.

2. Which included trainer Dan Florio who would get to know Marciano only to well over the ensuing years.

3. Apart from the one against Marty Monforte that was canceled almost immediately after the king defeat in order to add weight to the claim that Domonic was suffering with some form of injury.

4. These gatherings of like-minded sorts who advocated the abstaining from drinking alcohol as too much of this liqueur, so they believed would lead to ruin, would later lead to prohibition, the conclusion of which proved, ironically, that not enough liqueur would lead to ruin.

5. There are those who claim that Weill really didn't know what he had, or else he would not have allowed Rocky to leave New York and fight in Providence, these claims can be countered through sheer expediency for when Weill, and the rest of the world for that matter, knew exactly what he had later in his fighters career he still let Marciano return to Providence.

6. Even during Marciano's titled years Weill continued to put down and belittle his charge at every opportunity, even to the champions face.

7. Who was once a favorite of Ross Murray who built a gym at his estate in order for Richards to train when he was in the area, the same gym that Marciano himself occasionally used.

8. Included in the crowd are friends from Brockton, he knew they were coming through his constant correspondence with his beloved Barbara, many of Rocco's letters contain simply the seemingly mundane, hours of constant training, occasional trips out to publicity offices giving interviews, trips to shows to see, amongst others, entertainer Vic Damone; at times he would show his own childish awe at being in a city filled with celebrities, in one letter he notes to Barbara how he had seen a wrestler by the name of Jock Kelly, "Remember him," Rocky wrote, "He always wore the pants with the knee guards. That nite (sic) blood came from his head you almost cried." Some of the letters are revealing of his personality, like when he lets Barbara know that he is happy for her to go out so long as it is with her girlfriends because, "It's OK to go out with a bunch of girls anyplace you wish. I really can trust you anyhow. You should feel the same about me..." In reference to this very upcoming bout Rocky is keen to get home, but admits that he may be a day or two later

than he hoped, but "At least I'll be making good money from now on (I hope)." He ends some with the pseudonym he lives under at William Sloane House, John Oddo.

9. I wish more writers had thought of what stories these men could have told whilst they lived, such tales lost, not just of Marciano, but of a whole generation of boxing when it was at its peak.

10. Muscato's last four fights were against world class opposition for prior to his bout with Marciano he had lost to future world light-heavy champ and later challenger for Marciano's crown, Archie Moore.

part three   chapter twenty-seven

Carmine

"When I went into the ring against Rocky that night, the only thing I had on my mind was that I had enough in me to go the limit if the fight had to go that far. I wanted to put on a good show, like I always wanted to do. Who'd ever believe it? I figured the worst that could happen was to get knocked out. Actually I was figurin' on winning."

Carmine Vingo

Carmine 'Bingo' Vingo was born December 29th, 1929, twenty years and one day later he very nearly died. It is this morbid fact for which he is remembered today, that and at whose hands he nearly succumbed. Had he died the boxing world would have mourned the loss of a young, hugely promising fighter, at least for a while, soon he would have become nothing more than another statistic, a name dragged up when tragedy again struck in a boxing ring. Such was the fate of one Ernie Schaaf a New England heavy who had died in the very same ring as Vingo's near fatality after taking a beating at the hands of the giant Primo Carnera back in 1933 (*although later Schaaf's death would be attributed to a previous battering he received at the hands of future champion Max Baer*). Boxing may have also suffered another huge loss that night had Vingo failed to recover, for the sport may have lost Marciano too.

"As a boy my son he say to me, 'Poppa, I afraid, I afraid that one day I may hit someone and kill them!' " Thus recalled Piereno Marchegiano shortly after his son's rise to the heavyweight championship when recalling that dreadful night in Madison Square some three years before.

Had Carmine lost his greatest battle perhaps Rocky would have walked away from the sport; that at least is the prevailing view, however others felt differently, even his closest friend Allie Colombo later conceded that perhaps he would have carried on. "'The Rock' was a fighter pure and simple; nothing would have set him back for long. (1)"

Yet all that was fated to transpire was the furthest from the minds of those involved as the day of the fight rolled out on her inextricable course. Vingo, who at six-foot-four and scaling a solid and powerful 190-pound was a heavy on the rise, and a truly genuine threat.

So far he had taken part in eighteen professional engagements since turning pro in January of 1948, winning all but one (*and that reversal was to a young future fringe contender named Joe Lindsay over four torrid rounds*). He had, despite being labeled a rugged puncher, stopped just seven of those who had faced him, but he was still learning and maturing, today was his make-or-break fight, a semi-final at the Garden against a man who had begun to light up the boxing hemisphere with his last three performances.

"I knew that a victory over Rocky was all that stood between me and the rest of my life, win that one and our future (*his and his fiancee Kitty Rhea*) would be golden," remarked Carmine many years later (*in fact so sure was he of victory that he allegedly sent an unnamed cousin off with a couple-hundred-dollars to bet on the outcome*).

For Rocky too this fight, should it go his way, would be the culmination of all that had gone before in the previous two months since his ten forced, abysmal rounds against Lowry. His management had taken chances against Domonic, played safe with Richards, and again laid out a calculated risk with Muscato. Their charge had come through them all with flying colors. One wonders though, especially those bouts held in Providence, how many Al Weill had a hand in, certainly outside of New York Weill had to be cautious, not make it to obvious that he was still in control, so one assumes that Silverman and Almeida, as alleged above, were the ones steering the career of Marciano.

Al was sometimes over cautious, as would be seen later in Rocky's career when his fighter was really in the headlines. Weill then would almost coddle his fighter by wrapping him proverbially in cotton wool, particularly when he had a bad showing.

"I give 'em some easy pay days after a bad night, just to boost their confidence," Weill once mused to a reporter who was eager to find the secrets of good management. But sometimes that led to complacency, and a sense of false bravado, despite Weill's statement that he told his acquaintance's in Providence, "not to feed his boy set-ups", one cannot help feel that this is another of Weill's later statements used to revise the past in order to suit he, the king maker.

I doubt that Weill would have settled for the dangerous Domonic as the next bout after Lowry, yet there is no doubt that Vingo was all down to Al. He needed to take a chance now and he knew it, especially with New York's golden boy LaStarza looking anything less than impressive in his last outing. Thus with Marciano overshadowing Roland, the fight crowd in 'The Big Apple' needed to see what he could do again, this time against a boy that the locals knew, who they followed and saw running down their own streets, for if Rocky was going to win over fans outside of Providence, let alone Massachusetts, he needed to take out a few boys in their own backyards and, akin to a victorious barbarian general, win to him their army of adoring crowds.

So this was a fight that had to happen, it was a natural progression, winning and looking good doing it would move the victor onwards and upwards, defeat, then back to the beginning. For Vingo he could still rebuild his career, he had done it before, for Marciano, one felt however that defeat would signal the end of his at a time when it was beginning to catch on fire, this was his chance, he had to take it with both hands.

From the outset both fighters threw all limited ring craft aside and banged away, as reported James P. Dawson in the following mornings *New York Times*, "The savage fury of the Marciano-Vingo bout...presaged a knockout without the threat of serious consequences. They fought at a pace that would have done credit to lightweights in a slam bang, knock down and drag out battle.

"Marciano...piled into Vingo from the opening bell. The Bay Stater floored Vingo for a count of nine in a blazing outburst of flying fists; a left hook to jaw was the knockdown punch. Arising from this knockdown Vingo fought back desperately, trading blows with his rival, until a right to the jaw rocked Marciano and threatened to turn the tide of battle. Marciano recovered from this damaging blow, however and resumed the offensive in a burst of punching that had the crowd on its feet yelling wildly."

Years later Marciano still recalled that one punch, remembering it as the hardest he ever got hit in his life, "Walcott knocked me down and Moore knocked me down but they didn't hurt me. Vingo hit me a right hand and I blacked out but didn't go down. Just fell into a clinch...In all honesty that blow...was the worst I ever felt."

Dawson continued to recount the battle that Friday night which captivated and enthralled a crowd of some nine-thousand who had come to see if this boy from the little known city of Brockton was anything like he had been built up to be; by the end of the evening all in attendance would have to admit that he most definitely was:

> A duplicate second round followed. Head-to-head, toe-to-toe they fought like two lightweights instead of the heavyweight they are. Smashing drives thudded home to the body; wicked rights and lefts caromed (*sic*) off face, head and jaw. Neither gave nor asked quarter. They just fought all over the ring.
>
> In a furious melee, Marciano crashed another left hook to the jaw and down went Vingo, again (*see above left*) for a count of nine. But he seemed all right and indicated he was, by smashing a right to the jaw and staggered Marciano.
>
> Back and forth they waged their battle through the third, fourth, and fifth rounds, until it seemed human endurance could stand no more; one or the other must drop from the

combination of punch and exhaustion. But through it all Vingo fought back savagely. Through it all however, Marciano was the aggressor...

Both fighters were so engrossed in the battle that each was warned for low blows and erratic punching, although how referee Harry Ebbets could differentiate between the blows that were merely wild and the those that were believed to be intentionally foul is one to ponder over. Finally in the sixth-round, as Marciano reminisced, he unleashed a furious, "right-hand punch to the jaw -the same punch I knocked everybody out with. He went over back-wards and his head hit the canvass. It looked like another routine knockout (*most reports state that it was a short left that put the stricken Vingo down for the last time*)."

But it was far from another "routine knockout", for once it really looked like Marciano's fists would take a life. Referee Ebbets began the count; he reached three before realizing that the prostrate figure on the floor was in deep trouble[2]. Ebbets immediately waved the proceedings over and ushered New York physician Dr. Vincent Nardiello, who was sat in his customary position at ringside, to the ailing fighters side as quickly as possible.

Images of the moment that Nardiello came to Vingo's aid show just how much damage one mans fists can do to another, the stark image portrayed the prone boxers head being cradled in the arms of his trainer, Whitey Bimstein, a look of mourning etched deep onto the grizzled mentors visage. Vingo's eyes are closed, although hardly perceptible through the horrific mask of blood and gore that covered his limp, expressionless face, the Doctor is ready to administer an injection of adrenaline into Vingo's heart in the hope that this may bring him back to his feet. If ever an image were to be used to advocate a ban on boxing this would be it.

For the briefest of moments the hopes of all gathered about Carmine were raised as the fallen warrior revived temporarily and attempted to rise, but the reversal in his condition was fleeting. Suddenly he collapsed back down, unconscious, comatose. It was a condition that he would linger in for almost three long, agonizing weeks.

Marciano was completely unaware of the drama unfolding in the ring, for as soon as his hand had been swiftly raised in victory he had abandoned the stage, returning to his dressing room, he saw neither the frantic administrations of the Doctor, nor his stricken adversaries removal from the ring via stretcher to his dressing room where he awaited the ambulance (3). It was after Marciano had showered and the soon to be customary invasion by the press ensued that Rocky finally realized what was going on when he was appraised by a journalist.

As Rocky recounted in his ghosted autobiography serialized in *The Saturday Evening Post* shortly after his retirement, "Allie and Charley Goldman and me went right to the hospital (*about two blocks away*). There was this woman sitting there. She was sobbing so hard she had a handkerchief in her mouth, and I knew she was Carmine's mother (4). I just stood there and looked at her and said, 'I'm sorry.' She didn't say nothing. I didn't know what to do. A Nun came by and I looked at her. I was hoping she would say something. She touched my arm and says, 'We're praying-all praying for this boy'."

Dr. Nardiello, who had accompanied Vingo to St. Clare's, gave a hurried press conference in which he announced the injuries that the unfortunate Carmine had sustained, "...examination revealed a contusion or swelling of the brain...Vingo's condition is very serious and the outcome cannot be determined for 24 to 48 hours...The brain swelling was on the right side and was the result of repeated blows. The contusion caused paralysis on the left side yet the paralysis might disappear as the swelling subsides...X-ray examination revealed no skull fracture. A spinal tap showed a cloudy fluid which indicates a possible mild hemorrhage. Vingo was given the last rites as in accord with the Catholic Church, just in case (*Carmine had already been administered with the Church's conditional absolution whilst he lay in his dressing room*)."

Marciano continued, "Maybe around three o'clock in the morning the doc told us to go back to the hotel. All the family was there-Uncle John and Uncle Mike and Uncle Dom and Pop. Barbara was there too (5). She and I looked at each other, and we both had tears in our eyes."

If Marciano's intended bride was emotional, one can only speculate at the intense feelings that swirled through the head of Kitty, that slim, beautiful, jet black haired future wife of Carmine who had stayed home in their small Bronx apartment whilst he went to work. She waited for him to arrive, oblivious at first to the night's events; on their small kitchen table she sat with a cake, a treat to celebrate Vingo's birthday the day before. "When Carmine didn't come home," she recalled, "I gave it to the dog. But somehow he didn't want to touch it."

Rocky Marciano remained in New York for several days after his family retinue had returned home, he stayed to be with Vingo and to seek absolution from the grieving family, "I swore...that if Carmine didn't pull through I'd hang up my gloves forever. The priest who gave carmine the last rites tried to console me, but I was heartsick and guilty in my own eyes." finally he went home to Brockton, yet still he kept up the vigil, every morning he stopped at St, Patrick's Church on Main street and prayed...

Notes:

1. Before Peter Marciano distanced himself from this project I had the opportunity of asking him as to whether what happened to Vingo changed his brother's fighting style or personality; 'The short and honest answer is no,' stated peter before continuing. 'H was intelligent enough to understand that he was in the business where this could happen. All of his fights after Vingo shows he continued to do what he did before.' He was sure to add, 'Did he feel badly, of course he did.'

2. Later there would be criticism, both of Ebbets, and Vingo's manager Jackie Levine, why had they not stopped the fight earlier, why had they allowed Vingo to be taken so close to death? Ebbets would justify himself thus, "I wouldn't have let him continue if he had have been able to get up...He seemed pretty strong at the end of the fifth but seemed to be tiring in the first minute of the sixth." Whereas Jackie Levine would claim that he was on the verge of stopping the fight when his fighter went down for the last time but for the fact that New York law of the time forbade a manager or second from entering the ring before a round was over and definitely prohibited the throwing in of a towel, both an absurd law, and even more absurd justification for allaying himself of blame. General consensus was that Carmine had fought himself into a state of utter exhaustion leaving him at the mercy of his stronger opponent and unable to protect himself from the final blow.

3. Despite rumors and reports that Vingo was carried to hospital by six men using a coat as makeshift stretcher, extant photo's clearly show Carmine being borne out on a stretcher by police personnel.

4. She had the added trauma of actually being in the audience, along with Carmine's elder brother and sister.

5. Marciano's family were regularly found amongst his retinue of followers now, some, like Barbara had been to every fight he had as a professional, his future wife would later remark that she, "...died a thousand deaths every time I watched Rocky in the ring."

Afterward:

Rocky grew up relatively poor in the rough and tumble neighbourhood of Brockton Mass during the Great Depression. He was a very tough guy, a very physical guy and one who was no stranger to violence. He had plenty of fights growing up, as Nicky Sylvester and Izzy Gold who knew him best in those days attested. They said they got Rocky into more fights than he ever had in the ring and just left guys in a bloody heap. Now Rocky was not a bully but he would not hesitate to defend a friend who was being bullied. An ethnic slight (*so common back then*) could send him into a fist-flying rage and so could a competitive situation and, for sure, so could a dispute over money. So while he was not pathologically violent there was an innate instinct for physical aggression --- no doubt about it.

By the time he was in the army he knew that his physical powers were clearly out of the ordinary, although he had no serious intention of being a professional fighter. Baseball was his first love but even on the baseball diamond his pugnacious nature would surface. I'm sure you remember the story when he was trying out for one of Cubs' farm teams, he bobbled a grounder and the guy who hit it, a Southern reb, said pick it up you Nigger loving Yankee. With one left handed punch the Rock floored him and broke his nose.

With regard to the specific incident that sent him to the brig for some 563 days, my guess is that it must have been more serious than a solitary punch and accusations of stolen money, especially if his defence was that he was protecting himself from sexual assault. Transcripts of the hearings were burned in that 1972 fire, but I imagine that Rocky had a history of violent encounters (*which he euphemistically told the psychiatrist were arguments*) some of which we know of and others we don't. It seems that being sentenced for that kind of time would be more appropriate for knocking out 9 MPs rather than hitting a possible sexual predator in an English civilian house.

These stories of Rocky's physical prowess may have been embellished to Bunyanesque proportions after he won the title but there is probably, knowing what we know, an element of truth in them. The question becomes what are we to conclude of Rocky as a person, a human being. Unless you are a saint or a simpleton there are aspects and motivations of other people's lives that are forever unrecoverable. We are, indeed, often a mystery to ourselves. The famous Russian author Dostoyevsky said that "The spirit that moves a man is so deep, so mysterious and so inscrutable that no psychiatrist, no philosopher and no theologian will ever probe its depths." This should hardly be surprising since the mind is the most complex entity in the entire Universe. It is there we find all the seething mass of contradictions of human nature: generosity and greed, lies and honesty, courage and craveness, charity and malice, love and lust and a whole burning host of antipodes. It is these shades that make us such an enduring and compelling subject for novelists and playwrights.

Marciano was no exception to human corruption, nor was he bereft of honour and integrity. It doesn't pay at this stage to be his analyst except to draw, as I have, some very general conclusions. What redeemed him from his demons was boxing; a sport where he poured all his considerable energy, anger and intensity. It was in the gymnasiums slaying purgatories of exhaustion where he pacified that cold and numbing fear (*not physical fear --- he virtually had none*) that was born of being forever anonymous or working in the dreaded shoe factory that he felt broke his father's spirit. Rocky did not want to work at a menial job; he might have died of boredom, or acted on his frustration in some condemnable fashion. Instead he entered a profession that could excite and satisfy this inborn ferocity and in the process make him a bundle of loot without landing him in jail or worse. He knew he could fight, could knock a building down, tolerate adversities of pain and suffering that would crumble all but a Samson. From the beginning, said Allie Colombo, the Heavyweight Championship was our goal. It was here that his blue collar work ethic paid off; if it couldn't be baseball than let it be boxing. His body was his meal ticket to fame and prosperity. He believed in his power --- when he knocked out that large Texan back in his army days he remembered a feeling that came over him --- one that told him he could beat anyone in the world.

He was squat and physically graceless, his arms were short and stubby, and he lacked the august bearing of a Joe Louis, who looked like a heavyweight king. In his case the book cover was deceiving; it was the content inside that made all the difference. In Graham Greene's novel, "The End of the Affair" he relates that grace can descend on the most unlikely people. You don't necessarily qualify for grace by doing good works, going to church, saying your prayers or by acts of faith. Not that these practices are not beneficial, but God works in mysterious and inscrutable ways. I remember Ferdie Pacheco being interviewed about Marciano and saying that in every profession there is someone who is touched by God. Marciano, the Fight Doctor said, was one of the anointed being the greatest example of a human battering ram in boxing history.

I hope this doesn't sound like psychobabble but the ring, I believe, sublimated his more unpalatable qualities into something that society could both accept and celebrate: In effect legalized violence or brawling in which he was "King of the Hill." This dark side is hardly unprecedented for one who makes his living with his fists. In his early hobo days, Jack Dempsey was violent to the point of being homicidal. Forget about his bouts in the ring, his life and death struggles in saloons, the mines, the docks and hobo jungles are as much a part of frontier lore as the Old West itself. He opaquely admitted to doing things of which he was deeply ashamed. God knows what a biographer of John's intensity might have unearthed if Dempsey had been his subject. The same is true for Harry Greb, Jake LaMotta, Sonny Liston, George Foreman, Mike Tyson and a plethora of other famed pugilists. They earned their keep in the most violent and savage of all professions, their world was hard and cruel so why should we be surprised that their nature wasn't all gentle and light. If there is nobility in two stripped – down prize fighters trying to detach each other from consciousness it is because boxing does requires an abundance of skill, courage, fortitude and sacrifice. It why such champions are celebrated, it is why the memory of Marciano is among the most venerated in all of sports. I could go on but I think, for better or worse, you get my point.

Phil Guarnieri

(*Author of 'Inside The Ropes' - June 2011*)

To be continued...............

Made in the USA
Lexington, KY
03 October 2012